THE POPULAR BALLAD

THE POPULAR BALLAD

BY

FRANCIS B. GUMMERE

DOVER PUBLICATIONS, INC.
NEW YORK

This new Dover edition first published in 1959
is an unabridged and unaltered republication
of the First Edition.

Library of Congress Catalog Card Number: 59-65167

Manufactured in the United States of America.

Dover Publications, Inc.
180 Varick Street
New York 14, N. Y.

TO
A. M. G.

CONTENTS

PREFATORY NOTE

BY THE GENERAL EDITOR

THE extent of English Literature is now so vast that a comprehensive and scholarly treatment of it as a whole has almost ceased to be regarded as a task within the scope of a single writer. Collaboration has, accordingly, been resorted to more and more; and the method of collaboration hitherto employed has been to assign to each of a group of scholars a chronological period. This is, of course, a natural and useful principle of division. It brings out clearly the relation of the spirit of contemporary life to the literature of a period; and the considerations it involves will always be of prime importance. But it has certain serious defects. The separation of periods tends to exaggerate the differences between them, and to obscure the essential continuity of literary history. The Middle Ages, for example, are frequently treated as a static period, and the Renaissance is described as if the tendencies which characterized it began abruptly. The gradual nature of the transition is ignored, as is the fact that the roots of much that is regarded as exclusively

of the Renaissance are to be found in the intellectual life
of Europe for centuries before. Further, the persistence
and development of literary forms and modes of thought
cannot be justly exhibited in a scheme which of necessity
interrupts them at what are often arbitrary points.

The purpose of the series of which the present is the
initial volume is to attempt the division of the field along
vertical instead of horizontal lines. It is proposed to
devote each volume to the consideration of the characteristics of a single formal type, to describe its origins
and the foreign influences that have affected it, and to
estimate the literary value and historical importance of
all the chief specimens that have been produced in England and America. Biographical detail, except when it
has a bearing upon the modification of the type, will be
omitted, as sufficiently dealt with in the current manuals;
but bibliographies of the earliest and of the best accessible
editions of the works concerned will be given, as well as
of the more valuable criticism. It is designed to include
all the important literary species, so that the series as a
whole will constitute a fairly comprehensive survey of
the contents of our literature.

The advantages to be gained by this method of approach are obvious. It will be possible — for the first time,
save in the case of one or two popular forms — to view

the history of the growth, variations, and intermixtures of the genres of English Literature, disentangled from the mass of biographical and other detail which at present obscures the course of their development, and even their essential nature. It will bring into view forms which have an unmistakable identity, and which have had at times a remarkable vogue, but which have suffered partial eclipse from the accident of not having been employed by any writer of the first magnitude. It will reveal an unexpected flourishing of other forms in periods when they have been supposed to have practically disappeared. Thus the Picaresque is generally regarded as having culminated in the eighteenth century in writers such as Defoe and Smollett, while on more minute investigation it is found to be extremely active at the present moment, and to have recently produced at least one interesting new variety. Finally, one may fairly hope that the taking account of our literature along these lines will be an important step towards preparing material for that comparative study from which is to be expected the next great advance in our understanding of literary phenomena. The comparative method will indeed be employed in these volumes in the discussion of origins and influences; but beyond this one may discern a possibility for large and fruitful generalizations, when a

similar ordering of the material shall have been made
in the other European literatures.

The difficulties of the undertaking need not be ignored.
The defining of the type and the setting of it apart from
its nearer relatives, the contamination of types, the dis-
solving of the definable form into a mere pervasive
mood, the necessity of discussing a work from one point
of view at a time, leaving others to be dealt with in later
volumes, — these and many similar problems will call for
much exercise of judgment on the part of the individual
authors. But it will often be in the working out of just
such problems that most illumination will be cast upon
aspects and relations hitherto ignored. The comprehensive treatment of some great works which have been
the culminating points of previous histories is not here
to be expected. Thus " The Faerie Queene " must be
viewed as a link in the history, at one time, of Allegory,
at another, of Romance, at another, of Didactic Poetry.
But the sacrifice of one kind of unity and comprehen-
siveness thus entailed will be compensated for by the
light thrown from new angles; and it is a sacrifice of
something already frequently attempted.

The division of the whole body of a literature into constituent genres presents greater difficulties in the case of
English than in the case, say, of French. English writers

have been less accustomed than French to view their work as belonging to specific types, have been, on the whole, less conscious of form as such, more concerned with a subject-matter or a message. But to admit this is not to deny that the forms have been there, and have reacted powerfully, if silently, upon content. The extent to which this is true can be determined better at the close of our labors than at the beginning.

So also must we postpone till the work is nearer completion the much debated question of the evolution of genres, and the validity in this discussion of the biological analogy. No attempt in the present direction has yet been made on a scale sufficiently large to justify dogmatism as to the presence or absence of a clearly definable curve of evolution in the life-history of literary forms in English. A number of terms that seem to imply a belief in such a formal evolution have passed into the language of current criticism, and will doubtless appear in these studies. But the opponents of this theory may regard such terms as merely convenient figures of speech, not committing the writer to a prejudgment of the case for the debating of which he is at present only collecting evidence. What cannot be denied is the usefulness of segregating for purposes of special study the examples of the various literary types, and of the attempt to gather from these their essential characteristics, the modifications they

undergo from age to age and author to author, the
nature and degree of the excellence of each in its kind,
and their importance in the history of literature regarded both as a form of beauty and as a revelation
of the human spirit. And this is the main purpose of
these volumes.

PREFACE

GENTLE readers are advised to begin their reading of this book with the second chapter. The first chapter is for those who would quicken their faith in the ballad as an independent type of literature, as well as for those who wish to have all the conceded facts before their eyes. It must not be regarded, however, as a chapter of controversy, as canine, — if one may borrow the notion of an old English don who is quaintly said to have had "no tolerance for dogs, doubting their powers of self-restraint."

It is a pleasure to acknowledge the constant and helpful interest of Professor W. A. Neilson, the general editor of this series; to recall the encouragement, unfailing and unwearied for fifteen years, of Professor G. L. Kittredge; and to remember that these men, like the present writer though to so much better purpose, once learned the lore of ballads from Francis James Child.

F. B. G.

HAVERFORD, March, 1907.

THE POPULAR BALLAD

THE POPULAR BALLAD

CHAPTER I

THE BALLAD

I. THE MEANING OF "POPULAR"

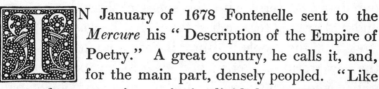IN January of 1678 Fontenelle sent to the *Mercure* his "Description of the Empire of Poetry." A great country, he calls it, and, for the main part, densely peopled. "Like most of our provinces, it is divided into Upper and Lower Poetry;" of the former, Epic is "the chief city" and Tragedy a lofty mountain range, while in the other district, the low countries, which are full of marsh, Burlesque is the capital town. Comedy, to be sure, "has a far more agreeable site; but it is uncomfortably near Burlesque." Between Upper and Lower Poetry are "vast solitudes," the region of good sense, little inhabited, though boasting an admirable soil. Two rivers water this vast empire; one is the river of Reason, and the other is called Rime, rising at the foot of the Mountains of Dream (*rêvérie*). There is an obscure Forest of Fustian; and far to the north are towns like Acrostic and Anagram. Well out in the sea are an Isle of Satire, and an Archipelago of Bagatelles containing numberless little islands, — "des madrigaux, des chansons, des

impromptu." And that is all. One searches Fontenelle's
empire of poetry in vain for anything that could answer
to the title and the purpose of this present book, for any
glimpse of what one now calls the popular ballad.

True, the popular ballad, or rather popular song, had
been discovered and named, a century before Fontenelle's
day, by one of his own countrymen. Montaigne had
opened critical eyes to the fact that poetry might exist
independent of books and of written records, had compared savage verse with the songs of French peasants,
and had praised for the first time what he was first to call
"poetry of the people." But it is not on Fontenelle's map,
the new world of poetry; and even in this day there are
critics who see no necessity for assigning to popular ballads a specific and clearly bounded portion of the poetic
globe. If one says, as one does say, that the popular
ballad is a poem meant for singing, quite impersonal
in manner, narrative in material, probably connected in
its origins with the communal dance, but submitted to
a process of oral tradition among people who are free
from literary influences and fairly homogeneous in character, one cannot be sure of general assent. There is no
subject on which men offer theories with such confidence as on questions about the origins and beginnings
of poetry; and the origins of the ballad have been debated almost beyond belief. Every one of the statements
just made might meet a challenge; and the challenge
cannot be ignored. The statements must all be proved,
or at least made reasonable, by facts. The facts, again,

must be rightly applied; and one is reminded of Rousseau's pious wish that two men, one very rich and one very wise, should together go round the world and study the human race. Just such a partnership of information and inference ought to be formed in a field of research where the capital and complementary faults have prevailed of collecting material without formulating a theory of what the ballad is, and of formulating theories about the ballad without intelligent use of the material. Difficulties begin with the mere nomenclature of the subject. It is not only what are popular ballads; but what is a "ballad," and what is "popular"? Popular is something which pertains to the people at large, and ballad is a song to which folk used to dance; yet nearly every variety of short poem in English has been called a ballad, from the translated songs of Solomon, " the Ballad of Ballads," through stirring lays in love or adventure and cheery lyrics of emotion, down to those feats in journalistic verse which filled the times of great Elizabeth with tales of a "monsterous pygge" or forecast of an earthquake.[1] Here, indeed, the danger of definition begins; for they were " popular" enough, these ballads in print, as Shakespeare bears witness, pouring sufficient satire on the news "but a month old" which they scattered abroad. His usurer's wife and his lyrical fish [2] need not bring

---

[1] The shepherd "lighteth no sooner on a quagmire, but he thinketh this is the foretold earthquake whereof his boy hath the Ballett." — Nashe, *Anatomy of Absurdity*, ed. Grosart, i, 33.

[2] *Winter's Tale*, IV, iii.

confusion into the case; but there were also printed
ballads about great men and great events, which, along
with the pedler or minstrel who sang them, and that
forerunner of the Grub-Street brotherhood who made
them, must be disentangled from popular ballads of the
traditional and unsophisticated kind.   Tom Nashe
would have "the acts of the ventrous and the praise of
the vertuous . . . by publique edict prohibited by such
men's mouths to be so odiouslie extolde," and rails
again and again at these "ragged rimes shuffled or
slubberd up" by some "stitcher, weaver, spendthrift or
fidler." Such ballads in print began to appear in England
about the middle of the sixteenth century [1] and by its
concluding decades were sold in thousands; they are not
quite the same quality as those popular songs made in
Paris and sung through the streets in the days of Mme.
de Sévigné,[2] which were called *vers du Pont-Neuf* or
ponts-neufs outright.   *Ponts-neufs*, although in the journalistic manner, have a more communal note, and were
sung by crowds, rather than read by the 'prentice or shepherd's boy.   Still, the line is not easy to draw; with the

---

[1] The oldest printed ballad of this sort now known in English is said
to be Skelton's *Ballade of the Scottish Kynge*, in black letter of about
1513; although the *Gest of Robyn Hood*, based on ballads, was probably
printed soon after 1500. The actual street ballads begin about 1540. For
earlier popular songs of the satirical and political order which were cir-
culated in manuscripts, see such collections as Wright's *Political Poems
and Songs*, 2 vols., Rolls Series, — e. g. ii, 224, where, about 1449, Talbot
is sung as a dog and the Earl of Suffolk as a fox "drevin to hole."
With this "ballad" cf. Child, no. 166, *The Rose of England*.

[2] *Lettres (Grands Ecrivains)*, i, 480, note 4.

journalism of the Elizabethan ballad-press was mixed a
deal of popular songs, reputable and disreputable, and
even, as the Register of the Stationers' Company can
show, here and there a traditional ballad of Robin Hood.
Songs made in the city, like the jingles of a modern con-
cert-hall, got into the country, and could serve as a charm
for every poor milkmaid to " chant and chirpe" under
her cow and so "let down" the milk.[1] Some of these
songs, we know, were pretty enough; but the ballad
of commerce tended to be scurrilous and lewd. Henry
Chettle, in his "Kind-Hart's Dreame," gives a vivid
picture of the singing and selling of ballads in Essex.
One Barnes and his two sons are described, these in their
"ballad-shambels " or booth, the old man outside leaning
on his crab-tree staff; the sons, "one in a squeaking
treble, the other in an ale-blown base, carowle out . . .
adultrous ribaudry." If there is any one line of the song
worse than the rest, says Chettle, "that with a double
repetition is lowdly bellowed," as, for example, —

> " He whipt her with a foxes taile, BARNES MINOR,
> He whipt her with a foxes taile, BARNES MAJOR,

'O brave boies,' saith Barnes Maximus. The father
leapes, the lubers roare, the people runne, the divell
laughs, God lowers, and good men weepe." Apparently
Chettle bewails the further degeneration of a degenerate
art; for in his dream Anthony Now-now, "an od old

[1] See *Whimzies* (1631), a curious pamphlet which hits off in alphabetical order the "characters" of London from *almanack-maker* down
to *zealous brother*. This is on the *ballad-monger*, pp. 8–15.

fellow . . . with a round cap . . . a side-skirted tawney coate . . . and leather buskins," after playing on his treble violl, sign of his profession, a "huntsup," sends messages to the "arch-overseers of the ballad-singers in London and elsewhere," lamenting abuses of the ballad press unknown in his day. But better or worse, these fellows who now hawked about the printed ballad, and now sang the scurrilous and lewd songs which Chettle cites, are responsible for none of the material with which we are concerned.

Even the minstrel of more romantic associations had nothing to do with the making of those typical ballads of tradition which form the bulk and give the quality in any collection of note. Minstrels before the Conquest, court poets like Deor and wanderers like Widsith, are out of the question. One glance at Elizabethan pamphlets is enough to fix the standing of that "rogue by act of Parliament," the ballad-singer; and what he was and what he sang in later time is even more decisive against his claims to traditional balladry. Before Elizabethan days, to be sure, in what is called the transition period, he was a far more important personage. He made money now and then.

> " Here lyeth, under this marbyll ston
> Riche Alane, the ballid man . . . "

runs a mocking epitaph which Wright and Halliwell put in the fifteenth century. But rich Allans had nothing to do with verse beloved and sung by the people; they were in a better trade, and dealt in more costly stuff. Warton

gives from monastery records a long list of gratuities to
minstrels; and he thinks that "some of our greater
monasteries kept minstrels of their own in regular pay,"
precisely as the lords and landed gentry kept them, and
even the towns.[1] There are gifts "to Lord Stafford's
mimes," as well as to "the mimes of Rugby." But this
association of minstrels with the castle and the convent,
with the aristocracy of wealth and power and with the
aristocracy of learning, is even more fatal to their connection with ballads than the proof of minstrel ribaldry
and a degenerate art. Minstrels, with loose folk of all
sorts, haunted the old fairs, as in the story of Earl
Randolph and his friends from Chester. They may have
ministered to popular mirth, these wandering players,
but they evidently affected strange ways, strange speech,
an esoteric craft, and doubtless despised such homely
traditional songs as the people sang at their village
dances and over their daily round of toil. It is significant
when Robert Brunne says that he writes his Chronicle
"in symple speche" and "for the luf of symple men,"
but not for *disours*, *seggers*, and *harpours*, who were evidently fond of "strange Inglis." Humble or exalted,
minstrels inclined to the modern, the difficult, and the
elaborate, in song. It is true that knights of the thirteenth
century disguised themselves as minstrels when they

---

[1] Minstrel, as a later official term, must often mean a performer on
musical instruments, town piper, or what not. John Selden's father,
says Wood, was "a sufficient plebeian and delighted much in music."
The parish register of West Tarring has "John, the sonne of John
Selden, the minstrell." See Arber, Selden's *Table Talk*, p. 3.

wished to spy, very much as Hind Horn, in the ballad, disguised himself as a beggar; it was going to the other extreme from knighthood. Yet both had the grace of song. When Johan de Raunpaygne, in the story of Fulk Fitz-Warine, takes this disguise, he goes in "very poor dress" and carries a great staff. For his good news he gets a cup of silver, but for a show of temper is nigh to be hanged. When his news turns out false, the noble victim remarks that all minstrels are liars. Johan's most remarkable feat, however, is his appearance before the king as a negro minstrel, — "blacked all over except his teeth." Here he carries a tabor to accompany his songs; and it is noteworthy that afterwards, in his true part as knight at a joust in France, entering the lists, he strikes this tabor so that mount and vale resound, and the very horses show their joy. The point is, that knight and minstrel had the same poetic dialect.

It is needless, however, to dwell on the life of minstrels at this time; it is clear that they are not responsible for the ballads. Banned by the Church, alternately petted and reviled by the lords and knights whom they amused, they practiced every art of the entertainer, and whether in poor or rich estate were at the farthest possible remove from the unlettered and artless simplicity which marks genuine ballads of tradition.[1] Professor Kittredge

[1] The woman ballad-singers of the seventeenth and eighteenth centuries need no investigation. There is a chap-book in the Bodleian library which purports to give the "confessions" of one of them. Her medieval prototype may be seen in the old manuscript illustrations.

thus sums up the case in a proposition, as he says, hardly
to be "controverted by any scholar who is familiar with
the subject. — It is capable of practically formal proof
that for the last two or three centuries the English and
Scottish ballads have not, as a general thing, been sung
and transmitted by professional minstrels or their representatives. There is no reason whatever for believing
that the state of things between 1300 and 1600 was
different, in this regard, from that between 1600 and
1900 — and there are many reasons for believing that it
was not different." He goes on to show that what the
minstrels did compose was work of an order totally
different from ballads.

Not the vocation of minstrels, but household and communal memory, has been the source of nearly all genuine
ballads of tradition. John Aubrey's words are seldom
quoted in full about that ancient way. Speaking of
old wives' tales, he remarks that "before Woomen were
Readers, yᵉ history was handed down from mother to
daughter. . . . So my nurse had the history of the Conquest down to Carl I. in ballad;" and two pages later he
quotes "what my nurse was wont to sing" from a ballad
about Rosamond. This is the old trail; but women are
all readers now, the schoolmaster has long been abroad,
and folk take the literary highroads. Mr. Thomas Hardy
gives the hint of this "end of an auld sang" in his account of the mother Durbeyfield singing ballads which
daughter Tess, with her superior board-school culture,
disdains. It is natural to think of minstrels carrying

ballads from land to land. Here is far-come stuff; there is the far-come carrier. Minstrels, one shows, carried this or that ballad from Germany to Sweden; one concludes that the ballad itself, the ballad habit, has been so imported. But common sense refuses to turn the primary instincts of verse and song and dance into a commodity first made nobody knows where and then distributed over Europe by these literary bagmen. So we come back to the vital question and the real facts: not only is it impossible to connect the traditional ballads with minstrel authorship, but we find that they belong demonstrably and absolutely to the people. That it was not the people who took and sang the minstrel's ditty, but rather the minstrel who intruded upon popular tradition, one learns from those "evening dances" of the young folks about village lindens or on open town squares in Germany, where girls offered the garland and youths improvised songs for the prize. Harmless enough at first, the custom came into disrepute and was forbidden by laws of the sixteenth century, which provide that professional singers, *spielleute*, who "help" in these dances, shall be imprisoned.

So the minstrel is ruled out of court. At first sight it seems that a better case can be made for the journalists themselves. Who made the ballad of occasion that Falstaff had in mind, Helena of "All 's Well," poor Pamela in Richardson's novel, and perhaps great Roland himself when he exhorted his men to fight so that no "bad songs" should be sung about them? These songs made

history. Selden, talking of libels as straws which tell the
way of the wind when "casting up a stone does not,"
remarks that "more solid things do not show the com-
plexion of the times so well as ballads." Or, on the other
side of the account, and as with newspapers of to-day,
while half the world tried to keep out of ballads, doubtless the other half tried to get in. Note the appeal [1]
of Geordie's wife, after she has saved her husband from
the block:—

> "'Gar print me ballants weel,' she said,
>   'Gar print me ballants many,
> Gar print me ballants weel,' she said,
>   'That I am a worthy ladie'"—

which may be a corruption of the wife's real remark, but
shows sufficiently the current feeling in the case. Suppose
that Geordie's wife really was printed in this way! Here
is the ballad. Who made it? Why should the journalists
not have celebrated such folk as well as the typical "cat
that looked out of a gutter"? Among all the printed
ballads, why could not this or that hit upon a traditional
theme and give it adequate expression? If Dekker, for
example, arrant playwright and man of the city, could
write the sweetest and most rural lyric of his time, why
not assume a few popular ballads of the best sort from
that early Grub Street? Isaak Walton's "cleanly" room
in "an honest alehouse" had "twenty ballads stuck about
the wall." The milk-woman who sang Kit Marlowe's
song for Piscator, named also "Chevy Chace" and

[1] Child, no. 209, B, 30.

"Johnny Armstrong" in her list. Captain Cox had "great oversight . . . in matters of storie;" he collected "histories" like "Robinhood, Clim of the Clough, the King and the Tanner, and the Nutbrown Maid," and "ballets and songs" like "Broom, broom on hill . . . Bony lass upon a green . . . and a hundred more he hath, fair wrapt up in parchment." [1] Are we to make arbitrary divisions? To this, of course, we reply that many traditional ballads were printed for the broadside press. But there is a closer thrust to parry. Two of the traditional and popular pieces which are found in Child's collection were actually printed, along with occasional but original verse, in Tom Deloney's "Jacke of Newbery," [2] a prose tale. Why not assume that Deloney made them? Now it is just here that the genuine ballad of the people vindicates its popular source as well as its popular vogue. Nobody can uphold even the probability that Deloney, the "ballating silk-weaver," as Nashe called him, whose undoubted work lies before us in much doggerel and a piece or so of some literary merit,[3] composed these two ballads printed in his tale. It is not merely because he says of "Flodden Field" that "the Commons of Eng-

[1] See Laneham's Letter from Kenilworth, 1575, in Furnivall's *Captain Cox*, Ballad Society Publications, London, 1871.

[2] *Historie of John Winchcombe, otherwise called*, etc., etc. — See the reprint of R. Sievers in *Palaestra*, xxxvi, Berlin, 1904, pp. 184, 195. Sievers concedes a possibility of Deloney's authorship of *Flodden Field*, but balks absolutely at such a case for the *Fair Flower of Northumberland*. "Beyond question," he says, "we have here to do with a genuine popular ballad of the north country." Page 121.

[3] *The Spanish Lady's Love* is still a favorite.

land made this Song,[1] which to this day is not forgotten
of many," though the phrase, as implying tradition and
a kind of communal authorship, is interesting enough;
one has simply to compare the two with Deloney's own
ballads, or to compare ballads of purely traditional
origin with journalistic ballads at large, to see that the
gulf between can be bridged by no assumption of the
same origins.[2]

So far as the ballad itself, then, is concerned, we have
cleared the field of intruders. The minstrel's making is
dismissed, and with it the ballad of commerce, the rout
of lewd and scurrilous songs and of harmless if mawkish
and sensational journalism. The ballad of our quest is
a narrative lyric handed down from generation to generation of a homogeneous and unlettered community.
Such ballads, of course, now and then finding their way
into the singer's basket and into the stalls, got corrupted
in the process; yet they show, even in this state, their
exotic character, as may be seen by the rude, stirring

[1] He calls the other also a "song," just as Sidney spoke of "the
old song of Percy and Douglas."

[2] Sievers, in his just quoted *Thomas Deloney*, pp. 130 ff., gives a few
of the differentiating qualities which sunder into three groups, first,
these "street-ballads," as he calls them, such as Deloney wrote, secondly,
the ballads of art, like *The Nut-Brown Maid*, and, thirdly, genuine
ballads of the people. Journalism is a better word for the first group.
Deloney, for example, reports in fairly vivid verse a great fire, the execution of Babington and other conspirators, battles at sea, and all the
rest. It is interesting, further, to see him in true journalistic spirit supply
a popular demand for sensations by falling back upon the old chronicles.
Some of his "reports" became universally popular, and were remembered into the eighteenth century.

verses of "Bewick and Grahame." But we still have
the adjective, that equivocal word "popular;" and on
the meaning of "popular" centres the main dispute.
Of all the definitions offered, and they are innumerable,
we can make two clearly sundered classes: the definition
by destination, and the definition by origins. Now it is
clear that only a definition by origins really defines. When
Aristotle sets off from actual, artistic, deliberate poetry
a mass of antecedent verse marked by improvisation,
song, and choral dance, or when Mr. George Meredith [1]
says that ballads grow "like mushrooms from a scuffle
of feet on grass overnight," one is on the trail, though by
no means at the finish, of a definition by origins; and
such a definition can be used for purposes of exclusion
as well as of inclusion in making up the ballad *corpus*.
If, however, one simply defines the popular ballad as a
narrative lyric which in course of oral tradition has come
into favor with the people, then there is nothing but the
law of copyright and the personal fame of Mr. Kipling
which could serve at some future day to exclude his
"Danny Deever" from a collection of English popular
ballads or to differentiate it from "Hobie Noble" and
"Jock o' the Side." There are three hundred and five
individual ballads in Professor Child's volumes; and in
his opinion the collection was complete. Mr. Andrew
Lang's ingenious plea [2] for "Auld Maitland" does not

[1] *The Amazing Marriage*, chap. xxxiv.
[2] See *Folk Lore*, xiii, 191 ff. The ballad is printed in the old edition
of ballads made by Mr. Child, but he calls it a modern imitation.

really affect the case. He thinks it a popular and traditional ballad; Mr. Child thought it spurious. Both agree
in the tests. So it is with inclusions. There are ballads in
Child's final volume no better than "Auld Maitland," not
so good, which the editor would gladly have jettisoned;
they are inserted, as he tells us, by the advice of Grundtvig, and on the chance that they preserve a few shreds
of tradition. Buchan's ballads from the north of Scotland are in some cases more than doubtful; but often
they may be sound; and so they find entrance. Dr.
Murray scoffs at the idea that "Thomas Rymer" grew by
"oral tradition" out of the romance. There will always
be challenges of the right of entry for this or that ballad.
The exclusions, on the other hand, are seldom matters
of dispute. "The Children in the Wood," the Agincourt
songs, both the Cambridge and the Harleian, and "The
Nut-Brown Maid" can come into no collection which
makes the popular and the traditional its test, — provided the test be firm. For these three-hundred-odd
ballads are either the surviving specimens of a genre, a
literary species,[1] which is called popular because in its
main qualities it is derived from the "people," or else
they are the somewhat arbitrary collection of poems

---

[1] "A distinct and very important species of poetry," says Professor
Child in his article on Ballads in Johnson's *Cyclopædia;* and he calls
fifteenth-century ballads "the creation . . . of the whole people, great
and humble, who were still one in all essentials." He rejects, of course, the
miraculous, mystic side of the Grimms' idea of popular creation; but he
insists on popular origins. Poor and imitated ballads of later time, he
says, "belong to a different genus; they are products of a low kind of *art*."

which had in some way become favorite and even
traditional, apart from print, with mainly unlettered
folk. In the first case they can be treated as a closed
literary account, and, like the medieval romance, the
ancient epic, as an outcome of conditions which no
longer exist and cannot be revived. In the second case,
while conditions of oral transmission may be changed,
there is nothing to prevent the daily production of
ballads which may become in time as popular as any
in our collections. Moreover, it is possible, under the
second case, that patient sifting of material might cut
away a quarter, a third, a half, of these ballads and give
them to poets of note and name.[1] In the interest of
mere stability, then, one would like to achieve a satisfactory definition by origins and so defend the genre,
fortify its frontiers, and establish a test and privilege of
citizenship in balladry. Is there such a thing as poetry
of the people as opposed to poetry of art? If there is
such poetry of the people, is the ballad to be counted as
belonging to it, or at least as derived from it?

II. COMMUNAL AUTHORSHIP

Poetry is now regarded as the concern of that person whom Emerson once called "the young man in
a library." True, the poet is anything but a pedant,
and much learning of the laborious sort has rather

---

[1] This process is frankly undertaken by Mr. Henderson in his recent
edition of Scott's *Minstrelsy;* he thinks, moreover, that the "chaff"
in Professor Child's collection "is out of all proportion to the wheat."

hindered than helped him. The Renaissance did away with that distinction of sterile medieval times which restricted the title of poet, even as late as Dante, to the writer in Latin; but it still fettered him forever to the printed page, as he had been fettered in older days to the manuscript. *Pedes*, says the Anglo-Saxon Ælfric in a Latin Grammar which he wrote for his country-men in their own tongue, "*pedes* are 'feet,' with which *Poetae*, that is, the learned *sceopas*, set their songcraft in books." Here is the real point. Here is where we begin to spell poetry with capital letters. The poet, to be sure, need not be learned, and his art is no longer a depart-ment of what the medieval man called grammar; but to set one's own songcraft in books, to take heart and fire from the songcraft in other books, is the case of the most inspired poet and the most original. Dante himself and his Vergil confess it; Chaucer, Milton, Gray, have vindicated the rights of the scholar in English poetry. So that, with a little harmless stretching of the terms, it may be said that all which now goes under the name of poetry, though not under the name of verse or song, is written by one of these young men in a library for an-other young man in another library. And there is nothing in the case to bewail; no modern Rousseau need beat his breast over the reign of books. Herder, the apostle of popular verse, who could on occasion wax sarcastic about the "paper eternity" of a modern poet as com-pared with the effect of a Homer "singing in the street," had to concede that the transcendent if solitary benefit

of the art of printing is "the invisible commerce of minds
and hearts" which springs from it.   Sainte-Beuve's
"ivory tower" is the reader's refuge as well as the poet's
stronghold; if one cannot now hear Homer "singing
in the streets," this loss is more than offset by the
gain of reading him in the study.   It is true that persistent
silence of appeal has robbed poetry of a part of its charm;
but the printed word still has a suggestive power.   As
Rostand prettily says, —

> . . . "La merveille
> Du beau mot mystérieux,
> C'est qu'on le lit de l'oreille,
> Et qu'on l'écoute des yeux."

Only romantic folly could turn its back upon the triumphs
of literature, strictly so called, and assert superiority for
illiterate verse.   Poetry made in the tower, the "library,"
has for compensation the range of all experience.   Its
emotion is wide as humanity; its reflection is cosmic.
Its maker, even in common phrase, is held to have something of the divine and the inexplicable, stands far above
his fellows, and looks out on the universe.   But how came
he to such height, such prospect?   He is standing on the
great edifice of poetry itself; and when one asks about
this, and not about the chosen few who inhabit its high
places, when one considers poetry as a human achievement, figures like the library and the tower are inadequate.   Poetry is a vast pyramid, widening, but losing in
æsthetic significance, as one approaches its base.   Sands of
time have drifted about it; the huge courses of its foun-

dation are buried forever from view in their full reach and plan, and only some happy chance of record or survival affords a glimpse of the lower masonry. Here, indeed, on the larger level, was no far view of time and space, no incitement to solitary but cosmic thinking; yet here, in compensation, were ampler room, closer touch with facts, and commerce with one's fellows. Opposed to that memorial and prophetic dreamer on the peak, there is seen, in the primitive stages of poetry, and in certain survivals, a throng of people without skill to read or write, without ability to project themselves into the future, or to compare themselves with the past, or even to range their experience with the experience of other communities, gathered in festal mood, and, by loud song, perfect rhythm, and energetic dance, expressing their feelings over an event of quite local origin, present appeal, and common interest. Here, in point of evolution, is the human basis of poetry, the foundation courses of the pyramid; in point of poetic process here is the social as opposed to the individual element. This festal throng and its rude choral verse are just as much a fact, apart from questions of value, as the young man in a library and his poem. The two pairs differ, not merely in degree of excellence, but in essence, in kind; and this distinction has been made from the beginnings of critical effort. Aristotle excluded improvised and choral song not only from the valued file of verse, but altogether from the poetic category; yet in these rude chants he recognized the sources of poetry itself. True, he begins actual poetry

only with the poet and the genius. "Æschylus dimin-
ished the importance of the chorus;" and behind him
looms up Thespis the founder; there is always some
figure of this kind about whom we sing the *deus ille fuit*,
the hero-myth in arts as in practical life. "Let us now
praise famous men . . . leaders of the people . . . such
as found out musical tunes and recited verses in writing," says Ecclesiasticus. And here, indeed, we seem to
have inverted the pyramid. Poetry is imitation of the
masters, we say; but we say no truth in terms of poetic
development. The masters are really successive focal
points, results, each of them, of a process of evolution,
summaries and not beginnings. They take at first their
tune, their occasion, their sympathy and sentiment, from
the chorus and the dancing, singing throng, precisely as
Aristotle points out; on this rhythmic and social material they stamp their individual art. In later stages
they begin with the literary traditions, the temper of the
time, public demand, which are subtler elements indeed,
but quite as communal and conventional in essence as
the old choral conditions. The pyramid allegory is so far
misleading that it fails to carry the constant interplay
of artist and throng in long reaches of poetic development, as if rather there had been a succession of pyra-
mids; it is true, however, in its general implication that
the course of poetry has run from a state where social
conditions were dominant, to a state where individuals
are so in the foreground of art and the chorus or throng
so deep in the background, that we talk only of poets, of

their poems, and no more of the undifferentiated mass, the raw material, whence they derive. Yet this raw material has always been recognized in a romantic and incidental way. Tibullus, in a pretty elegy, makes his primitive farmer the first to sing "rustic" words to a regular rhythm — *certo pede* — and first to essay the choral dance; while the earliest songs of labor, as he thinks, were those that first resounded to the country wife's spinning-wheel.[1] Mention and recognition are not all. Poetry of the people, as distinguished from the poetry of art, has come upon the record, a transfer mainly due to the Romantic School. Since Rousseau's day, the rich man and the wise man have really circumnavigated the globe; and the sciences of anthropology, ethnology, sociology, are the result, sciences which have made sure the old theoretical and critical antithesis of popular and artistic verse. Ethnology, indeed, has gathered an immense amount of savage or half-savage "literature," in which, under certain limitations, the scholar can see a reflection of poetry in its primitive form. The other sciences have given other help. It was a professor of sociology[2] who demonstrated the vast importance of this primitive verse in early stages of man's social career, and the great part played by choral rhythm in the making of society itself. The modern science of folklore,

---

[1] Discussions about the relative priority of epic, lyric, drama, were really settled by Müllenhoff, who showed that choral poetry, inclusive of all three, is the primitive form; and here the German scholar joined hands with Aristotle.

[2] Bücher, *Arbeit und Rhythmus.*

moreover, has actually revealed amid byways of civilized
life a host of survivals in song, dance, chorals of the
festal year, refrains of labor and the march, all point-
ing to a time when such verse was found everywhere
in Europe, and sprang from social conditions under
which the universal gift of improvisation was still
mainly unchecked.

No sensible critic now quarrels outright with these
conclusions of ethnology and folklore. None denies either
the survivals or the mass of surely indicated but vanished verse made among the people by the people, rather
than, as is the process of authorship, outside of the
people for the people. Improvisation of verses in a singing, dancing throng is a fact assured for a vast range
of times and places. The critic contents himself by saying with Aristotle that these improvisations are not poetry
and do not even result in the popular ballad; the gap,
he says, between popular verse and popular ballads has
not been bridged. It will be well, therefore, not to take
the matter for granted. We must look at two or three
positive statements by way of proof that homogeneous,
unlettered communities have existed at times and places
which are not remote ; and we must find out what
sort of verse resulted under these conditions. Radloff,
who studied, at the closest possible range, the life of
certain tribes in southern Siberia, found that if isolation
from other influences be granted, the homogeneous folk
is a fact. "An almost inconceivable uniformity," he says,
marks the tribe. In five volumes of patient record and

unerring critical skill, the author presents, not a theory of popular poetry, but the body of it in actual presence, and a careful account of the conditions under which it is produced. More than this, he shows that wherever contact with literature was felt in any force, there the folk song and the ballad, along with that knack of improvisation which produced them, declined, and were in a fair way to disappear before the poetry of the learned poet. No sociological parallels are absolute; but this popular "literature" observed amid the steppes of southern Siberia can at least establish a probability for the same kind of literature under similar conditions in medieval Europe. But Radloff's account is not an isolated case. The same tale is told over and over again; it is merely a matter of chance in the extent to which old ruins have been spared and modern survivals have been accessible. Isolation is a prime preservative in popular verse. How far George Borrow [1] really knew his Basques and their songs may be a question; but his account is borne out by more exact inquiry. They have, he says, *no poet or poetry ;* but all of them sing, and they sing "songs, ballads, and stanzas," — the latter, no doubt, improvisations of the common European type. The music is martial and fine; " but such words! Nothing can be imagined more stupid, commonplace and uninteresting," — that is, uninteresting to George Borrow. Here and there, how-

---

[1] *Bible in Spain*, ii, 393 f. See also F. Michel, *Le Pays Basque*, Paris, 1857, pp. 214 f., and Bladé, *Dissertation sur les Chants Héroiques des Basques*, Paris, 1866, pp. 6 ff.

ever, something of demonstrable interest, if not of poetic value, springs from popular improvisation; and for this reason our third case is perhaps the most instructive of all. On the remote Faroe Islands, where the community even now is homogeneous to a remarkable degree,[1] where the old dances, with joined hands, in a great circle, are still danced to the tune of a traditional ballad which all must sing, and where on occasion every member of a festive throng must still improvise his stanza, conditions of a century ago favored communal verse in a measure seldom found with folk of such an advanced stage of civilization. The ballad was and is sung by this people "not, like dance-music, simply to order their steps," but "by its meaning and contents, to waken certain feelings. The dancers by their gestures and expressions . . . take pains . . . to show the various contents." They sang, to be sure, many old songs about Sigurd, the hero of Icelandic literary traditions. This, however, was not all. They could also make a new ballad, in most dramatic fashion, at the dance; as, for example, when some fisherman has had a mishap with his boat, sturdy companions push him out into the dancing throng, and first one and then another stanza is improvised upon the fatal theme, until a complete story of the situation, with much repetition, we may be sure, uproarious refrain, and considerable dramatic action, is attained. If the

[1] The modern instances are taken from N. Annandale, *The Faroes and Iceland*, Oxford, 1905, pp. 42, 62 ff.; the older account is from Lyngye's *Færøiske Quæder*, etc., Randers, 1822, pp. viii, 14.

song wins general favor, so the good missionary says, it is remembered and sung from year to year, — a genuine traditional and communal ballad.

There can be no question, then, of the facts. Popular improvisation at the dance has been the source of certain traditional lyric narratives; and ethnology could pile up similar evidence from her stores of observation among less civilized races all over the world. But there is no need to draw further upon these records. Everybody must admit the existence of this poetry of the people made under conditions radically different from those which determine the making of artistic poetry. Concession to the popular muse goes even farther; and one admits that only a while ago she was knocking at our doors. Europe, until a very recent date, still rang in all rural places to the echo of refrain and chorus made by labor in house or field, by festal mirth at the dance, at wedding and harvest-home, and by communal sorrow at the funeral. Soldiers even now sing their iterating and cumulative chorus on the march. Although a careless challenge is now and then offered to the idea that "popular" can be in these cases an adjective by origins, critics are fairly content to hand over all this choral, iterative, and nugatory verse to the antiquarian or to the folklore enthusiast and bid him label the stuff as he sees fit, provided he do not call it poetry. It is masterless in every sense, "orphan" making, as the Elizabethans would say; no Burns, no Villon and Dunbar, a pair whom recent suspicion accuses of making many of the

actual ballads, will claim it. But the "people" sing
other verses. The Norwegian peasant does not only
improvise his *stev ;* the Italian girls, as they gather
olives, can sing something else than the *stornelli* which
fly back and forth from tree to tree; the Bavarian youth
and maiden, facing each other at the dance, have or had
other songs than their isolated stanzas of praise or blame
exchanged on the spur of the occasion; the Faroe folk
not merely improvised verses about luckless fishermen,
but chanted old lays of Sigurd; and the cottager of
England or Scotland, besides rough chorus of harvest-
home, knows or did know certain anonymous verses, of
the same kind and spirit, to be sure, but with such use of
literary or romantic stuff, such an æsthetic appeal, and
such a satisfactory coherence of parts, as to make the
critic prick his ears. "What are these?" he asks. "Ballads," he is answered; "the popular ballad of Europe,
traditional for five centuries." But the critic at once
asserts a difference in the two kinds of popular verse.
He concedes to the throng its odds and ends of rime,
its rude refrain, its iterated and unmeaning choral; he
claims these ballads as poems, and begins a search for
their poets. They own, he thinks, a shaping hand. They
differ absolutely from any mere collocation of verses
made in alternate suggestion to the rhythm of refrain
and dance. They have a narrative often traced to literary
sources, and are informed by that epic purpose impossible as outcome of mere festal improvisation. Trained
to test his material by classical standards, the critic is

sure that ballads are popular only by destination and not by origin. If they lie in the world's literary waste-basket along with really popular trash, it is simply because they have lost their original signatures.

It must be conceded that the critic makes out a good case, so long as one listens only to his side of it; and the other side seems very remote. Students of popular poetry pile up proof of communal makings, of Siberian flytings in verse, of Faroe improvisations; for our immediate problem, however, these arguments seem like "Bohemian villages," and the critic not only puffs finely into space the notion that folk anywhere out of wonderland — or Siberia — can make anything like a coherent poem by festal collaboration, but proceeds to trace such an actual ballad as "Tam Lane" in great part to Burns, and to assign the whole of "Kinmont Willie" to Scott. With consummate ease he tracks[1] a lyric of Schiller through all sorts of popular corruptions, or a mawkish bit of sentimental verse into a dozen varying versions all claimed by the "people;" and he thinks he has solved the problem of traditional ballads, and cheerfully assumes that this study of poetic distortion by the lower classes represents the facts of oral tradition in homogeneous communities now unknown. He laughs at Siberia and the Faroe Isles. But candid readers must bear with Siberia and the Faroe Isles, must put aside the temptations of Burns and Scott, and must admit that the ballad has two handles. There is the "popular" handle, joined

[1] See John Meier, *Kunstlied im Volksmunde*, 1906, pp. xiv, ff.

in the piece with elements for which modern poetic methods cannot account; and there is the "æsthetic" handle, joined also in the piece with characteristics due to something better than rustic improvisations. Lusty pulling in these contrary directions has been going on for decades, like a tug of war; the question itself gets little advance by such treatment, and it is time to approach the ballad in some more rational way.

III. COMMUNAL POETRY OTHER THAN BALLADS

Briefly stated, and without regard to any theory, the question of popular ballads amounts to this: at their best, they were sung and transmitted from generation to generation by people who were mainly of the absolutely unlettered class, who neither read anything nor wrote anything, and who were demonstrably, as well, the makers and transmitters of those chorals and refrains and improvisations which everybody concedes to popular origin. On the other hand, a good popular ballad differs from these refrains and improvised stanzas in that it has coherence in structure, definite contents, and what is surely an æsthetic if not a literary appeal. Either, then, the ballad, which carries such popular elements as the refrain or chorus and those peculiarities of structure which we shall presently examine in detail, is originally a product of the people under conditions of improvisation and choral dance, but ennobled and enriched on its traditional course in such a way as to endow it with something of the dignity of art; or else it is originally a poem, made like any other poem, but submitted by tradition to influences which give it a "popular" character. It is either the choice and glory of wild flowers or a degenerate of the garden. Each of these explanations of the ballad is reasonable in itself, and does not conflict with common sense. One of them must be right, the other wrong. If the former is right, the present book can deal with a definite subject and be based upon compact and complete material, — the collection of Professor Child. If the second explanation is right, all boundaries of the subject are obscured, the material is questionable, and a haze at once fills the air, that haze to which we are accustomed in "Thoughts on Poetry" and kindred works of great amiability and scope. Decision of this question, therefore, is not merely a pedantic or academic affair; it is vital, inevitable. For reaching a decision, two plain lines of inquiry are indicated. It is in order to study the ballad itself, to get an accurate idea of its elements in all their bearings, and to determine whether these are to be referred, as older critics would put it, to nature or to art, to the people or to the poet. It is also in order to study the actual ballads, muster them in every way, and find out what they reveal in regard to their sources.

If, indeed, this revelation of sources were complete, if the ballads of Europe could be followed as individual poems back through all their changes to their original form, the ballad question would be solved at once; but the bridge is broken, and connection must be made in

some other way. To begin with, the medium of transmission is an uncertain one at best, — oral tradition,
seldom reduced to written record. Again, ballads as a
body, and in the shape in which they now lie before us,
go back through the fifteenth century; and there they
cease. Older and lost versions, to be sure, are easily
traced through the thirteenth century. The Robin Hood
cycle must have been forming then; and another cycle,
bracketed with the greenwood ballads by the author of
"Piers Plowman," celebrated the deeds of one of the
last great feudal lords, Randolph, Earl of Chester, but
has been totally lost. Analogy tempts us to conceive the
songs about Hereward to have been ballads of the same
type; so that it is usual to speak of English ballads as
running back to the Conquest, as well as to believe that
the ancestors of men who sung their Hereward and their
Randolph must have had, before the Conquest, in spite
of changed conditions in speech and verse, something
not unlike the ballad beloved of the sons. But all this
is in the realm of conjecture, however plausible and
right conjecture may seem to be. As actual material,
ballads are not to be found in any number in England
before the fifteenth century. Thence come the best
Robin Hood versions. The Percy folio manuscript,
written in the seventeenth century, and oral tradition in
Scotland for the past hundred and fifty years, will account for nearly all the rest of the collection. These are
the actual ballads; and with one insignificant exception,
nothing of the same kind, nothing resembling them in

structure, metrical form, and style, can be found in
earlier records.[1] The doors of a medieval library were
shut inexorably upon the popular muse; poetry was a
part of "grammar;" traditional song lived and died with
the humble generations whom it consoled.

It is clear, then, why ballads cannot be found upon
the literary record before this time; but, since they belong
in any case rather to oral tradition than to script or
print, one asks why a tenacious popular memory, re-
gardless of records, does not stretch beyond that baffling
period of literary readjustments well into the traditions
of medieval Europe. Again, there is a plain and convincing reply. Poetry made in the vernacular, and orally
transmitted, depends for its preservation upon such linguistic stability as will enable it to pass from generation
to generation without the changes of word and form
that make it both unintelligible as language and impossible as verse. Such linguistic stability begins about the
time when we date our oldest English ballads; both
Barbour and the author of "Piers Plowman" mention
them in the fourteenth century, and the versions which
have come down to us are only a little later in origin.
Moreover, though this subject is extremely difficult,
the naming of "Piers Plowman" reminds us that with
the early fifteenth century, and in the face of a most

[1] As paper came to be used for manuscripts popular verses stood a
better chance of record. Such random stuff as sailors' cries and other
popular rimes is found in the Trinity Coll. MS. R. 3, 19, which is paper,
and dates from Henry VI's reign. See Wright and Halliwell's *Reliquiae
Antiquae*, i, 2 ff.

remarkable popular revival of the old Germanic rhythm, English prosody was nevertheless settling into the system which has obtained in all our modern verse. It is hard, so far as metres are concerned, to make an equation between Chaucer's fling at *rom-ram-ruf* and the "Piers Plowman" fling at "rimes of Robin Hood;" but the "rimes of Robin Hood" were there, they were in the new metres, and they prevailed.

The bridge is broken, then, between our popular ballads and their supposed medieval representatives; but can we not mend the bridge, or rather, can we not recognize the lost planks and piers as they have been used again in another and still existing structure? One is constantly hearing of ballads as the basis of many a medieval record, as the source of many a medieval poem. Obliging hands have even "restored" these ballads by a few simple dissections, excisions, insertions, combinations, inferences, conjectures, and appeals to the open mind. From this restored material to the collections of modern days is an easy leap, — provided one takes the restored material on trust. But this is precisely what one must not do. There is no objection, to be sure, in calling much of this older and mainly inferred poetry by the general name of ballad; but in very few cases is it clear what the ballad really was in terms of its structure and its origin. Traditional ballads are obviously and absolutely different from those songs made by the professional minstrel, mainly for a political end, some of which have survived from the twelfth century in England; these were ephe-

meral, popular in the sense of the Limburger Chronicle
when it records sundry songs as "sung this year" by
the German people and hurried into oblivion along with
the excitement or passing interest which they served.
What was "sung this year" is exactly opposite to what
the folk have sung steadily through a long series of years.
Political songs, rimes of the moment upon whatever
topic attracts popular attention, cannot pass as traditional
ballads. Moreover, the uniformity of the Middle Ages
must not be pushed too far; there was a diversity of
talent as well as a variety of product; and when a song
or a ballad, otherwise unknown, is mentioned, its nature
is not lightly to be assumed.

Still less confidence is in order for cases where one
suspects a "ballad" to be lurking behind some metrical
portion of the old chronicles or some particularly vivid
piece of narrative, or some event embedded in the popular epic. It is well known that the brief notices of the
Anglo-Saxon Chronicle are broken for the year 755 by a
most dramatic and detailed story, recognized by Ten Brink
as a later interpolation and claimed as the summary in
prose of "an English lay." It is good ballad stuff, no
doubt; but no ballad style or structure, no hint of rhythm
or repetition or refrain, is left; and one is rather reminded
of the swift, relentless narrative pace, if not of the artistic perfection, in an Icelandic saga. The actual poetry
of the Chronicle, moreover, as we shall presently see,
though it has been sundered into "learned" and "popular" classes, has absolutely nothing in it which can be

compared with traditional ballads, — the "popular"
poem on the death of Edgar for an example. One hears
of Alfred's love for "Saxon" poetry, and of Dunstan's
preference — an enemy charged him with it — for
*avitae gentilitatis vanissima carmina et historiarum fri-
volas . . . incantationum naenias:* but what were they?
"Heathen popular songs," saith mine author; but the
answer is not definite for ballad purposes. Absolutely
no Anglo-Saxon verse which has come down shows a
shred of structural and formal identity with the actual
ballads; there is no strophic division, no refrain, save
in the song of Deor, — and that pretty lyric denies balladry in every syllable. Something like the ballad, it has
been said above, our ancestors must have had; but
nothing can be restored and little can be guessed. Certainly neither "Maldon Fight" nor a poem from the
Chronicle like "Brunanburh" can pass as a traditional
ballad. Immediate as an echo, self-conscious, the latter
is a summary and challenge of English patriotism, sung
from a watch-tower. They are both made on the epic
pattern dominant everywhere in Anglo-Saxon verse; and,
indeed, the uniform style and the slight differences in
metrical form which all that poetry reveals make one of
the marvels of literature. Such a lyrical subject as "The
Wife's Complaint," for instance, should lend itself admirably to the ballad style, and ought to differ structurally from epic; but how traditionally epic are its phrases,
how sophisticated its variations and metaphors, how
intricate and interlaced its stichic verses, and how remote

it is from actual singing, compared with the simplicity of
style, the choral suggestion of structure, the repetitions,
and the irresistible lilt, in a real traditional ballad of later
time but similar theme! In the first case a banished wife
says that while many happy lovers throughout the world
are still locked in embraces, she must go at daybreak —

> "Under the oak to the earth-caves lone,
> 'There must I sit the summer-long day,
> there must I weep my weary exile,
> my need and misery. Nevermore
> shall I cease from the sorrow my soul endureth,
> from all the longing this life has brought me !'"

She gives a romantic touch to her landscape, which is
as dreary as that of Mariana in the moated grange:—

> "'Dim are the dales, the dunes are high,
> bitter my burgwalls,[1] briar-covered,
> joyless my dwelling.'"

Contrast with this the ballad,[2] later of record by nearly
a thousand years, where a mother has been "carried off,
four days after bearing a son, to serve as nurse in the
elf-queen's family."

> "'I heard a cow low, a bonnie cow low,
>   An' a cow low down in yon glen;
> *Lang, lang will my young son greet*
>   *Or his mither bid him come ben.*

> "'I heard a cow low, a bonnie cow low,
>   An' a cow low down in yon fauld;
> *Lang, lang will my young son greet*
>   *Or his mither take him frae cauld.'*"

---

[1] "Citadel-hedges," what should be her "castle walls."
[2] Child, no. 40, *The Queen of Elfan's Nourice.*

Let the lyrics go, we are told; surely there are ballads
in the national epic itself, and surely they stretch through
our old colonial or heathen literature back in majestic
line to the chants about Arminius and the rout of Roman
legions in the forest of the fatherland. True, we have
no continuity of heroes, as with Scandinavian Sigurds
and Brynhilds,[1] from late ballads back to early epic; but
the break is easy to explain. What cannot be explained
is the exact nature of those "ballads" which doubtless
served as basis for the epic in both Scandinavian and
English, of those *cantilenae*, songs called by whatever
name, which once carried the tale of legendary Beowulf,
developed the myth of Sigurd, and spread far and wide
the deeds of historical Charlemagne. How is one to make
a precise statement about them and connect them, for
purposes of poetic classification, with that actual mass
of ballads, wonderfully uniform in structure and style,
which make up the later Germanic group, — English,
Scottish, Scandinavian, German? Something, surely,
can be confidently said about the older songs. "It is
probable," says Gaston Paris,[2] "that the verses were
grouped in stanzas, and were alliterative with the Germans, assonant for the Romance." They had the refrain,
and were so far choral. They fall into two chronological

---

[1] Professor Ker calls *The Winning of Thor's Hammer* a ballad
as it stands. *Epic and Romance*, p. 130. See, however, his distinction between epic and ballad, as a difference in kind due to style,
pp. 147 ff.

[2] His results still hold with little change from later criticism. See
Romania, xiii, 603, 617; *Histoire Poétique de Charl.*, pp. 11, 21, 48, 69.

classes: first comes the rude *cantilena*, flourishing from
the seventh to the tenth century, "improvised, and contemporary with the facts," made by warriors and sung
by warriors about their own deeds.   Anglo-Saxon and
earlier Germanic fighting men, thinks Gaston Paris, had
at first no class of minstrels to sing for them; every
man could improvise and sing his own verses.   The
second period is that of the professional poet, the *jongleur*,
minstrel, court bard, who worked up the old material
into coherent and protracted lays.   On this foundation
rested the later epic; and it is not hard even in the third
stage to recover many a hint of the first.   Survivals of
the old warrior improvisations are to be found, with little
change due to an epic setting, in Roland's famous speech,
with the refrain remnant at its close, inciting his comrades to play the man, show no fear, give no occasion
for reproachful and scandalous songs on their cowardice,
and above all to bide faithful to their lord the king; in
the cry of the Saxon warrior at Maldon, true to his dead
chieftain, as to the old Germanic strain; in the appeal of
repentant Wiglaf in the Beowulf.   Doubtless all these
might be traced back to the improvised boast-song of
the Germanic clansman in hall or camp, at the feast
before the fight, with a refrain of his comrades, *truci
cantu*, as Tacitus calls it, a wild choral ringing through
woods and hills to the amazement of the silent Roman
legions.   A distant and confused echo of this warrior improvisation may even linger in balladry, as when Johnny
Armstrong calls to his men, —

"Saying, 'Fight on, my merry men all,
    I am a little hurt, but I am not slain;
I will lay me down for to bleed a while,
    Then I 'll rise and fight with you again,' " —

or when the Percy and the Douglas pledge their word
for a battle to the death. This is legitimate conjecture;
but it is no proof of identity as to old song and later ballad. Occasion, subject, spirit, may be alike; but what
of structure, style, and poetical form? Tradition, again, is
a prime factor in ballads; it chooses and moulds its material in its own way. The battle is over, the captains and
the kings depart, and the very shouting of the warriors'
chorus dies away; reminiscent, not too sure of details
even while it adds them, tradition sings the fight centuries later in no dramatic and immediate style. "Old
men," says the "Cheviot" ballad, —

"Old men that knowen the grownde well yenoughe,
    Call it the battell of Otterburn," —

and it is probable that both the famous ballads, different
as they are, describe one and the same event. Professor
Child thinks that Sheale's copy of 1559, or thereabouts,
is much more modern than "the rude and ancient form"
of the "Cheviot" which Sidney heard, a decade or so later,
sung by the "blind crowder" of his famous avowal. If
this is the work of tradition between the actual making
of a ballad like the "Cheviot," as it must have been sung
immediately after the fight, and its estate at the time of
Sheale's record, or between the "Cheviot" and "Otterburn," what is one to say of analogies between our popu-

lar, traditional ballads and the old sources of the *chanson de geste?* How much was left of warriors' improvisations and choral in the "ballad" that served as stock-in-trade for the gleemen of Germanic days; and how much was left of this ballad when the poet of the epic had wrought it over in a process not far removed from modern poetic composition? For the Beowulf is surely the deliberate work of a poet; its art is far higher than the art of that epic in embryo made five or six centuries later by some humble rhapsode from the ballads of Robin Hood. Anglo-Saxon poetry, Anglo-Saxon speech, were of a more elaborate type than the Norman;[1] and the rude lay of warriors was already prehistoric, or almost so, for the best period of our early colonial literature. Difference in structure and rhythm, a strange tongue, and the intervening waste of years have all combined to make Anglo-Saxon poetry seem the rude product of a rude folk. A vivacious English scholar not long ago described his ancestors as "stuffing their bellies with acorns," and singing lays that accorded with the diet. Gurth does not count, though he was surely as intelligent as any Norman hireling; but one suspects that Cedric's forebears were superior in literary taste to the Front-de Bœufs and even the Bracys of an earlier day. Anglo-Saxon poetry asked a fairly intelligent listener, and it was the work, even in what we call popular epic, of an artist, a poet. Long before the Beowulf of our version, there must have existed on the Continent, among groups

[1] Greenough and Kittredge, *Words and their Ways*, p. 84.

of kindred tribes whose speech would show some divergence, a common poetic dialect, the language of wandering minstrels and of all that intertribal journalism which
can be inferred from a Widsith. In this poetic dialect,
perhaps most developed after England had become the
intellectual clearing-house of Greater Germania, material of all sorts could have been fused, and themes and
styles could have been exchanged, somewhat as in the
latyn corupt or *corumpus* [1] of the thirteenth century
minstrels and traveling folk must have passed the literary time of day.

The point is that from *cantilenae* to epics like the
Beowulf, from warrior improvisation to court composition, the process is open, central, and, to a large extent,
official. It was on the highway of what then counted
as literature. It excluded that long tradition which loves
the bypaths and has nothing to do with court, army, the
stir of national life. Precisely here the analogy breaks
down which would range the ballad of oral, communal,
unsophisticated tradition with such warrior lays as
formed the basis of the Beowulf. Fortunately a passage
in our old epic tells us [2] precisely how such songs of the
fighting man and the aristocratic gleeman were made.
Jocund riders, coming back from the scene of a notable
fight, produce a lay which is indeed improvised, but which

---

[1] See *Fulk Fitz Warine*, Warton Club, 1855, pp. 127, 168, and
Wright's note.
[2] See vv. 865 ff. It is to be hoped that the word *gilphlœden* is not
strained in the interpretation.

draws upon Germanic legendary verse for a setting and for an edifying contrast of character. A king's thane, a warrior, who "has taken part in many a poetic contest," and is "skillful in improvisation," who furthermore is "mindful of songs," has a stock of phrases at command, and "holds in memory a mass of old sagas," of tradition, "finds fresh words" and makes a new story "based on the new facts." And thus "the warrior cleverly repeated the adventure of Beowulf, and successfully told the story, linking word with word." So the process is described, and as no strange one. It must have been a general habit and a common source of heroic song; events passed by improvisation immediately into verse, but by the aid of skilled and fairly noble singers. In the passage just quoted, other song follows the lay of Beowulf and Grendel; conforming to that love of types so prominent in Germanic verse, and to a Platonic, not Aristotelian, idea of morals in poetry, the singer in eulogy of his hero goes on to compare Sigemund for virtue, and to contrast Heremod for vice,—figures famous in Germanic tradition which do not concern us here. The introduction of them shows the epic poet's reflective tendency; he must allude and suggest rather than narrate; his historical, ethical, and comparative instincts are utterly alien to any popular ballad. What we learn from him is the formula of improvisation and tradition, by fighting-men of rank or by actual court-poets, in the making of such songs as served for source of his epic. These two classes are on the same plane in the

Beowulf perspective.[1] Improvisation and tradition, to be sure, is also the ballad formula; but a gulf is fixed between song and ballad even wider than the distance between a remote village fisherman and an international hero. This gulf, moreover, is quite as formidable with regard to style and structure. We shall presently see that the main structural feature of popular ballads is simple repetition with incremental changes, utterly void of metaphor, which advance the statement of fact, and help the narrative, however slowly, on its way. The main characteristic of "literary" Germanic, and particularly of Anglo-Saxon, poetic structure is crossed and broken repetition with variation, which emphasizes only the previous fact by the use of kennings, or striking metaphor, but does not advance the story. Springing from the same primitive source of exact verbal repetition in chorus, the art of the epic and the art of the ballad have taken widely sundered courses, and the divergence was marked enough at the dawn of Germanic history. For Anglo-Saxon times the actual writing of epics had influenced narrative art; epic repetition, or summary, condenses, whereas ballad repetition, oral in its record, repeats literally and at length. To sum the case, Anglo-Saxon epic, in its didactic vein, its reflective tendency, its comment on the action, its consciously pathetic tone, its attitude towards nature, its control of material and cor-

---

[1] That our court-poets, like *jongleurs* in France, revised and combined songs made by the warriors themselves (see G. Paris, *Hist. Poét. de Charl.*, p. 121), is probable enough. It is mainly professional songs that get on record.

relation of parts, its organic conception, its descriptive power, as well as in its reliance on the lays of song-loving warriors and courtly bards, was so far from primitive methods of the old choral throng, so alien to the ways of tradition, that even a Beowulf can do nothing for those who would trace English popular ballads to their source.[1] Woden and his runes had long reigned over the world even of earliest Beowulf material; to find the forerunner of the traditional ballad, one would have to track old Norse Thor to his hiding-place, a banished god, and would have to discover a forgotten mass of choral and homely verse. Can this be done? Can we connect our individual ballads as they lie before us with the old communal song of medieval Europe?

This, too, is an impossible achievement. Of course, those old songs and refrains of the people did not die with the occasion which called them forth. They not only lived in tradition, but sprang up with every need of the daily round of life. Unwritten, just as ordinary experience is unwritten, they filled with song and dance the whole festal year. The ritual of a hundred superstitions, ignored by the great, added to this store of rude

[1] The repetitions of a message, or the like, are more artistic in the Beowulf, more varied, than one would expect. In the fifteenth book of the Iliad, on the other hand, Iris delivers to Poseidon almost literally the message of Zeus. So in the ballads ; for example, in *Child Maurice*. Contrast Wulfgar's cleverly paraphrased report of Beowulf's message to Hrothgar, vv. 340 ff. This constant artistic effort after picturesque variation is quite above the ballad reach, and demands, like the kindred "thought-rime" in Hebrew poetry, intellectual effort on the part of the hearer.

and choral verse. In a sense now totally unfamiliar, song resounded through the whole communal life; and all life, apart from court and camp, was of this simple, homogeneous, communal kind. The choral and communal song of the Middle Ages was undoubtedly the ultimate source of our ballad as a poetic species; and yet it is impossible to seize upon any one phase of that old poetry and connect actual ballad with actual choral verse. There were many kinds of choral verse, as one can tell in general from medieval allusions as well as in particular from the variety of old English compounds with the words *leóð*, lay, and *lâc*, game, dance, ritual. On every side we hear tantalizing echoes of these chorals from men and women, from high and low estate, from camp, from the conventional garden where aristocratic folk amuse themselves, from the "ladies foure and twenty, and yet mo," whom the wife of Bath's knight saw dancing by the forest, or other four and twenty ladies playing ball with song and graceful steps, from the village, from the church itself, from old pagan holy places new sanctified by episcopal benediction. But no one can or will tell us what they sing; at best, as we shall see, the information is misleading or vague.

There were chorals of war. Germanic warriors rushed into fight singing refrains to their gods of battle; and doubtless their sons on English soil did the same thing. The repeated cries seem to have carried sense and to have excited the singers by something more than mere noise. Ammianus Marcellinus says that the Goths,

hurrying into battle, "with discordant noise sang (*stride-
bant*) the praises of their ancestors;" and when Taillefer
chanted his solo at Hastings, there was no doubt a good
chorus to back him, as well as a right Saxon refrain to
greet him with defiance, however hoarse Saxon throats
must have been after the *treper, è saillir è chanter*, as
Wace recounts it, of the night before. Hymns, too, were
choral, with a dramatic dance. Songs and dances of the
May go back to immemorial ritual and ceremonies in
worship of Nature and the revival of her powers at the
springtime; a Russian scholar, who has studied the
ritualistic songs of his race, comes to a theory of poetic
origins embraced in the formula of "ceremony to song,
song to poetry." [1] It has been maintained, furthermore,
that the primitive German hymn was like that song of
the Arval Brothers in Rome, — cries to the god in repetition and refrain sung by a dancing throng. Chorals of
labor, too, rise everywhere in medieval life, and still
exist in survival. In fact, nearly all emotional expression
was once public and concerted in its utterance, and loved
the rhythmic fall of feet as well as of voice; but the
obviousness and range of this rude song forbade its
preservation except in the traditional way. Of bridal
and funeral songs, originally bound up with the dance,
there is evidence of every sort; but actual record occurs

[1] Anichkof, as reported by Dr. Arthur Beatty in his valuable study
of the St. George Plays, in *Trans. Wisconsin Acad. Sciences, Arts and
Letters*, xv, 11, October, 1906. See also J. G. Frazer, *Lectures on the
Early History of Kingship*, 1905, pp. 164, 178; and E. K. Chambers,
The Mediæval Stage, vol. i.

only in cases where the accomplished warrior-poet or
the professional minstrel was concerned. Young men,
the flower of their clan, rode round the tomb of Beowulf,
chanting his praises; and the strikingly dignified conclusion of our epic echoes their very words. Of a similar
song chanted by warriors of Attila, but quite in the
Gothic manner, we have a Latin paraphrase. But this
is no choral and communal song; again, we have to
think of a Widsith or a Deor, or rather, in these cases,
of song-skilled warriors like him of Hrothgar's court,
who chanted the fight with Grendel. Contrast the account given by Jordanis [1] of another royal death and
funeral song, where soldiers bore their slain chieftain
from the fight. "Then one could see the Gothic squad-
rons, even amid the rage and rush of battle, showing
the last honors to their king, and singing with inhar-
monious [2] voices their songs of grief." With which, now,
of these funeral songs, the sonorous, stately praise or the
wild choral wailings, are we to connect later ballads of
grief like "Bonnie James Campbell" and the rest? The
answer is prompt enough. So far as the evidence goes,
with neither of them. In the one case, style, structure,
manner, differ absolutely from the style and structure of
the ballad. In the other case, we have no record.

The festal year, too, was full of choral song; and here
one assumes, with great show of truth, the origins of

[1] The two accounts are respectively in chaps. xli and xlix.

[2] Doubtless Jordanis means by this word what Julian meant in his
contemptuous account of Germanic songs; it is the rude but rhythmic
choral of a throng.

the older ballad. But in what one recorded case? High-born folk loved the *carole*, and sang as they danced; many a picture in the old manuscripts shows them at their play, and Gawin Douglas [1] gives us a hint of what they were wont to sing: —

> "Sum [sang] ryng-sangis, dansys ledis, and roundis,
> With vocis schill, quhill all the dail resoundis;
> Quharso thai walk into thar carolyng,
> For amorus lays doith the Rochys ryng:
> Ane sang, 'the schyp salys our the salt faym,
> Will bryng thir merchandis and my lemman haym;'
> Sum other syngis, 'I wil be blyth and lycht,
> Mine hart is lent upon sa gudly wight.'"

These are not narrative ballads; one thinks rather of an origin for love-lyric, and of that scene in Chaucer's "Parlement of Foules" where a roundel, or triolet, is sung to Nature in a "note" which Chaucer describes as "made in France." The *ballade*, not our ballad, had its source in these amorous chorals; although both own the common choral feature of repetition and refrain. Actual ballads were sung by the "people" themselves, at dance and play; witness the famous passage in the "Complaynt of Scotland," contemporary with recorded traditional ballads which it names. For older times there is plenty of general information, but no particular fact to which one can link a ballad of the collections. Ballads which dealt with prominent persons or events were beyond all

[1] Prologue of book xii of the Æneid, 193 ff. To lead the dance was to lead the singing, as the *foresinger* of German dances testifies; but this was a later stage of the original choral.

question made in the choral throng; there is no more venerable fact of poetic production. "And Miriam the prophetess, the sister of Aaron, took a timbrel in her hand; and all the women went out after her with timbrels and with dances. And Miriam *answered* them, Sing ye to the Lord, for he hath triumphed gloriously; the horse and his rider hath he thrown into the sea." If one objects to the aristocratic tinge, the high rank, in this "ballad" as well as in the song of Jephthah's daughter, one can turn to another scene, where "it came to pass . . . when David returned from the slaughter of the Philistine, that the women came out of all the cities of Israel, singing and dancing, to meet king Saul . . . *And the women sang one to another in their play*, and said,

> "Saul hath slain his thousands,
> And David his ten thousands." [1]

There is popular refrain; and the narrative improvisation can be inferred. It is all democratic and communal enough. Like these women, too, Gothic matrons and maidens streamed out from their village in a throng to greet Attila with songs, dancing the while and waving their uplifted veils. A distinctly historical ballad was not only sung in choral by Franks of the seventh century, but, so the chronicler declares, was actually there "composed by the women as they danced and clapped their hands." Women, indeed, seem everywhere ad-

---

[1] 1 Sam. xviii. For the other extract, Exod. xv, Lowth has some excellent comment on the "answered:" *De sacra Poes. Hebr.*, ed. Rosenmüller, pp. 205 ff.

dicted to this choral composition of verse; and in the
case just mentioned the song became traditional. *Com-
ponebant*, however, is a rare word in these reports; and
the fact of composition has to be inferred by analogy
with the Frankish song, the ballad of the Faroe fisherman, and many convincing cases from ethnology. Tradition is all that can be inferred from Barbour's well-
known statement about a certain fight in Eskdale.
Particulars, he remarks,[1] he need not give, because —

> "Young wemen, quhen thai will play,
> Syng it emang thame ilke day."

So with the forged chronicle of Croyland when it says
that "women and maidens sang in their dance" the
exploits of Hereward. In neither case, however, is incidental improvisation to be denied.

The fact of ballads seems clear enough for old times,
and choral composition is to be inferred; but we have
restored no bridge from our balladry back to the original
individual versions. We found no real stay in old epic,
and no direct choral origins. We shall find as little help
in the mention of actual sources, or in the suspicion of
them, obtained from early historians; the "ballads"
which they name, or quote, or seem to quote, cannot be
defined save in the most general terms. They may have
been genuine traditional ballads, even choral fragments;

---

[1] *Bruce*, ed. Skeat, E. E. T. Soc., p. 399. For other cases, and the
Frankish song just cited, see the present author's *Old English Ballads*,
Introduction, pp. lxxvi ff.

they may have been songs of the gleeman and the professional bard. What, to begin with, were those ballads of Randolph, Earl of Chester? What were the Hereward songs, and all the outlaw cycles? Who made them? And even if we could trace them to tradition, could we be sure that they were structurally of the traditional type? Were they of the minstrel or of the people? Or were they made in the old warrior fashion by the men who themselves did the deeds and lived the stirring outlaw life? Minstrels are not a remote conjecture for some cases. Randolph is actually said to have been rescued by a "rabble of minstrels," to have given them privileges, and to have been sung by them. Waltheof, contemporary with Hereward as well as with Eadric the Wild, was sung, says Freeman, "in the warlike songs of the tongues of both his parents;" but one of these songs is preserved and is plainly by a minstrel, a scald, with no trace of the popular ballad about it. The account of Waltheof's doughty deeds at York given by William of Malmesbury, a fine bit of description, Freeman thinks to be plainly taken "from a ballad." What sort of ballad? Henry of Huntingdon takes an account of the battle of Brunanburh from a "ballad," too; but the source in this case is easily recognized as that fine battle-poem in the Chronicle, and is no ballad at all. William of Malmesbury tells explicitly of his own use of ballads, and comments on their value as historical material. He distinguishes carefully between earlier trustworthy information that he got from written documents and the evidence that he

must now take from "ballads — *cantilenae* — crumbled
by the successive rubbings of time." What were these
cantilenae? Three centuries later, Blind Harry, Henry
the Minstrel, was singing "the things commonly related"
of William Wallace before men of high rank, and getting
"food and raiment" for his pains. Maior, the old historian, will give only "partial credit" to such writings.
But the extant "Wallace" with its learned style, its
couplets of description often as crisp as Chaucer's, is
absolutely without the popular note; if a minstrel wrote
it he was a learned man. So, too, the direct inference
of traditional ballads in Malmesbury's case is open to
very grave doubt. Professor Child, discussing the ballad
of "Gude Wallace" and its obvious source in the poem
ascribed to Blind Harry, suggests that this poem itself
was founded on earlier ballads not unlike "Gude Wallace" itself, the wheel thus coming full circle. But in
the case of kings and prominent men, the old court poet,
the minstrel, is always to be suspected. Even Layamon, who heard many old songs in his story-haunted
land by the Severn and let them mingle with his book-
lore to make the tale of the "Brut," usually suggests
a gleeman of some sort when he alludes to popular
verse. He tells,[1] for example, of songs of praise when
"the king's eldest son came to the hustings and was
lifted to king;" when a king returns to his army, and

[1] See, in the order of citation, verses 14641, 19212, 22077, 30608, and
9538. "Said in song" is the "carping" such as Thomas Rymer used,
the ideal gleeman of Scottish tradition.

"horns were blown and gleemen sang;" while a victorious army was marching home under Arthur, "and then sang the men wondrous lays of Arthur the king, and of his chieftains, and *said in song*, never in world was king like Arthur;" in a charming little scene on shipboard, how "the sea and the sun, wind and the wide-sea, were glad, and the flood bore the ships, and the singers (*scopas*) were singing;" and how, after a treaty of peace, "there were in this land blissful songs." Only one of these cases is obviously choral. It was always the gleeman's business and profit, so the famous conclusion of "Widsith" shows, to sing in praise of great men. Blame, too, was his business as a journalist, when it was at long range. Two centuries after Layamon, in the so-called prophecy, really a retrospect, of John of Bridlington,[1] the Scottish king, David, is held up to obloquy as one who is going to be sung and harped for his evil courses; and the exposition notes that minstrels, "as they were wont to sing the deeds of good warriors, must sing also the shameful and luxurious doings of this David." These prophecies and their like became popular enough. Contemporary satire attacked

---

[1] The text is interesting. *Psalletur David luxuria festis*, says the prophecy; and the exposition: *quia sic solebant ministralli dicere opera strenua et bellicosa bonorum militum, ita de isto David facient gesta luxoriosa.* — Wright, *Polit. Poems*, i, 143. For a mixture of various prophecies, popular enough and traditional, see the third "fytt" of *Thomas of Erceldoune;* chap-books embodying these were common in Scottish farmhouses down to the nineteenth century. — Murray, *Romance and Prophecies of Thomas of Erceldoune*, E. E. T. S., 1875, pp. ii, xlii.

high places; the commons were quick enough to hold a king responsible for dearth, injustice, and all manner of wrongs, and liked to sing or quote sharp verses of complaint. It is sheer folly, however, to range this sort of poem, popular as it may have been, with traditional ballads; and even on lower levels, in the satires on the monks and friars, the complaints about landlords, the moan over taxes, which come down to us as the voice of an oppressed people, we are simply to see the verse of some humble poet who makes himself the mouthpiece of the folk. We do not call the vision about Piers the Plowman a series of popular ballads. Traditional ballads tell a story, or else give a situation, story and situation each for its own sake; the lyric element is confined to what one may awkwardly call the singable qualities; and any ulterior purpose, any subjective hint, even when subjectivity is of the throng, takes a poem at once out of the ballad file.

Even on strictly narrative ground, and in a case where identity of subject-matter is supposed to link an acknowledged ballad to a lost source of chronicle or poem, we can draw no final conclusion. Identity of subject cannot carry with it identity of structure and form. The popular ballad of "Sir Aldingar" tells a story agreeing in many respects with the account which Malmesbury gives of Gunhild, daughter of Cnut and wife of the German Henry III; "nor can we doubt," says Professor Child, "that William is citing a ballad." But we hear in the fourteenth century of such a ballad in professional

hands. In 1338 the prior of St. Swithin's at Winchester
entertained his bishop by letting a minstrel, a *joculator*,
sing in hall the ballad of Emma, Gunhild's mother,
who triumphed in her ordeal for adultery. During the
progress of this ordeal the spectators are represented as
praying for the queen and exhorting her to be firm.
A refrain, *Dieu vous save, Dame Emme*, seems to belong
to a version of this ballad and was sung by the common
laborer in the days of "Piers Plowman." [1] If we had no
better evidence, we should be tempted to hand over "Sir
Aldingar" to Herbert the minstrel.

It is the old dilemma. In the lack of actual material,
any theory can be proved. If the minstrel is favored by
one account, other evidence is soon found to over-
whelm and bury him out of sight. From the earliest
medieval times, "ballads" were made and sung in dancing by the throng, and from the earliest medieval times
songs about men and events were made by the minstrel.
From the nature of the case, communal verse was not

---

[1] See Warton, *Hist. Eng. Poetry*, ed. 1840, pp. 81, 82, who is quoting
"an antient register of the priory." The name of the minstrel is given,
— Herbertus, — and he sings also a local ballad of Colbrand whom Guy
had conquered just outside of the city. It is noteworthy for the popular
side of these ballads that, as Warton remarks, the Colbrand story
"remained in rude painting against the walls of the north transept of
the cathedral till within my memory." Further, one is interested in
Warton's quotation from the directions of William of Wykeham in regard to his scholars at New College. They were to have a fire in the hall
after dinner and there sing songs, recite poems, and the like. These
cantilenae were to include the chronicles, *regnorum chronicas*. (Warton, p. 84.)

recorded; but the recorded verse of the minstrel is never
of the sort found in our traditional ballads. To say that
this antithesis proves the communal source of ballads
is manifestly wrong. Only a reasonable probability
springs from the facts at our command on these lines
of investigation, and proof must be sought elsewhere.
Some of the material, indeed, which has been arrayed
for the support of communal origins, proves too much.
The two flytings of English and Scotch soldiers in the
war of 1296 are mere taunting songs, with little trace,
save in the second, of a choral; and they have, of course,
no epic touch whatever. Fabyan's account of the songs
that were made after Bannockburn "in daunces, in the
carols of the maidens and minstrels of Scotland," is
damaged, not so much by the collocation, which probably means that everybody was making songs about
the fight, as by the specimen of the verse itself. Marlowe
inserted it, as "a jig" made "by the fleering Scots," in
his "Edward II." The refrain is popular, a kind of
water-chorus used by sailors and oarsmen; and what is
it doing, one may ask, in *that* galley? The text is unepic;
it is of the taunt or flyting order; it is remote from
balladry of the traditional kind; and it is suspiciously
like the work of that "professional song-writer of his
age," as Wright calls him, Laurence Minot.

> "Skottes out of Berwik and of Abirdene,
>   At the Bannokburn war ye to kene" . . .

runs his taunt on the vengeance taken by the third
Edward for the second Edward's disgrace. This verse

of Minot's, too, has a kind of refrain; it is very singable;
the vocative note is dominant, and narrative is reduced
to mere allusion. There is no traditional touch. It is
what was "sung this year," journalistic lyric. Very
similar is Fabyan's fragment: —

> "Maydens of Englande, sore may you mourne
> For your lemmans ye have lost at Bannockisburn,
> With heve a lowe.
> What, weeneth the king of England
> So soone to have won Scotland!
> With rumbylowe."

Perhaps the maidens of Scotland are responsible for
the gibe about lost lovers; but at best this is only a burr
of political song that has stuck to the coats of chronicle.
It does nothing for the traditional ballad.

Minot ceased to sing about 1350; in 1388 was fought
the fight responsible for two of our finest ballads. Here
tradition has done its perfect work; but what of the
original stuff? The alliteration in the "Cheviot" and
in "Otterburn" is noticeable, along with remains of a
peculiar stanzaic arrangement. Minot hunts the letter
with positive frenzy. "Sir Edward oure cumly king" is
close to the Robin Hood phrase. Did some minstrel like
Minot make the ballads? Again one must leap to no
conclusion of this sort. It is true that the bulk of the
old border ballads, along with the Robin Hood cycle
and a few others, must be put in a class far advanced in
narrative skill and scope beyond the traditional domestic
ballads that best represent the type; but the former are
cast in the ballad mould, differ in spirit, rhythm, metre,

style, both from old minstrel songs and from lyric
of the Minot variety, and, moreover, can be attributed
to a definite source on fairly definite authority. The
border ballads seem to have been made, as Mr. Andrew
Lang pointed out, by the borderers themselves. As with
warriors of Germanic and early English days, so these
fighting men made their own songs. Leslie [1] says they
"delyt mekle in thair awne musick and Harmonie in
singing quhilke of the actes of thair foirbearis thay
have leired or quhat thame selfes have invented of ane
ingenious policie to dryve a pray and say thair prayeris."
The bishop's Latin is really more to the point, with his
*cantiones,—quas de majorum gestis, aut ingeniosis prae-
dandi precandive stratagematis, ipsi confingunt.* This
is unequivocal; *ipsi confingunt* is plain talk. The borderers, then, made songs about their ancestors' raids
and about their own; so do primitive folk all over the
world.[2] Warriors, particularly, who have the communal
feeling as in the intense clannishness of the border, or
in the days of Germanic bands united by that most
characteristic Germanic institution, the *comitatus*, sing
their deeds with the same inevitableness that marks the

[1] See his *Historie of Scotland wrytten first in Latin . . . and translated in Scottish by Father James Dalrymple*, 1596, edited for the Scottish Text Soc., 1888, i, 101 f.
[2] See, below, the ballad *Lads of Wamphray* discussed for its earlier
marks of structure and style. In the *Defense of Poesy*, just after the praise
of "the old song of Percy and Douglas," Sidney says: "In Hungary
I have seen it the manner at all feasts and other such meetings, to have
songs of their ancestors' valor."

doing of them. It is thus possible to put "Otterburn" and the "Cheviot" in line with songs which fighting men sang about their own deeds in England a thousand years ago; but the line is only a vague and faint tracing, it concerns only a small group of ballads in the collections, and it touches only the subject-matter and the conditions of making, not structure, style, and metrical form, not the qualities that go to mark off one poetic species from another.

The first glimpse of actual ballad structure and the ballad's metrical form, which is to be met in English records, has an interest of its own; but even this does little towards solving the ballad problem. We see, to be sure, how those border ballads in their original shape could have been improvised under choral conditions; for here at last are the ballad style, the rhythm, probably the refrain, and, moreover, direct testimony that the fragment was a favorite in really popular tradition. The tale must be told at length.[1] Cnut, with his queen Emma and divers of the great nobles (*optimatibus regni*), was coming by boat to Ely; and, as they neared land, the king *stood up*, and told his men to row slowly while he looked at the great church and listened to the song of the monks which came sweetly over the water. "Then he called all who were with him in the boats to make a circle about him, and in the gladness of his heart he bade them join him in song, and he composed in English a ballad (*cantilenam*) which begins as follows, —

[1] From "Historia Eliensis," ii, 27, in Gale, *Hist. Script.*, i, 505.

"Merie sungen the muneches binnen Ely,
Tha Cnut ching rew ther by.

"'Roweth, cnihtës, noer the land,
And herë we thes munechës sang.'"

The chronicler turns this into Latin, saying then, with unmistakable reference to popular tradition, " and so the rest, *as it is sung in these days by the people in their dances*, and handed down as proverbial."

We may chip and cut, with critical knives, from this pretty story as we will. Cnut himself may go, precisely as Alfred is sundered from his proverbs; and the modern look of the words may take them well hitherward out of the eleventh century; what remains is a fragment which is not only one of the earliest pieces of verse to break away from the stichic order of Anglo-Saxon poetry, but is in the metre and the rhythm which belong to the best popular ballads. The story of Cnut's making is highly interesting as a true process if not a true fact; for it was evidently a method of poetical composition which excited no comment and was familiar to the twelfth-century writer of the chronicle. If verses were improvised then, under choral conditions, in the rhythm of the traditional ballads which begin to be recorded a couple of centuries later, there is every reason to think of such a process and such a result lying behind that formula of *ipsi confingunt* which Leslie, an eye-witness, affirms for border verse of the sixteenth century when our best traditional ballads were making. Better even than the making, than the improvisation along with choral

song, is the popular transmission of these verses of the
king; the singing and dancing by the people, the traditional note, are even more to the purpose. Grundtvig has
shown that the quoted lines are very probably the burden
or chorus of the song itself, which may have carried them
throughout, along with the improvised narrative verses [1]
which followed, or else let them alternate as full chorus
after each new stanza; and he gives many similar cases
from old Scandinavian tradition.   Of the song itself there
is so little left that little can be inferred. It may be a
mere refrain, a rowing-chorus such as one finds, however
irrelevant it seems there, in the Bannockburn verses, and
in many Danish ballads; but one would like to hear
the rest of the piece as "still sung by the people in their
dances." The main point is that here for the first time
occurs that two-line stanza in which so many of the oldest
English and Scandinavian ballads are composed.[2] In
a sense, Cnut's song is the beginning of recorded English
balladry; [3] but it is balladry from the warrior caste,

[1] Grundtvig thinks the missing verses were epic, and told of Cnut's
conquest, — a chronicle-ballad in the grand style.

[2] Nearly all English ballads are either in this measure, — couplets
of four accents in each verse, — which seems by Professor Usener's
showing to have been the prevailing measure for early popular poetry
everywhere, or else in the so-called "ballad" measure, a stanza of four
verses with four accents in the first and third, and three in the second
and fourth. The couplet is undoubtedly the older form; and if we add
to it the refrain as alternate verse, we have also a stanza of four verses.

[3] Some tradition of Cnut's improvisation was obviously connected
with the words of a favorite song at rural dances; and so came the cir-
cumstantial account.

and of the chronicle or epic type, rather than of domestic tradition; and while it gives a glimpse of the transmitting folk of the countryside, its story of origin is obviously conventional and based upon surmise.

IV. SPECIFIC MARKS OF THE BALLAD

Between definition by origins and definition by destination no choice is to be reached by attempting to follow our popular ballads back through the fifteenth century and so to connect them with song and heroic lay of medieval times. It remains, then, to study the ballad itself, and determine whether it was primarily of a piece with those forms of verse which are conceded to popular origins. What are the specific marks of the ballad? What is there in the structure, the style, the setting, and the conditions of it, which must refer it either to ennobled popular improvisation or to degenerate art?

Before these questions are answered, however, there is a bit of house-cleaning to be done. Rubbish left by the romantic school is still to be swept away, and facts must be set in their place again, whence they have been pushed by the modern school of common sense in hysterics. There is no miracle, no mystery even, to be assumed for the making of the ballad, which was composed originally, as any other poem is composed, by the rhythmic and imaginative efforts of a human mind. The differencing factors lie in the conditions of the process, and not in the process for itself. Again, all that can be recovered by a reconstruction of these conditions is the

poetic form, the ballad as ballad, and not the original
poetic product. It should be cried from the housetops
that no one expects to find in the ballads of the collections anything which springs directly from the ancient
source. Apart from literary influences, there is the great
factor of oral tradition, which has made over and over
again the stuff of communal song. Stripped, then, of
these old reproaches, our search is anything but a fantastic attempt. Nothing could be more practical and
sensible than inquiry into the origins of that poetic
species which oral tradition has chosen as the form of
its favorite narrative themes, and nothing could be more
scientific, by way of determining these origins, than a
study of the form itself. Confusion of the two problems,
form and product, is absurd. Nothing is done for the
study of the ballad as a literary species when one has
attributed "Kinmont Willie" to Scott and the better part
of "Tam Lane" to Burns; one has simply settled two
interesting questions of detail, and has merely proved
that the form of the ballad can be fairly well imitated.
The problem of the species still remains; and it remains
unsolved even after the next and obvious step of assuming that all ballads are simply the late appropriation by
the lower classes of poetry once made for the upper
classes or for the learned and the reading world. An ingenious study [1] has recently appeared to show how illiterate folk even now appropriate in this way some poem,

[1] John Meier, *Kunstlieder im Volksmunde*, Halle, 1906; see pp.
xix ff.

changing and corrupting it almost beyond recognition. Nobody denies this process. Here, for example, in the question-column of a widely read newspaper,[1] is a query which the editor does not answer. Where is the poem, asks a correspondent, "in which these lines occur?

> " I thank whatever gods there be
> For my unconquerable soul.
> I have not shrunk or cried aloud
> Beneath the bludgeonings of fate.
> My head is bloody but unbowed.
> I am the master of my fate,
> I am the captain of my soul."

To such a case, at the shortest possible range of tradition and in a world of printed things, has come Henley's poem! The grasp of thought and phrase, the lapse in stanza and rime, are very interesting; the inquirer is an educated person. On lower levels, as Child points out, and under oral conditions, the confusion lays hold of word and idea; "they cast their glamourie o'er her," in "The Gypsy Laddie," becomes "they called their grandmother over;" and the "consecrated cross-eyed bear" of the little girl's hymn comes into mind. But this Malaprop theory of the ballad as a distorted poem of art will never do. It is very simple. German editors tell of "folk songs" that are simply Schiller or Uhland with a difference, and sometimes a very great difference. And there is Dr. John Meier's case of a mawkish poem which he thinks is to settle the ballad question out of hand. In these verses, written about 1781 by a German

[1] Philadelphia *Evening Bulletin*, Nov. 16, 1906.

nobleman named Von Stamford, "Fair Annie" is spinning to a song of pure drivel, which she exchanges for dialogue even more drivelish as a young knight comes up and asks her to go to his castle. She rejects his silks and satins, but counters deftly by asking him to put down his name for a contribution in relief of a distressed neighbor. She describes the distress, and bursts into tears; the knight —

> . . . "husch! im Wagen
> Befahl davon zu jagen" . . .

and the poem ends with advice for all girls under such temptation to use the same means of escape. The number and variety of versions of this mawkish poem which sprang up among unlettered German folk can only wake our wonder. But what do they prove? Precisely what is proved by the game of gossip, where a story is whispered from ear to ear in a large circle of players; by the versions of any oral tradition, verse or prose; and even by the manuscript copies of a widely read poem. They solve no problem of origins; they only illustrate the process of transmission. So we go back to our inquiry after the specific marks of the ballad, and essay the various tests which are commonly supposed to determine it.

Ballads, then, like folk song, chorals of labor, and popular verse generally, are handed down by oral tradition; and we have seen that this traditional quality is thought by some writers to be the only ballad test. But it leaves the question of origins untouched. It accounts for the many variants, the versions more or less diverging in stuff and style, of a given ballad, and for all the peculiarities which that sort of transmission must bring about; but it will not account for the original ballads or for most of those specific qualities which set them off from poetry of art. Whosoever tries to make tradition account for these things, stretches its powers beyond all belief; and a far simpler explanation is at hand. Tradition, of course, is an absolute test in exclusion; the popular ballad of our collection must be, or, like the old printed versions, must once have been, transmitted in this way; but all traditional verse is not ballad, and much of it differs radically. A recent printed collection of deplorably low songs can be put to good use in illustrating this difference. We see not only how four or five genuine ballads stick fiery off from the sooty mass, but also how this underground spreading of songs, which are written in many a case by known authors, fails to divest them of the personal and artistic note. Like that mawkish, sentimental, feebly didactic poem which became, save the mark, a "folk song" in Germany, so a wanton song by Burns or another, impossible for decent print, spreads with changes, and often very great changes, among lovers of the unlovely, until between a couple of versions here, or between these and a copy in some manuscript collection, there is hardly relationship left. So it is with ballad versions. But this vital distinction remains, not only that the song can be traced to its author back from the various versions under popular control, and that the ballad cannot be so traced, but also that the song, in all its windings

and variations of fact and phrase, still bears the mark
of individual authorship and differs in no specific way
from its original, while the ballad, however far it be
followed back, is still a poem specifically different from
the poem of known authors. In other words, both cases
of variation are due to mainly oral, traditional record,
but no trait of the ballad as a species, whether in structure,
in style, in form, or in general spirit, is due to this variation so as to disappear as one approaches its supposed
personal source. Tradition in itself will not explain the
ballad.[1] What it does explain we shall see in the
chapter on Sources.

This impersonal quality of ballads as a species is in
no way disturbed by the use of the first person. The
cases are comparatively few, and the "I" is even then
extrinsic, perfunctory, not personal in a real sense. Ballads of the broadside kind, telling of adventure by bands
of men, armies, or the like, use the first person plural.[2]
The singer of the ballad pretends now and then to have
seen the characters and heard their talk:[3] "By Arthur's

[1] There is no need to point out the personal note of the folk song as
compared with the impersonal note of the ballad. For particular contrasts, however, one may note *Bonny Bee Hom*, Child, no. 92, and its
related "song," *The Lowlands of Holland;* further *Jamie Douglas*,
no. 204, and the song *Waly, Waly*. Folk songs, kittle cattle to shoe in
any case, are uncommonly baffling in English records.

[2] So nos. 164, 285.

[3] Nos. 92, 55, 188, 163, A, 38, 183; see also 108, and 111, — a
"minstrel ballad" out and out. The minstrel is audible enough, and
his "I" is very bold, in ballads like the *Rising in the North*, 175; but
in 182 he is only the singer, not the maker.

Dale as late I went," or "On the dawning of the day, I heard two brothers make their moan," or "As I came in by Dunidier," or "As I was walking all alone." More remotely, as in the very old ballad of "Robyn and Gandelyn," the singer hears "a carping of a clerk," that is, the story of a bookman, a scholar, an authority; and he proceeds to tell what he heard told. What he tells, however, is a genuinely popular and traditional ballad with its refrain. So with the dream-opening, so familiar in medieval literature; "As I was cast in my first sleep" is the beginning of a disordered ballad, "Young Andrew." The harmless character of this "I" of the singer or reciter comes out admirably in the fourth stanza of "Lord Lovel" — the version of the Percy papers, taken down from singing: —

> "He called up his stable-groom,
>   To saddle his milkwhite steed;
> Dey down, dey down, dey down derry down,
>   I wish Lord Lovill good speed" . . .

There is an amusing interpolation of the singer in "Young Beichan." Still less significance attaches to the "I" of a dramatic story such as is told by the victim of "Alison Gross," or begun by Mary Hamilton;[1] in the latter case, and in "The Flower of Serving Men," "I" turns into "she." In quoted stanzas, indeed, the egotism does not count; and nobody grudges the reciter of long-winded ballads his occasional "I tell you in certain." The ballad ego, on the whole, has nothing to say to the question of origins.

[1] No. 173, E. See also 36, *The Laily Worm*, which is "pure tradition."

Traditional, objective, impersonal, as they are, ballads must also tell a definite tale. Although this is a test common to all epic verse, it acquires peculiar significance for the ballads on account of their community of interest, which gathers scattered versions from all times and lands into groups that again seem to form an almost definite and coherent whole. No account of these mutual relations, however broadly sketched, can do justice to them in comparison with a single but comprehensive study like Professor Child's introduction to "Lady Isabel and the Elf-Knight." And yet, for all the community of material, and for all the rigid objectivity in treatment of it, ballads cannot be set off in these terms from narrative and objective poetry of art. Ballads, like folk tales, share some of their stories, their subject and motive, with literature, and at times in a relation of dependence. "King Orfeo," of course, is the old story of Orpheus and Eurydice; Hero and Leander were made to tell their tale of woe again in southern and northwestern Europe; "Sir Hugh" and the Prioress's story in Chaucer deal with the same essential facts, and spring practically from the same legend. Ballads have, as a rule, better claims to priority than the romance can offer; but there are undoubted instances where, so far as material is concerned, ballads derive from the romance. It is true that ballads as they lie before us seem to exist for the sake of their story, and for no other pervasive purpose; but ballads have not always been what they are. Despite its rank as necessary condition, narrative is not a fixed, fundamental, primary fact in the ballad scheme. The ballad was not exclusively epic from its start, as was the heroic lay. The greatest ballads affect us not by the story itself but by the way in which the story is told; and this "way" is not narrative art at high pitch. Narrative art at high pitch we get in the prose sagas of Iceland; they are literature, literature "just on the autumnal verge;"[1] the moment that one brings even the best ballads into contrast with these sagas, one ceases to boast about narrative art as the test of balladry, and one casts about for other explanation of the charm which pervades a "Babylon" or a "Sir Patrick Spens." It will not do to say that ballads are artless narrative, and charm by their artlessness, while the saga is art itself; artless narrative is best studied in the popular tale. This *märchen*, again, itself as old as any æsthetic propensity in man, will do nothing for the origins of balladry; it follows an entirely different line and springs from an entirely different impulse, as any observer can determine for himself who watches the same group of children, now

---

[1] Ker, *Epic and Romance*, p. 235. The sagas, he says, pp. 241 f., "are the last stage in a progress from the earliest mythical imagination and the earliest dirges and encomiums of the great men of a tribe to a consistent and orderly form of narrative literature, attained by the direction of a critical faculty . . . the great victory of the Humanities in the North, at the end of a long process of education." If, now, Professor Ker remarks that "the ballad poetry of the Faroes is derived from Icelandic literary traditions" (pp. 324 f.), he must limit this derivation to narrative material, and — see above, p. 24 — make even that only partial. The ballad genesis is more plainly proved for the Faroes than for any other modern people.

playing "Ring round the Rosy," or what not, singing
and shouting in concert with clasped hands and con-
senting feet, now sitting silent, absorbed, while some one
tells them a story. As with the manner, so with the
material. No test can be obtained for the ballad by a
comparison of its matter with these tales which have long
formed the flotsam and jetsam of European narrative.
The actual community of subject in ballad and folk tale
is limited. Ballads rest primarily on situation and deed
of familiar, imitable type; the popular tale, untram-
meled by rhythmic law, by choral conditions, tends to
a more subtle motive, a more striking fact, a more
unexpected, memorable quality, and a more intricate
coherence of events.

Stories and poetical forms, moreover, stand in no
mutual relation of cause and effect. The point is clear that
when one has traced the story of a given ballad, one has
by no means settled the origins of ballads as a poetic
genre. Professor Child's introduction to "Lady Isabel
and the Elf-Knight" shows the manifold migrations of
a ballad-subject, and Professor Bugge's essay[1] on the
Orpheus and Eurydice motive disposes of the idea that
in such cases the ballads and the legend itself were both
branches of an old myth. But grant that a ballad, "Harpens Kraft," was really made about the year 1400 by a
Scandinavian singer, who got it from a traditional German
version, into which he put certain features, which, in
their turn, came from Scotland or England to the Danes;

[1] "Harpens Kraft," in *Arkiv for Nord. Fil.*, vii, 97 ff. (1891).

suppose that all this ballad material goes back, through English versions of the late thirteenth century, to a romance composed about 1200 by a Breton poet, who retold it, "with Celtic touches," from the old medieval Latin tradition, whither it had come from the classics! So we run a fine chase, through wild country, and are more or less sure — until the next hunt—that we have kept the trail notwithstanding very feeble scent; the fox nobody dreams of finding.[1]   Actually, too, we have acquired valuable information about the migration of a good story. But of the origins of that particular form of poetry to which this subject turned when it was embodied in ballads like "Harpens Kraft," or the Shetland "King Orfeo," we have learned no more than we have learned of the origins of epic, of romance, of popular tale. We still confront the problem of the ballad as a poetic genre.

V. THE BALLAD STRUCTURE

The differencing quality of the ballad of tradition lies not in its subject, which may be anything, not in its setting, which may be anywhere, but in its actual structure. Structure, moreover, must not be misunderstood as style. Manner, style, what is vaguely called the note of ballads, is indeed characteristic and may be unique; but it is not the fundamental fact. The ballad, of course, like any real lyric, must be sung, it must have a tune; and this tune, usually rustic, unsophisticated, is provo-

[1] See the chapter on Sources.

cative as well as reminiscent of accompanying steps; but the same thing is true of many a song utterly foreign to the ballad. The ballad, as its name implies, was originally inseparable from the dance; but other forms of verse were also choral, and the proof of origin in the dance itself must be made, and presently will be made, by more direct proof than this wavering line of connection. So, too, with that other "rustic" note of simplicity, the use of common words in common order, and the lack of all figurative and tropical language; while characteristic of the ballad, this is not its essential mark of structure. Simplicity, moreover, is a very equivocal word. The Icelandic sagas are simple, and so is a lyric of Wordsworth; but the ballads are not simple in this artistic way. William Blake wrote simple lyric verse, and he has the ballad note of repetition; but his lines about the piper piping down the valleys give no ballad effect, while a single phrase —

"O sunflower, weary of time," —

beautiful as it is, carries an inference of pathos and reflection that the ballad never knew. Indeed, it is the thought and meaning of the ballads which are simple, rather than their expression; for while Matthew Arnold wrote very wildly about the ballads' "slang," he was right in attributing to them a dialect of their own; and this dialect is not simple in the severest sense of the word.

Rudeness or roughness, whatever quality superficial

critics contrast in ballads with the smoothness of art, is
even farther from the mark. It is true that they plunge
often into the heart of the subject, without a word of
explanation. "It begins in the fifth act of the play,"
was Gray's admiring comment on a version of "Child
Maurice;" and Dr. Johnson thought that Gray himself stole ballad thunder for the opening of his "Bard."
"This abruptness has nothing new in it. . . . Nay, we
have it in the old song of Johnny Armstrong." But
roughness of the stylistic sort, rude rimes and metres,
are not essential. Cromek[1] says "it was once the opinion
of Burns that a poet of a nice ear and fine taste might
compose songs without the incumbrance of rhyme. He
was led into this error by the seeming dissonance of many
of them in this necessary appendage." But imperfect
rimes do not even characterize the ballad in general, and
are often apparent only to the eye; it need hardly be
added that rhythm in actual ballads, as they were
sung, is always exact to a fault, however the record may
distort it.

Neither the vague test of simplicity nor the false test
of imperfect rhythm and rime will do. We must look
deeper into the case, and find tests that are organic.
The refrain is an organic part of the ballad; it is of great
structural importance; and under certain conditions it
comes close to the requisite test. It establishes beyond
all doubt the lyric and choral origins. Ballads were

[1] *Remains of Nithsdale and Galloway Song*, London, 1810, p. vi, —
quoting from another work.

at first always sung,[1] and always had a refrain;[2] the refrain is incontestably sprung from singing of the people at dance, play, work, going back to that choral repetition which seems to have been the protoplasm of all poetry. Refrains, of course, hold fast in oral tradition, but tend to drop from the record, where text and narrative verses play the only important part. If, now, one finds a ballad made up of verses and a constant refrain, is it not fair to assume that both belong to the same source, and that written composition of the text is far less likely than improvisation in the throng, which is demonstrably responsible for the refrain itself? Indeed, the fact of ballads made in this way stands beyond doubt.[3]

[1] For the singing of a given ballad, say *The Fair Flower of Northumberland*, no. 9, see Deloney, work quoted, p. 195; the maidens "in dulcet manner chanted out this song, two of them singing the Ditty and all the rest-bearing the burden." This is before king and queen; but the process was doubtless the same as in humbler cases. "The oxygen and hydrogen," announced a lecturer heard by royalty, "will now have the honor of amalgamating in the presence of your Royal Highness."

[2] This is proved by Professor Steenstrup, *Vore Folkeviser*, pp. 75 ff. Out of 502 Scandinavian ballads which he examined, only 20 lacked a refrain. In English, owing to the increase of chronicle ballads, the figures are not so striking; but they tell the same tale. Of the 305 ballads in Child's collection, 106 show in some version evidence of chorus or refrain. Of some 1250 versions in all, about 300 have a refrain; but among the old ballads in couplets, out of 31 only 7 lack the refrain as they stand, and even these show traces of it. In the German ballads refrains are even less evident; but the tendency to chronicle ballads, which of course are recited and need no refrain, and the preponderance of rival folk song, explain easily this decadence of the choral element. Wolf has placed beyond doubt the popular origin of refrains: see his *Lais*, etc., pp. 27, 191.

[3] See the Faroe ballad described above, p. 24.

Basing one's assertion on these elements of recurrent refrain and alternate improvisation, one could safely define the ballad, by origins, as a narrative lyric made and sung at the dance and handed down in popular tradition. This formula, of course, strictly valid only for vanished and primitive days, would imply in later stages a dwindling of lyric and choral elements in favor of epic; and it would agree with facts. All Greek poetry, and there is no higher type, began in some kind of singing; poetry everywhere so begins; and the sundering of music and words is a recognized process which would keep pace with the decline of purely choral verse, the rise of individual poets, and the increase of passive interest in story and idea for themselves. Improvisation, once almost universal among peasants and rural folk throughout Europe, is conceded by Aristotle, in an empiric way, as the basis of poetry; theoretically, too, it is only composition in a rude; unreflective stage. The ease of applying communal improvisation to the ballad problem is obvious to any one who reads Professor Kittredge's comments [1] on the process.

Doubtless, now, this ought to serve as a definition of ballad origins. It shows what ballads may, even must, have been. But it is not an adequate account of ballads as they lie before us, of ballads in their bulk and actual text, of the "Child Waters," the "Sir Patrick Spens," the "Twa Sisters" of our collection. The early texts, we say, were mainly improvised by dancers in intervals

[1] Cambridge Ed. Child's *Ballads*, p. xxiv.

of the choral refrain; this is a reasonable supposition, but so far it is only a supposition. It has been denied outright, and other explanations have been given. The texts, one could answer, are not really needed for choral purposes, and, allowing for the difference in time and place, might well have been suggested to a rustic poet by the refrain itself, somewhat as on higher levels of art a crude bit of popular verse suggested "Childe Roland to the Dark Tower Came," or as, by Pater's pretty imagining, a great hymn to love sprang from the repeated *Cras amet* of a Roman festal throng. A rough but efficient criticism might set aside hundreds of stanzas in our ballads which could never have been improvised by a throng of dancers. True, these could be referred to the refining and ennobling process of tradition; but that again is a guess. Why not take the obvious way, giving the choral to the chorus, and the poem to the poet? The simple artistic refrain, from Theocritus and Catullus to Spenser, and the more complicated forms of roundel and triolet and ballade, have something to say to this sweeping claim that ballad texts are derived from purely choral and popular origins. If we are to give the poem itself, whether directly or indirectly, to the chorus, — and that is what the definition by origins really means, — we must find better reason for such an award than mere juxtaposition of refrain and text. This juxtaposition, to be sure, creates a presumption that they spring in the first instance from one and the same source; but such a presumption is offset by the protest of com-

mon sense against the idea of ballads like our "Child
Waters" deriving from the improvisation of a choral
throng. We must face the extant, present facts. Take,
for example, "The Maid and the Palmer," [1] a ballad
known in Faroe, Danish, Swedish, Finnish, found in
the Percy manuscript, and recollected from tradition, as
a fragment, by Sir Walter Scott. The refrain and first
stanza in the Percy version may follow in spite of possible revolt on the part of readers: —

> "The maid shee went to the well to washe,
>   Lillumwham, lillumwham!
> The maid shee went to the well to washe,
>   What then? What then?
> The maid shee went to the well to washe,
> Dew ffell off her lillywhite fleshe.
>   Grandam boy, grandam boy, heye!
> Leg a derry, leg a merry, mett, mer, whoope, whir!
>   Drimance, larumben, grandam boy, heye!"

Relieved of this "burden," we read with interest the text
in its rapid two-line stanza, its dialogue, and its swift
conclusion; if the burden were printed throughout, we
should not read the ballad at all. Those, however, who
sang this ballad, sang the burden with delight. In Scotland it had another burden, a short, articulate one, a
compromise, fused with the text. Now we are just as
sure that the origin of this varying burden or refrain,
purely choral in purpose, was different from the origin
of the epic text, as we are sure that under certain conditions the refrain was the main consideration in the

[1] No. 21.

piece. It is quite possible that many a stanza of independent origin came to be used as refrain for a new ballad. There is the dilemma. Analogy, and even the history of ballad literature, raise, as was said, a fair presumption of common choral origins for refrain and text; the texts themselves often protest against it. We can come to no conclusion until we get some proof of choral origins for the texts themselves.[1]

If we can but lay both presumption and protest aside, study the ballad as a whole and in all its range, text as well as refrain, and fix careful attention upon its structure in every case, we are confronted by certain facts which will lead to definite results, however they may seem at first to beget intolerable confusion. We find ballads, and parts of ballads, where the text is really little more than a progressive refrain. We find ballads which combine this dominant choral structure with simple and straightforward but quite subordinate narrative. We find, again, fairly long ballads which are simple narrative throughout. And, lastly, there is the combination of certain narrative ballads into a coherent epic poem.[2] Chronology of the usual kind has nothing to say in this matter; the epic poem, later and more finished in form, is actually of older record than most of the ballads; and we must

---

[1] It should be added that the history of ballad refrains is still unwritten and presents enormous difficulties. A theory is easily made; its application to facts such as are presented by the Faroe, Icelandic, and Scandinavian burden, often longer than the ballad stanza itself, is difficult to a degree.

[2] *The Gest of Robin Hood*, no. 117.

forget the tyranny of dates. This done, the confusion disappears. It is clear that ballad structure, like the structure of a language, is not stable; and it can be shown that the evolution of the epic out of the simpler dramatic form is a thing of growth easily followed back from stage to stage. The making of the original ballad is a choral, dramatic process and treats a situation; the traditional course of the ballad is really an epic process which tends more and more to treat a series of events, a story.

Before the facts are produced upon which this explanation of balladry must lean, it is well to outline the development in general terms. What is meant by an "epic process"? One must not think of mere epic expansion, such as those *eoiae*, or "like" poems, of Hesiod, said to have been expanded from the separate items in a catalogue of women, or of medieval narratives that may have been suggested by the *ubi sunt* formula, or of the possible working out of old memorial verses. Let us take a more familiar illustration. When an Italian peasant tells a comrade, or a group of comrades, about something which has lately befallen him, the onlooking alien can frequently get the "story" without understanding a word that is said. Action, often directly imitative, is constant; certain sentences recur again and again, along with their proper gestures; and the event itself is reproduced in all its phases as closely as conditions admit. Evidence without end shows that communities in early stages of culture, or in remote places, like the Faroe

Islands, where primitive conditions long survive, are wont to reproduce events and scenes in this same immediate and dramatic fashion; but since a group, not one person, is "telling the story," concerted action and harmonious words are achieved only by a consent of movement and of voice. Hence the fundamental fact of rhythm and chorus. The words, or " text," will be primarily repetition of a pithy, comprehensively descriptive phrase,[1] while the action, already known to all, will admit of variety from the start. Taken in length and breadth, such a "transcript" of events will be best called not a story but a situation, and it will long be limited by the exigencies of dramatic reproduction. Coming back now to our Italian, it is easy to think of him late in life recalling and recounting to his friends the event in question; it is easy to think of his children telling it again to a still later generation. But we know that in the personal reminiscence, and still more in the tale at second hand, dramatic conditions will be sensibly reduced, and epic details will spring up like a young forest about the parent tree. What led to the event, what complicated it and heightened it, what came after it, what sort of man the hero was, and what interplay of character and circumstance: these are details, not to speak of reflective elements that wait so closely upon

[1] So in songs of labor, and in the games of children which imitate these songs, words exactly fit the action: "thus the farmer sows his seed" stands for an older "thus we sow," etc. Compare the pretty Reapers' Song in Peele's *Old Wives' Tale*.

reminiscence, which now will seem necessary to the teller
and interesting to the audience. Violently descriptive
acts, as of the immediate impression, can have no place;
and such action as does occur will be limited to the
climax, to the critical situations. Precisely such a parallel
as was found in primitive literature for the Italian's
immediate "story" is at hand in more developed literature for his reminiscence and for his children's account
of it. So the dramatic, choral *cantilena* of warriors who
fought their battles over again in song passed into the
chanted narrative of the early minstrel. The "we"
of a chorus becomes the "he" or "they" of the rhapsode. Gaston Paris finely remarks that earliest epic verse
both creates and confirms the historical sense of a community, tones down the spontaneous, passionate, momentary elements, regulates expression, and paves the
way for epic of a nobler sort. Traditional ballads, sung
in the homogeneous communities of Europe, helped to
create the social memory; and until this epic process
worked upon lyric and dramatic material, song was
evanescent. Ballads still bear the mark of immediate
relation to their theme, so that no particulars of time
or place or person need to be given. Statistics, as Child
remarks, when too exact, are enough to throw suspicion
upon a ballad. *Le roi a fait battre tambour*, — "the
king" is enough. Nearer epic perfection, however,
ballads must particularize with "Edward our King,"
or fasten upon the type, as in Charlemagne and Robin
Hood. In the earlier stages of this epic process, it is in-

evitable that aristocratic personages should fill the stage,
a fact that has made some students of the ballad hesitate
to allow it any but aristocratic origins. But the social
group is naturally represented by its leaders, the prince,
the knight, the warrior. It is only in very recent development that the humble or common man is put into the
foreground of story and play; and as a rule, conforming
to the fifth and last stage of the development outlined
by Gaston Paris, this hero is told in prose. Summing
up the epic process, then, we may say that it gradually
absorbs the situation into the narrative, the chorus into
the text.

 This is surely a reasonable assumption. It is simple
and clear. But one must make it even more reasonable;
and simplicity is not always a good feature in explanations
of so complex an affair. The defect of nearly all theories of literary evolution lies in their attempt to make
an assumed movement or process work steadily, singly,
and untroubled by other influences. Quite the contrary
must have been the case. It is preposterous to assert
that at such a date and in such a place ballads were at the
x-position, and just two centuries later, in such another
place, had advanced to y-position. But it is fair to
assume a general progress, however crossed and baffled
by other forces, from direct impression rendered in a
"situation" to traditional reminiscence rendered in
narrative; and if the facts of balladry can be shown
to conform to such a general theory of progress, not, indeed, in close ranks marching like an army, not even as

an infallible series of accretions, but as a succession of
changes in structure revealed by actual specimens of
the ballad itself, then the principles of science entitle
that theory to precedence over mere cavil and criticism
without stay of facts or warrant of research. For this
theory of epic progress falls into line with two great
tendencies in man's artistic career, — with that social,
gregarious habit of reproducing events, which begins
in the mimetic, choral situation, and on its own lines
is developed into triumphs of the later drama,[1] as well
as with that personal, reminiscent habit which follows
hero or hero-group through long reaches of time and
many changes of scene for the edification of a listening
throng. There was in primitive life a time to dance, and
there was a time for passive curiosity, for getting information and reminiscence. Choral poetry in some shape,
and also some form of epic, seem to be of equal birth and
equally prosperous development. Each borrows something from the other; drama must still have its complicated story, no longer the simple situation of its prime,
while story will boast of its spectacular, dramatic features. Epic, as every one knows, cannot part with dialogue; like Thucydides in history, the writer of novel or
romance, even of verse-epic, gives as much as he can of
the actual speech of his characters. So with the ballad.
Dialogue, easiest form of improvisation, was the evident
development from choral song, alternating with a general
refrain; dialogue and refrain make up many a ballad

[1] See E. K. Chambers, *The Mediæval Stage*, for these beginnings.

still.   Repetition, of course, — for a primitive choral
must be all repetition, — was the protoplasm; and it can
be distinctly traced in the dialogue of older ballad versions.   Supplying the refrain, "Sheath and Knife" ends
thus: —

> " 'There is ships o' your father's sailing on the sea,
>   (*The brume blooms bonnie and says it is fair,*)
>   That will bring as good a sheath and a knife unto thee.'
>   (*And we'll never gang down to the brume onie mair.*)
>
> " 'There is ships o' my father's sailing on the sea,
>   (*The brume blooms bonnie and says it is fair,*)
>   But sic a sheath and a knife they can never bring to me.'
>   (*Now we'll never gang down to the brume onie mair.*) "

This element of dialogue in the ballads is very important, and deserves careful study for itself.   It has its own
hint of choral origins.   Abrupt, dramatic openings, with
a dialogue only partially explained, are characteristic;
but the choral influences are best followed in a more
pervasive and definite guise.   At this more sweeping
proof of our proposition we are now to look; but it may
be said generally that the course of the popular ballad
is from a mimetic choral situation, slowly detaching
itself out of the festal dance, and coming into the reminiscent ways of tradition in song and recital.   Of that
primitive choral ballad nothing is left but the traces of
its course and the survival of its elements in later stages
of evolution.   In its original fluid and quite choral form,
the ballad could no more be preserved as a poem than
molten iron is preserved as such in the casting.   Only

after it had cooled and hardened into some consistent shape, in some particular mould, could it be handed down as a definite ballad, sung or recited from age to age. Naturally the reminiscent elements increased; the process of transfer from dramatic to epic influences resulted in one instance and at a very late stage in the "Gest of Robin Hood." But the ways of the English and Scottish ballad were mainly those of a survival; it had fallen on evil times, and shrank everywhere from the onrush of letters; so that most of our traditional versions remained in a far older stage of progress than the "Gest" or even than its component ballads, often, indeed, in close neighborhood to choral origins. — But this is theory, statement. How do we know it all? What are the facts which prove such structural and specific changes along the traditional line?

VI. CHORAL AND EPIC ELEMENTS

There is a division, easy to note, between the structure in longer narrative ballads, like those of the Robin Hood cycle, the "Cheviot," and "Otterburn," and the structure in shorter ballads of tradition. Reversing the course, we can follow that epic process from chronicle to situation, from what seems to be a mature stage, marked by length of treatment, rapidity of narration, coherence of parts, and individual recitation, back to a stage marked by brevity of treatment, dominance of a situation, lack of narrative movement, and preponderance of choral singing. In this process, too, another element, which is the fundamental element in all primitive forms of poetry, should come and does come more and more into prominence, — verbal repetition. The maturer the stage of poetry, the less repetition and the more facts; reversed, the fewer facts, the greater amount of repetition.[1] More than this, the two stages in ballad structure, the earlier of course with some modification of original choral elements, can be found side by side in a single traditional ballad. It will be profitable to study such a ballad at length. What has been claimed as the story of Hero and Leander appears in a group of ballads widely distributed through Europe, but fullest and oldest in the Low German. The best version comes from the neighborhood of Paderborn,[2] and the following is a literal translation of it.

> "There once were two kings'-children,
> They held one another so lief !
> They could not come together,
> The water was far too deep.
>
> "'Sweetheart, art thou not swimmer?
> Sweetheart, then swim to me.
> I will set thee up two tapers
> Shall make a light for thee.'

[1] The exceptions to this rule are only apparent, such as recurring phrases of epic; refrain lines in artistic forms of lyric, like rondeau or triolet, which were really developed out of popular iteration; repetition in dialogue, as in early French poetry; and the recent outbreak of repetition as a kind of prose rhythm in Maeterlinck and D'Annunzio.

[2] Reifferscheid, *Westfälische Volkslieder*, p. 1. — For French and Italian forms see *Le Flambeau Éteint*, Crane, no. 111, and Nigra, p. 68, with references to the Spanish.

" A false old witch she heard them
  In her sleeping-room, ah me !
She went and put out the tapers:
  Sweetheart was left in the sea.

" 'T was [1] on a Sunday morning
  When folk were gay and glad, —
All gay but the king's daughter;
  She shut her eyes so red.

" ' O mother,' said she, ' mother,
  My eyes they trouble me;
May I not walk a little
  By the edge of the murmuring [2] sea ?'

" ' O daughter,' said the mother,
  ' Alone thou must not go;
Wake up thy youngest brother,
  And he shall with thee go.'

" ' Alack, my youngest brother,
  'T is such a losel child;
He shoots me all the seafowl
  Along the ocean tide.

" ' And e'en if he spared the tame ones
  And only shot the wild,
Yet all the folk will tell you —
  'T was done by the king's child.

[1] *Et was*, matching the *et wasen* of the first stanza. Here is the fresh start. For we now come to the second part, made up of two situations; with the coherence of these, compare a similar case in *The Lass of Roch Royal* (Child, no. 76) and *The Mother's Malison, or Clyde's Water* (Child, no. 216). See note on p. 90, below.

[2] "Murmuring" is artistic. Swedish versions make her ask first to go " walk in the garden," and then " to the white sea-strand," where " white " matches our adjective here. The Frisian has simply " by the edge of the sea."

  "'O mother,' said she, 'mother,
    My eyes they trouble me;
    May I not walk a little
      By the edge of the murmuring sea?'

  "'O daughter,' said the mother,
    'Alone thou must not go;
    Wake up thy youngest sister,
      And she shall with thee go.'

  "'Alack, my youngest sister,
    'T is such a losel child,
    She plucks me all the flowers
      Along the ocean tide.

  "'And e'en if she spared the tame ones,
    And only plucked the wild,
    Yet all the folk will tell you —
      'T was done by the king's child.

  "'O mother,' said she, 'mother,
    My heart is sore in me:
    Let others go to the churches,
      I will pray by the murmuring sea.'

  "On her head, then, the king's daughter
    She set her golden crown,
    She put upon her finger
      A ring of the diamond stone.[1]

  "To the church went up the mother,
    To the sea the daughter went down;

[1] It is interesting to note the different kinds of repetition. Swedish versions describe the heroine's dress; when she asks leave to go to the garden, and then to the sea, she wears "the scarlet white, likewise the scarlet blue;" when she goes to the shore, it is "in scarlet white, likewise in scarlet black." One frequently finds the demand of structure or of rhythm leading thus to a kind of verbal confusion.

She walked so long by the water
The fisherman she found.

"'O fisher, dearest fisher,
    Great wage can now be won;
Set me your nets in the water,
    And fish me the king's son.'

"He set his nets in the water,
    The sinkers sank to the ground;
He fished and he fished so truly,
    'T was the king's son that he found.

"And then took the king's daughter
    From her head her golden crown, —
'Lo there, O noble fisher,
    Thy wage I pay thee down.'

"She drew from off her finger
    Her ring of the diamond stone, —
'Lo there, O noble fisher,
    Thy wage I pay thee down.'

"And in her arms she clasped him,
    The king's son, woe to tell,
And sprang with him into the billows:
    'O father, O mother, farewell!'"

We have in this ballad two well-marked and clearly
divided parts, although the whole makes a perfectly
good story. The first part is a complete, straightforward
narrative, very brief; the second part is a kind of supplement, a protracted situation, and very long. Swedish
versions, to be sure, give the first part in greater detail:
the swimmer's start is described, his weariness, his confusion when the lights go out. A page of the court sees

him drown, and brings the news. Execration, in an
"aside," disposes of the witch for time and eternity.
But short or long, nothing of this first part, the narrative,
is really needed for the second part, the situation, save
the drowned lover; and any lover, provided he is distinctly drowned, will serve. Juliet far outshines Romeo.
Nor, again, is there so much interest in the narrative part
as in the supplement, the situation part, which really
consists of two situations closely joined by motive, time,
action. In many cases this arrangement, which is typical
in most of the short English ballads, could be called by
some such name as "the split situation," — not eupho-
nious, to be sure, but convenient. We shall often meet
it.[1] Going back to the Hero and Leander case, we find
that as between narrative and situation, the main divisions of the ballad, not only is the suture evident, but the
style and structure of the second part mark it off from
the first part. The first part is fairly epic, telling its
straightforward story; the second part is full of what
may be called incremental repetition. There is nothing
straightforward about it; the story, if that word may be

---

[1] This "split situation" marks the first breach of the dramatic
unity of time, and the entering wedge of narrative. The trail of it can
be followed even into long and awkward chronicle ballads like *Hugh
Spencer* (no. 158) and *Sir Andrew Barton* (no. 167); in a short ballad,
The Great Silkie (no. 113), the situation has an effective combination
with retrospect and prospect, the latter worthy of Heine. Ordinarily
the "split situation" appears in such ballads as nos. 76 and 216,
mentioned above, p. 87, note. Compare also *Prince Heathen* (no. 104),
hardly a "fragment" as Child calls it, the popular *Lord Lovel* (no. 75),
and many ballads of the same plan.

used, keeps lingering, still lingering, and then leaps to a
new part somewhat like those clocks whose hands point
only to the five-minute intervals on the dial. A great
deal has been made of this leaping, springing movement
of ballads, the omission of details, the ignoring of con-
nective and explanatory facts, the seven-league stride
over stretches of time and place which in regular epic
would claim pages of elaborate narrative. Far too little,
on the other hand, has been made of the lingering, of
the succession of stanzas or of verses, mainly in triads,
which are identical save for one or two pivotal words,[1]
delaying and almost pausing on the almost pausing
action, and marking a new phase in the grouping of
persons and events. And practically nothing at all has
been made of the combination of these two features as
a formula of the situation-ballad which points unerringly
back to choral conditions, to a dance where the crowd
moves to its own singing, and where the song, mainly
repetition, got its matter from successive stages or shifts
of what may be called a situation rather than a story.
Literal repetition yielded, for the sake of progress, to
this repetition with increments, developing the situation;
and incremental repetition came soon to be the close
pattern of ballad stuff. Refrains may stay or vanish;
in the record they cease to appeal to voice and ear, and

[1] Troubling eyes and the wish to walk — repeated, with a slight
change in the answers from "brother" to "sister," in two stanzas —
shift in the third increment of the triad to sore heart and the need to
pray. The second of the two situations condenses the repetition.

seem a waste of energy; but incremental repetition can wane only by the slow process of "making over," by excision and connection, from one version to another. Hence its great significance. It supplies a visible link between oldest choral repetition and actual text; and in the ballad just quoted it furnishes, now by its presence and now by its absence, a capital illustration of the evolution of epic out of choral conditions.

For it is beyond doubt that the situation in ballads is older, more characteristic, and more essential, than the unmixed, smooth-flowing narrative. As was pointed out in the preceding section, all ballads of tradition carry with them the marks of two great interests that have ever been active on the æsthetic side of man's life. One is the natural desire of everybody to hear a good story; and the other that equally natural desire of the normal man to gratify his social and emotional propensities by singing, dancing, and enacting, along with his fellows, a familiar or exciting situation. The adjustment of these two claims is neither simple combination, as in our "Hero and Leander," nor that cheerful but clumsy fusion found in the Shetland traditional ballad of "King Orfeo." [1] It is a matter of evolution; choral and dramatic elements ruled in earliest stages, while epic prevails at the end. In the ballad now under consideration, the epic preface is a summary, an accretion,[2] a later thought, and therefore can easily fall away. It does fall away. Many

[1] No. 19.
[2] See note on *Two Brothers*, below, p. 123.

versions drop it altogether, or rather, as Reifferscheid
concedes, *never had it to drop*. Abrahamson, who heard
this ballad sung by a housemaid in Denmark about the
year 1750, says that she always began with the daughter's
request, with abrupt dialogue of the situation, and with
no preliminary narrative.   In like manner the Lettish
version begins: —

> "Ah, how sore my head is aching,
>   Ah, my head is aching sore; —
> Let me, mother, darling mother,
>   Let me wander by the shore."

Such, too, is the opening of many other versions.

This addition of epic details to verse which in the first
instance springs from a choral and ceremonial source, is
familiar upon other fields. So common is repetition in all
religious rites, that its vogue in poetry is now and then
ascribed to a liturgical source rather than to the obvious
communal and festal influence. It is the choral, public,
communal origin of all liturgies that explains their repetition; and their epic part must be explained along with
the epic of ballads. Charms or incantations have a brief
narrative introduction, a kind of Olympian credential,
often detachable from the charm itself; but in such a
ritual as the hymn of the Arval Brothers in Rome, all is
choral and fairly resonant with the steps of the dance.
There can be no question that this is the original form;
why should narrative come into the ancient rite? It is
worth noting, too, that the inscription which preserves
this hymn, in its invocation to Mars, gives most of the
verses three times in laborious repetition; iteration must

have been a serious matter when so much of it had to be cut in stone. All poetry which begins in these public rites, in funeral and marriage and whatever festal occasion, has an insistent note of repetition, at first literal and then incremental. As one recedes from choral conditions, direct reference to the dance, as in the Arval Hymn —

"Leap o'er the threshold! Halt! Now beat the ground!" —

is apt to fall away, and narrative comes in to explain and justify the rite itself. Precisely so with old ritual and what passes as its myth, with magic ceremonies, mainly a mimetic dance, and the legend or legends which explain the rite in epic fashion and give a reason for the faith that is in it. The primacy of ritual is sustained by a mass of ethnological evidence. Often several legends are found to explain the same ceremony; and trustworthy authorities regard the former as derived from the latter.[1] Beatty's study of the St. George Plays in England makes it almost certain that the underlying and original function was a magic, dramatic ritual, full of dance, song, and mimetic action, to symbolize the awakening of the powers of nature. With Christianity the legend, such as it was, needed a new form; and the story of St. George was adapted to the old play, changing so far to fit the original rite as to make the hero first a victim to hostile powers and then the subject of a revival or resurrection. Frazer, in his "Golden Bough," has brought abundant evidence for our general thesis. A myth is never the

[1] See Beatty, work quoted, pp. 313, 323. And see above, p. 45.

basis of ceremony, — epic, in other words, never gave birth in the first instance to drama. The dramatic fact may be developed by the epic process into narrative of whatever kind; and myth is a projection of early rites.

Such was also the case with ritual of a later and more domestic sort. The old Corsican funeral songs were called not only *lamenti*, but *ballati*, because of the dance that modern generations know no more. "Make wide the circle," ran an ancient lament, "and dance the *caracolu;* for this sorrow is very sore." The dance vanished, but the *vocero* remained; and it long held the incremental repetition of choral grief. Later rose the epic or historic elegy, the panegyric. Traces faint enough but sure of this custom can be found in our own ballads. A kind of *vocero*, with haunting refrain and the usual epic, explanatory stanzas, is to be found in "Bonny James Campbell;"[1] while incremental repetition marks the choral part of "The Bonny Earl of Murray,"[2] in no sense a primitive or even unsophisticated ballad, but interesting for the detachment of narrative from situation and for the echo of an old lament.

> " Ye Highlands and ye Lawlands,
>   Oh where hae ye been?
>   They have slain the Earl of Murray
>   And they layd him on the green.
>
> "'Now wae be to thee, Huntly!
>   And wherefore did you sae?

[1] Child, no. 210. The wife's lament, though different in two versions, is characteristic of the real *vocero*.

[2] No. 181.

I bade you bring him wi' you,
But forbade you him to slay.' [1]

" *He was a braw gallant,*
  And he rid at the ring;
And the bonny Earl of Murray,
  Oh he might have been a king!

" *He was a braw gallant,*
  And he playd at the ba';
And the bonny Earl of Murray
  Was the flower amang them a'.

" *He was a braw gallant,*
  And he playd at the glove;
And the bonny Earl of Murray,
  Oh he was the queen's love.

" Oh lang will his lady
  Look o'er the Castle Down,
Ere she see the Earl of Murray
  Come sounding through the town." [2]

We shall also see how the riddle, at first mere question
and answer in the circle of dancing folk, is taken out of its
first setting and embodied in a little epic or tale. One does
not need, however, to rely on these analogies to show that
the epic or narrative part of ballads is detachable from

[1] This dramatic turn in the narrative is supposed to be spoken by the
king to Huntly, whose followers killed the Earl in February, 1592.

[2] The smoothness and pathos of the ballad, and the source of it in
Ramsay's *Tea-Table Miscellany*, give it a sophisticated if elegant note,
as compared with the version B (from recitation), with its homely *vocero*
touch at the end. Nevertheless, the triad and the incremental repetition
are of the true traditional type, and the groundwork of the ballad is both
popular and of genuine, if remote, choral origin.

the older situation, and so to prove that the ballad of
situation is offspring of the festal dance. The latter process stands out clearly for itself. In the long reaches of
time, to be sure, very few ballads that were actually composed at the dance have come down to us. Two considerations should always be borne in mind. Such a ballad,
apart from its occasion, would have little of what we call
literary merit, and would not commend itself for written
record; and where it did find record, the tendency to
suppress repetitions would be almost irresistible. The
only real preservative of this choral repetition is when it
passes into the actual structure of the ballad and so for a
long time defies the epic impulses of smoothness and proportion. Nevertheless, traces of actual choral repetition
can be found. Not only is it certain that ballads were
made in the festal throng; some survive that were used
for the dance, and these afford in their structure clear
evidence of actual dramatic and choral origin. The
Ditmarsh folk of Holstein, whose old dances have been
carefully described,[1] had a certain *springeltanz* which,
despite a corrupted and abbreviated text, shows incremental repetition of the type just noted, and a situation

[1] Neocorus, *Chronik*, ed. Dahlmann, i, 177, who says the people have
fitted nearly all their songs to the dance "in order to remember them
better" and keep them current, gives this interesting account. The
"foresinger" plays a great part, with choral answer and refrain; but
there are whole ballads where all the persons sing as they dance. This
is precisely the case with old French dances; but while the latter are all
"aristocratic" to the point of making their modern investigators doubt
the existence of "popular" customs, here are genuine communal dances
and songs of the "folk." See above, p. 24.

akin to the first situation of the second part of the Hero
and Leander ballad.   It is the formula of "asking permission" to go somewhere or to do something,[1] — in this
case, to join the festal dance itself.

> " 'The summer days are coming,
>   The pleasant summer tide,
>   And lasses and lads are dancing
>   In the dale,' — so spake the wife.

> " 'Dear mother, little mother,
>   To the evening dance I'd go,
>   `Where I hear the gay drums beating,
>   Where I hear the pipers blow.'

> " 'O nay, my daughter, never that,
>   To sleep thou'lt go, thou'lt go. . . .'
>   .   .   .   .
>   .   .   .   .

> " 'O mother mine, that makes me woe,
>   That makes me woebegone;
>   And come I not to the evening dance,
>   To death I would be done.'

> " 'Nay, nay, O nay, my daughter,
>   Alone thou shalt not go;

[1] Getting permission to go and visit a dangerous gallant or other
fascinating person is found in the continental versions of the *Lady
Isabel* group; see Child, i, 26, and "relative-climax," below, p. 102.
Compare also for English ballads the incremental repetition of this
formula in *The Cruel Brother* (no. 11) and even in the less popular class like *Katharine Jaffray* (no. 221).   It is effectively used in tragic
ballads represented by the German *Christinchen ging in'n Garten*,
Reifferscheid, no. 2, and in the whole class of which *The Maid Freed
from the Gallows* (Child, no. 95) is type.

> But waken up thy brother
> And let him with thee go.'

> " 'My brother is young, is but a child,
> And him I'll never wake;
> I'd rather rouse another man
> With whom I'm fain to speak.' "

Further escort was doubtless suggested and declined; but the fact remains that here, in an actual dancing ballad, however imperfectly recorded, is the situation, and practically nothing more. The mother prophesies evil, but submits, — reminding one of the mother in Her Nithart's verses;[1] and the daughter merely goes to the dance, meets a knight, and is kissed and claimed as partner by him. That is all this dance-ballad needed. In a Danish version,[2] however, which has lost its connection with the actual dance and come to serve other interests in the course of tradition, narrative and tragedy triumph. It is the king who meets fair Signelille; the queen hears, then sees her; and promptly poisons her with a cup of wine. A story, from whatever source, has first attached itself to

[1] *Deutsche Liederdichter des* 12–14 *Jhdts.*, 3d ed., p. 104. Note the daughter's wish: —

> " Mother, let me wend
> Afield with the merry band,
> And let me dance the ring !
> 'T is long since I have heard the girls
> New ditties sing."

That is, they are singing new songs at the dance, after the medieval fashion.

[2] Grundtvig, iii, 165. There is a hint of this old "choosing partners" motive at the end of the *Revesby Sword Play*.

this simple situation, and then has dominated it. Such a development of epic out of dramatic and choral interests is natural enough, and can often explain differences between related versions of a given ballad. Thus " The Bonny Lass of Anglesey," [1] in its two Scottish versions, is mainly narrative and has only traces of incremental repetition; the lass tires out a number of dancers in a match made by the king, and wins her "fifteen ploughs," her mill, and for husband the fairest knight in the court. In the corresponding Danish ballad,[2] however, the main situation is the dance itself, where a king's son offers one gift after the other, only to be refused, until he pledges honor and troth. Then follows the story, still, to be sure, with incremental repetition and the refrain of a dancing ballad, but with distinctly epic interest and in this case a very romantic conclusion.[3] Now the actual stories differ considerably in what seem to be varying versions under different names; while the dance, as Grundtvig says, may be regarded as the characteristic and stable feature, — one may add, the original feature. No better case of incremental repetition, along with refrain,[4] as sole material of the ballad, could be found than in this first half, which echoes the very steps and motions of the dance, —

> "'Christine, Christine, tread a measure for me!
> A silken sark I will give to thee.'

[1] Child, no. 220.
[2] *Liden Kirstins Dans*, Grundtvig, v, 119 f.
[3] Compare the romantic conclusion of *Tærningspillet*, below, p. 118.
[4] Omitted in the verses quoted here.

> " ' A silken sark I can get me here,
>   But I'll not dance with the Prince this year.'
>
> " ' Christine, Christine, tread a measure for me,
>   Silver-clasped shoes I will give to thee.'
>
> " ' Silver-clasped shoes I can get,' " etc.

The same refusal, in the same words; and next a clasp
of gold, half of a gold ring, a pair of silver-hilted knives,
each with the refusal in answer, — and then " honor and
troth." Knowing how common is the gift of improvisation
with unspoiled rural folk everywhere, one sees how easily
this sort of dialogue could spring up at the dance, stayed
upon a lively refrain, and ending with the end of the particular situation. The next departure is epic and traditional, — a story to explain or comment on the situation.
Such is the case in our Danish ballad. In the Scottish
version situation and story are fused to the loss of nearly
all the choral features; but very different is the case with
a ballad of no æsthetic value, indeed, but of the highest
importance for the significance of its dramatic situation
and its primitive form of structure, — " The Maid Freed
from the Gallows." [1] Here one can really think himself
with the earliest ballad-makers. The song is formed by
incremental repetition alone; it has no epic preface, no
narrative, but such as can be guessed from the situation;
it is dramatic from beginning to end. It has no refrain,

[1] Child, no. 95. Professor Kittredge, in the one-volume ed., p. xxv,
uses an American version of this ballad to show how easily mere choral
singing of a crowd, with slightest touch of invention, could improvise a
ballad.

and needs none; the whole piece might be called an incremental refrain in dialogue. It deals with a situation, common to many ballads of Europe, which brings out the "climax of relatives;"[1] and it is of course derived, in the length and breadth of its vogue, from oral tradition.

> " 'O good Lord Judge, and sweet Lord Judge,
> Peace for a little while !
> Methinks I see my own father
> Come riding by the stile.
>
> " 'Oh father, oh father, a little of your gold,
> And likewise of your fee !
> To keep my body from yonder grave
> And my neck from the gállows-tree.'
>
> " 'None of my gold now shall you have,
> Nor likewise of my fee;
> For I am come to see you hang'd,
> And hanged you shall be.'
>
> " 'O good Lord Judge, and sweet Lord Judge,
> Peace for a little while !
> Methinks I see my own mother
> Come riding by the stile.
>
> " 'O mother, O mother, a little of your gold,
> And likewise of your fee,
> To keep my body from yonder grave,
> And my neck from the gallows tree.'
>
> " 'None of my gold now shall you have,
> Nor likewise of my fee;
> For I am come to see you hang'd,
> And hanged you shall be.' "

[1] See below, pp. 120 ff.

Two more triads deal precisely in the same way with
sister and brother; it is clear that this line could stretch
farther than the eight kings in "Macbeth," and that no
faintest spark of "invention" is needed for such a song
once the first stanzas are achieved. Only its definite situation, its grouping of persons, its distinct if monotonous
narrative progress, and the climax, presently to be
quoted, sunder it from the great mass of cumulative
songs, some of which serve the same purpose of a festal
dance.[1] But when the singer chose, or the supply of relatives ceased, this little dramatic ballad of a situation
found its end to general satisfaction, — as follows: —

> " 'O good Lord Judge, and sweet Lord Judge,
>   Peace for a little while !
> Methinks I see my own true love
>   Come riding by the stile.

> " 'O true love, O true love, a little of your gold,
>   And likewise of your fee,

[1] These cumulative songs are conceded generally to the popular muse.
Most of them are mere repetition save for a single increment to the
stanza. See *Beginnings of Poetry*, pp. 201 ff. As for ballads, version K
of *Lamkin* (Child, no. 93, ii, 333 f.) can be continued as long as female
names will last. No. 274, *Our Goodman*, is a jocular cumulative ballad;
it is highly interesting to note (Child, v, 90) that "the lace-makers of
Vorey are wont to recite or sing [the counterpart of] this ballad winter
evenings *as a little drama*." So, too, in Lorraine and in Provence. The
old dancing-song of the East Frisians is an extremely interesting case of
cumulative repetition (cock, ox, cat, dog, dove) used in figures of the
dance, as distinguished from the incremental repetition of this *Maid
Freed from the Gallows*. The latter is more dramatic, and is farther
removed from the memory-tests of cumulative verse. — See *Buske di
Remmer* in Böhme, *Liederbuch*, pp. 378 ff.

To save my body from yonder grave
And my neck from the gallows tree.'

" 'Some of my gold now shall you have,
And likewise of my fee;
For I am come to see you sav'd
And saved you shall be.' " [1]

This ballad of " The Maid Freed from the Gallows," in its European variants, is extraordinarily widespread and popular; [2] in remote Finland there are fifty versions of it. Now and then a narrative has been prefixed to explain the situation, as in the long Sicilian version; but the core of the thing is the situation itself. The setting varies at will. A girl is drowning, or is to be carried off by pirates; she appeals vainly to father, brother, sister, mother, but all refuse to save her, to ransom her, to sell a red coat, a house, a castle, what not; and they tell the sailors to "let her drown," until finally the lover is willing to sell himself as slave to the oar and so redeem his sweetheart. Whatever the details, incremental structure, combined with the climax of relatives, is the essential and

[1] This happy ending commended itself in two versions of *Mary Hamilton* (no. 173), turning the edge of tragedy. In X, however, the true-love refuses, a mere interlude, and the ballad has its usual end. An inversion of this same situation, with even clearer and quite persistent reference to choral conditions, is *La Ballerina*, an Italian ballad, where a woman will not stop dancing "for the reported death of father, mother, brother, sister, husband, but when told that her boy is dead, asks the players to cease." — Child, v, 231.

[2] See Child, iii, 516 ; v, 90, 231; Reifferscheid, notes to *O Schipmann*, pp. 138 ff.; and the discussion by Liebrecht, *Zur Volkskunde*, pp. 235 f.

invariable element; choral origins are made certain by internal evidence, by traditional connection with the dance, and by the important test of survival. For this ballad in at least one of its English versions, in a Faroe version, and in sundered groups like the Danish and the Magyar, is still used as an actual game or dance, now for children and now for older folk.[1]

Here is the real connecting link between ballads as they appear in our collections and that choral, communal origin towards which so many probabilities have pointed. The process cannot be reversed. To make the dance or game a terminal and accidental application of verse written for epic purposes is to ignore obvious facts. Ballads named from the dance are so named by origins and not by destination. In late stages of development, to be sure, a popular play, a folk drama, as it is called, could be founded on a popular ballad, as in the fragment, printed by Professor Child from a manuscript older than 1475, and evidently based on the ballad of "Robin Hood and Guy of Gisborne." But this "dramatic piece" is at the end of a long process of evolution in folk plays and, like the ballad itself, has few if any choral elements left.[2]

[1] In the Faroe version, still used for the dance, as many relatives can be interposed before the lover-climax as the players please. It is really a game, with two parties: the girl and her friends, and the pirates. The dance ends when, after the refusal of all the friends and relatives to intervene, — that is, to dance with her, — the girl is "rescued" by her betrothed, and the two dance together a final figure. — See the ballad in Hammershaimb, *Færøsk Anthologi*, i, 268 f.

[2] The Robin Hood plays "are subsequent to the development of religious drama," and "are of the nature of interludes, and were doubt-

Robin Hood plays were presented in London and other cities, and even before the court of Henry VIII; and it is probable, as Chambers points out, that this Robin was at first only the Robin of French *pastourelles*, and later identified with the popular ballad hero. The primitive play, festival, rite, are never derived from any stage of the ballad, legend, myth; these, it is generally conceded, spring in the first instance from the dramatic and communal presentation. Apart from possible liturgical sources for certain phases of the ballad, we may be content with its manifest origins in the dance. Dances, as overwhelming evidence, ethnological and sociological, can prove, were the original stuff upon which dramatic, lyric, and epic impulses wove a pattern that is traced in later narrative ballads mainly as incremental repetition. Separation of its elements, and evolution to higher forms, made the dance an independent art, with song, and then music, ancillary to the figures and the steps; song itself passed to lyric triumphs quite apart from choral voice and choral act; epic went its artistic way with nothing but rhythm as memorial of the dance, and the story instead of dramatic situation; drama retained the situation, the action, even the chorus and the dance, but submitted them to the shaping and informing power of individual genius. Only in these earliest and rudest ballads of the actual choral dance, and in their late sur-

less written, like the plays of Adan de la Hale, by some clerk or minstrel. . . . They are, therefore, in a less degree folk-drama than sword-dances and the like." — E. K. Chambers, *The Mediæval Stage*, i, 178.

vival as children's games, are the original elements visible in what is approximately the original combination. European ballads of the dance, in their dramatic form, lingered with remote homogeneous communities like that of the Faroes, or among the happy folk of Holstein before the innovations came which Neocorus so feelingly deplores; even in the record these ballads have been submitted to the merest touch of epic explanation. The Faroe ballad of relatives, for example, took its situation directly from life; rovers who carried off girls are still held in vivid remembrance on the islands; and it is with a shudder as of real peril that the piece is still enacted and sung. Visitors of long ago, and visitors of yesterday, tell of the force with which the Faroe folk realize this simple situation, their dramatic fervor and their intense interest in their parts. To feel the ballad as one dances it is the primary stage in its development,[1] not the final lapse into decay; such customs bring one close to the real situation, the real event. If Chambers is right, the homely but affecting ballad of "Andrew Lammie"[2] "used in former times to be presented in a dramatic shape at rustic meet-

---

[1] That the cante-fable, a late and artistic, if often successful affair (such as *Aucassin and Nicolette*), cannot be the protoplasm common to folk tale and ballad, as Mr. Joseph Jacobs suggested, is evident. The ballad in its beginnings is contemporary, choral, rhythmic; the tale is reminiscent prose. Combination of verse and prose is always late, always artificial or artistic, and is impossible for choral conditions. See *Beginnings of Poetry*, pp. 71 f., and such hints as Child gives, i, 46, and elsewhere.

[2] Child, no. 233. Compare, too, the dramatic singing of the *Twa Brothers* at the St. George play: see below, p. 123.

ings in Aberdeenshire;" and it is probable that a like tale could be told of many another ballad now known in none but its reminiscent and traditional versions.

Similar considerations must prevail in view of the survival of a primitive stage of ballads in the games of children. Survivals of this sort are really a rescue and not a funeral rite. They revive the past of communal festivity as in other forms they revive the past of a ritual, an old ceremonial dance. For whatever reason, too, these very games are now passing away in their turn; but such as they are, these diversions of boys and girls were once the æsthetic expression of a whole adult community quite as homogeneous in its unlettered life as the crowd of children at play is homogeneous in terms of inexperience and youth. In a survival we are always looking at things through a reversed spy-glass; the primitive folk looked through the right end, and what this mere game represents was once poetry, music, drama, bringing the fate and mystery of life into larger outline and more majestic groupings. It is not romantic nonsense to say that the choral effect, even now, of a few simple words sung many times over by many voices, has an æsthetic appeal quite independent of verbal associations. In poetry we moderns — modern in the sense that an Athenian at his Euripidean tragedy was modern — demand the "lyric cry;" under the conditions which ruled when earliest ballads were made, men needed the choral cry. Distinct from both is the reminiscent, less exciting and more satisfying, quite objective story of the epic, — the middle way, neither "cathartic" like the drama nor a relief of personal emotion like the lyric. Ballads tended from dramatic beginnings into this middle way.[1] The ballads that we have are not, in bulk, of the primitive dramatic type, where all that directly interested the community fell into mimetic action with song. Tradition had doubtless selected and preserved some of the best ballads of situation; a few, purely dramatic, had survived with the dance; but an impulse not purely dramatic and choral had come into play. Set in words and song, the situation could shift for itself; and it was easy to improvise a few verses which ·developed the situation by description instead of by action, and thus to answer demands of an epic interest.

It is not hard to imagine this epic interest in a very humble and initial phase. The too familiar sight of a Faroe girl carried off by those "Frisian pirates," and appealing in turn to her relatives, passed directly into choral expression bounded by the situation itself. Striking, full of poignant interest, the simple iterated verses were soon sung for their own sake, and at once responded to an external demand for more facts.[2] A mother, we will say, sings them to her children, in reminiscent mood;

[1] Popular tales had taken this route from the start; and it may be presumed that, different from ballads, they had always been concerned with things remote in time or in space. The ballad was immediate.

[2] "The Frisians bent to their oars," so a slight narrative puts it; the girl wept, and cried in the refrain, "Let me not pine in Frisia." Then the dramatic situation begins, with wonderfully uniform incremental repetition throughout, as detailed above.

the situation is no longer present, the persons no longer in evidence; and the children wish to know who the girl was and how she came to her plight. Or the story is still sung in a group, but as reminiscence; meeting the external desire for more details, improvisation of new stanzas, still holding fast to the old formula, develops, as poetic "invention," a higher type of verse. So the ballad, if noteworthy, might go its way from year to year. It is clear that nothing in this ballad of the Frisian pirates needed to be borrowed or imported; as we learned, the case was too familiar, and is said still to cause a traditional shiver of fear among the Faroe folk. "To be take in Fryse," or to Frisia, was no word of jest, as with Chaucer. Here, in any case, was material enough to fill and form the original ballad mould, to create the poetic species. That all manner of interesting stories, found, imported, and perhaps even invented, could subsequently be run into this mould is natural as a process and plain enough as a fact. But the species itself, the ballad as a poetic form, was subject to the usual laws of growth and change. Sung as a choral favorite, such a piece as the "Frisian Pirates" would not only improve in its traditional course, but, according to the conditions of its vogue, would fall into one of two great classes. It might remain as a ballad of situation, short, dramatic, choral. It might also go the epic way, find rather an audience than a throng of active, singing folk, lose its refrain, attract other details, motives, parts of story, grow in length and breadth, vary in good versions and bad versions, and come finally upon the record, now as a sterling traditional narrative, or even chronicle, and again as popular broadside printed by the cheap press and sold in the stalls. Let us look for a while at the first class.

Here the situation retains its sovereignty, and keeps the ballad brief, abrupt, springing and pausing, full of incremental repetition, and mainly in dialogue form. Pages of description and comment cannot take the place of the ballad itself; and there is no better example of this old type than "Babylon,"[1] recovered from Scottish tradition. It is neither so near its choral origins as to lose, like "The Maid Freed from the Gallows," all epic body and nearly all æsthetic appeal, nor so far from those origins as to have become a mere recitation of events. The refrain should be read aloud through the entire piece; singing would be better; and the incremental repetitions, marking out the vital and specific ballad from its epic introduction and end, should be felt, as far as possible, to be mainspring, and not dead weight, in the poetic mechanism.

> "There were three ladies lived in a bower,
>   *Eh vow bonnie,*
> And they went out to pull a flower
>   *On the bonnie banks o' Fordie.*
>
> "They hadna pu'ed a flower but ane,
> When up started to them a banisht man.
>
> "He's ta'en the first sister by the hand,
> And he's turned her round and made her stand.

[1] Child, no. 14.

" 'It's whether will ye be a rank robber's wife,
Or will ye die by my wee pen-knife?'

" 'It's I'll not be a rank robber's wife,
But I'll rather die by your wee pen-knife.'

"He's killed this may, and he's laid her by,
For to bear the red rose company.

"He's taken the second ane by the hand,
And he's turned her round, and made her stand.

" 'It's whether will ye be a rank robber's wife,
Or will ye die by my wee pen-knife?'

" 'I'll not be a rank robber's wife,
But I'll rather die by your wee pen-knife.'

"He's killed this may, and he's laid her by,
For to bear the red rose company.

"He's taken the youngest ane by the hand,
And he's turned her round, and made her stand.

"Says, 'Will ye be a rank robber's wife,
Or will ye die by my wee pen-knife?'

" 'I'll not be a rank robber's wife,
Nor will I die by your wee pen-knife.

" 'For I hae a brother in this wood,
And gin ye kill me, it's he'll kill thee.'

" 'What's thy brother's name? Come tell to me.'
'My brother's name is Baby Lon.'

" 'O sister, sister, what have I done!
O have I done this ill to thee!

"'O since I've done this evil deed,
  Good sall never be seen o' [1] me.'

"He's taken out his wee pen-knife,
  And he's twyned [2] himsel o' his ain sweet life."

With the parallels and the relations of "Babylon" we are not now concerned.[3] It may belong to a group of ballads which all derive from the narrative of an obvious complication; it might spring, like the "Frisian Pirates," from fact. The motive of it has been used powerfully but repulsively by Maupassant in one of the stories of his "Main Gauche." We deal now with the specific ballad form. That the situation is fairly explosive in its tragic outcome must not blind us to the fact that it is a situation. Who the three ladies were, why the brother was banished, all the essentials of a narrative, in short, are wanting. Maupassant in his kind of art, the Icelandic saga in its kind of art, would have worked all this out. The longer, romantic ballad itself would have come to terms, however briefly and awkwardly, with persons, place, time. Here

[1] "By." — The rimes, and perhaps the verses themselves, are quite disordered here.
[2] "Deprived," "sundered."
[3] Besides the Scandinavian versions named by Child, i, 170 ff., see Axel Olrik, *Danske Ridderviser*, i, 115 f., and "Torkels Døtur" in Hammershaimb, i, 45 f. The incremental repetition in the latter is constant and typical; for example, "they sleep till the sun shines on their bed: they sleep till the sun shines on their bedstead," — a stanza for each statement. In the stable, again, —

  "She looses one steed, she looses two.
  The best she places the saddle on."

The refrain, too, belongs to the actual dance.

no persons are described; as merely "a banished man,"
the hero's name is indifferent; the place is a fortuitous
and meaningless part of the refrain; the time is vague.
The simple force of this "Babylon," the effective character of its lingering repetition followed by the crash of
revelation, must not make us forget that here is not even
the art of narrative. Here Lessing's famous distinction
breaks down. Poetic as it is, this ballad presents no story,
no epic nucleus; but its art, like the art of painting, of
sculpture, lies in the moment and in the moment's scope.
The figures must all be before us at once, a situation
inevitable under conditions of the dance; and they must
all tell their tale in a single action. Indeed, with the dance
quite ignored, forgotten, the ballad and its staying, hem-
ming refrain still give the effect of collocation in space
rather than of succession in time. If normal dramatic
time be put by the old rule at four and twenty hours, the
normal time of the situation ballad ought not to exceed
twenty-four minutes. To accent this impression one has
only to contrast with "Babylon" a purely narrative ballad
of the best type, say "Robin Hood and the Monk," or
"Robin Hood and Guy of Gisborne." Here are long
stories. Personality and character are described. Robin
is handsome, blond, has a "milk-white side;" he is a
muscular Christian, indeed, for while an inch of his body,
so the Gest assures us, is worth an ordinary whole man,
he is gentle, pious, will harm no woman, worships the
Virgin Mary with a kind of passion, risks his life to hear
Mass. He is the poor man's friend. Even particular habits

of his are described. Yet, just as "Babylon" is at some remove from actual choral conditions, — for one must not stretch the hint of a dance in that taking of the sisters' hands and turning them round, — so the Robin Hood ballads, while far gone in epic, still keep their distance from the narrative of lettered art. What they have accomplished for epic purposes by changes in structure, and that is the point now in view, lies mainly in the reduction of the element of incremental repetition, that is, by the removal of what seemed a needless obstruction, as well as by the filling of those gaps and omissions which critics persist in explaining by the psychology of authorship and which are so clearly due to oldest dramatic form. The filling up, indeed, is more easily accomplished than the cutting out; you turn any drama into a novel by liberal supplies of "Hamlet smiled sadly, and remarked," or "Sobbing convulsively, Ophelia handed him the letters; then, with supreme effort of self-control, . . ." For transition from situation to story, the rhapsode had his own devices. Medieval reciters used a change of voice, or other trick, to denote the various persons in the poem.[1] So, too, by actual word and phrase, by an explanatory stanza or line, the shift of persons and scenes can be indicated, as in one of the homely but pathetic English ballads: —

> "Now we'll leave talking of Christy Grahame
> And talk of him again belive;
> But we will talk of bonny Bewick
> Where he was teaching his scholars five."

[1] So with Greek rhapsodes.   See Creizenach, *Geschichte des neueren Dramas*, i, 32, with references to Vinesauf's *Poetria*.

Other devices are familiar enough, and will be considered in the proper place; but even here,[1] with gaps well filled, the excisions are not so noticeable, and the tendency is still to situation, dialogue, and a touch of incremental repetition to mark the important moment. Repetitions are not yet felt, in Cowper's phrase, "to make attention lame." In point of fact, even the epic process at its farthest point in ballads, and with all its desire to push a narrative or cover a gap, is less potent to crowd out choral memories than the lyric, emotional and reflective impulse. This lyric impulse really creates a third class of ballads, just halting and trembling on the border of pure song. Here belong "Barbara Allan" and "Lady Alice;"[2] while the pretty sentiment, the long-range sympathy, of "Bessy Bell and Mary Gray"[3] have converted it in England "into a nursery rhyme." "Ballad *or song*" is Professor Child's account of it. These ballads of lyric tendency have repetition, but not of the incremental and dramatic kind.[4] They need not be regarded in the present

[1] *Bewick and Grahame*, Child, no. 211, is a stall-copy, a corrupted but not utterly spoiled version of a noble old ballad. Long as it is, it is really a ballad of two situations, and in the first of these the incremental repetition is very effective. See below, p. 126.

[2] Child, nos. 84, 85.

[3] *Ibid.* no. 201.

[4] It occurs, however, as if "dancing for joy," in the pretty fifteenth-century carol of *Christ and his Mother* : —

> "He came al so still
> There his mother was,
> As dew in April
> That falleth on the grass.

> "He came al so still
> To his mother's bower,

case, which is concerned with incremental repetition as the touchstone and test of original ballad structure, prominent in the ballads of situation, and dwindling as narrative gets the upper hand.

VII. INCREMENTAL REPETITION AS FINAL PROOF OF POPULAR ORIGIN

Incremental repetition made up the whole frame of "The Maid Freed from the Gallows," simply because such ballads were still part and parcel of the dance.[1] Disengaged from the dance, ballads of situation like "Babylon," "Lord Randal," "The Twa Brothers," held their ground stoutly and kept narrative at arm's length. This leaping and lingering, with the group, so to speak, fixed, and the parts of it shifting about, created its own æsthetic appeal; and even the somewhat mechanical system of triads came to be regarded as true ballad progress. Except in the chronicle ballad, which felt that grim work was cut out for it, and therefore took the nearest way, or tried to take it, the structural fashion of increments held firm.

> As dew in April
> That falleth on the flower.

> "He came al so still
> There his mother lay,
> As dew in April
> That falleth on the spray."

Incremental repetition of the refrain (as in the short version of *Lord Randal*) is common in all lyric.

[1] Incremental repetition is here treated as characteristic of Germanic ballads. It occurs, of course, elsewhere, even in Armenian popular verse. French ballads have it in plenty; and further study would doubtless trace it through all the Romance tongues, and give it due importance.

Alien material had to fall into this mould; "Sir Lionel," "Hind Horn," are cases in point, and the latter ballad is most instructive when compared with the related "gest." So vital is this incremental system in the structure of ballads, that it not only dominates the main progress of a borrowed story, but even treats a detail of this story so as to make it conform in pattern with the rest. In " Kemp Owyne," [1] which nobody would claim for choral origins, one kiss in the popular tale becomes three kisses in the ballad, with incremental repetition of gifts, — belt, ring, brand. Parallel cases are innumerable, — for example, in a Norwegian ballad,[2] the three draughts of Lethean effect which make Little Kirstie, now the hill-king's queen, forget her former home. It is easy to see how this structure would be almost inevitable for the ballad of situation, provided the situation still tended to absorb narrative and block an epic process which was bound to conquer in the long run. This epic process is first seen at the beginning and the end of a situation. A most popular ballad, spread, as Grundtvig says,[3] "over the whole north," tells of the princess who plays tables or dice with a boy, first her necklace against his old hat, where she wins, then her gold crown against his old coat, winning again, then herself against his hose and shoon, — where she loses. The three casts have each three stanzas in strictest form of incremental repetition, except that two are in dialogue, and the third in narrative. Next, in rapid dialogue, with

---

[1] Child, no. 34.   [2] Landstad, pp. 435 f., stanzas 16 ff.
[3] Danish version, *Tærningspillet*, iv, 402 ff.

pairs of stanzas and no narrative at all, the girl offers silver-clasped knife, silken sarks, horse and saddle, at last the castle itself, to be free, but in vain. Four stanzas of romantic conclusion then reveal "the best king's-son on earth," and turn the despair of the princess to joy.

We see the set of the tide. Explanations prefixed to this dramatic nucleus will soon give the desired details; events will be added, connected; and narrative will soon absorb the situation. Epic interest, here gratified only by those concluding stanzas, will prove stronger than dramatic interest in the lingering game and in the climax of bribes.[1] Incremental repetition, ceasing to dominate the whole ballad, now passes from general structural form into a sort of formula of situations or topics which have become traditional and recur as old favorites in the new narrative ballads. Like the refrain, it will linger best in those ballads that belong to genuine popular tradition, and it will disappear utterly from such a ballad as "Lord Delamere," [2] where tradition is at a last stand, and the popular maker, with his drawling, perfunctory "Ritoora-loora-la," is disgustingly evident.[3] In genuine ballads it survives almost constantly in one of three forms:

[1] For brevity of narrative, intense and effective, yet retaining scraps of dialogue, see *Le Pont des Morts*, Crane, no. xix.

[2] Child, no. 207.

[3] Stall-copies, of course, can be fatal to incremental repetition, while it will linger in popular recitation of the same ballad. Compare versions A and D of *James Harris, the Dæmon Lover*, no. 243. See also Professor Child's remark (ii, 180) on "a copy of *Lord Thomas and Fair Elliner* written over for the ballad-mongers, and of course much less in the popular style."

it appears as necessary, effective expression of the situation; as perfunctory mark of style, a mere manner, by
no means inevitable; and as the ballad commonplace.[1]
Setting aside the small group of which "The Maid Freed
from the Gallows" is type, we have a large and important
class where situation is still dominant in one of its characteristic features and incremental repetition is a matter
of course. Besides cases like "Babylon," there is the
ballad where a "relative-climax" is a part and not the
whole of the situation. Thus a wounded soldier calls
vainly for water from father, mother, brother, sister, getting it at last from his sweetheart. This, of course, is
developed by incremental verses. Precisely the opposite
case occurs in " Clerk Saunders;" [2] of seven brothers
who surprise their sister with her lover, six will spare him
for this reason or that, but the seventh does what he

[1] There is but one other way to account for this structural peculiarity
of ballads and at the same time discard popular origins. It might be
urged that the formula, let us say, of the relative-climax was brought,
as any good story is brought, from popular tales or wherever else, and
applied in ballad verse. The result would be incremental repetition.
Pleased with the smoothness and easy course of such structure, ballad-
makers would use it on other occasions, and so it would get its vogue.
But such an explanation flies in the face of all the evidence that we have
gathered. It leaves unexplained that decrease of incremental repetition
with the increase of epic elements. It ignores the obvious connection of
ballad and dance. And it jars absolutely, fatally, with the facts of poetic
evolution, where repetition, the common and original choral stuff, taking
different lines of change, rules at first in popular verse, yields to epic
necessity, and finally disappears amid the triumphs of full artistic
control.
[2] No. 69.

thinks to be his duty. Another case combines relatives
with a scheme of colors: a woman's father dies, — she
will dress all in red; the mother, — make it yellow; the
brother indicates green; and the sister white; "but if
my dear husband dies, I will dress in black." [1] As might
be expected, the climax is multiform; but it falls most
readily into the system of triads, like those three cries for
help, best shown in the German *Ulinger:* [2] the first cry is,
Jesu, Marie Sone, the second *Maria, du reine Maid,* vain
both, but the third and successful cry is to *allerliebster
Bruder mein,* who rescues or else avenges his sister. The
nearest and dearest may even be one's self. In the critical
part of "Sir Andrew Barton," where the mast must be
climbed, first it is the retainer, then the sister's son, none
dearer, and finally Sir Andrew himself. In "The Cruel
Brother " [3] the climax is an omission, — with fatal conse-
quences. This formula is combined with that of the
"legacy," a favorite end of tragic ballads; in "Edward " [4]
effective repetition leads from "poor wife" through "old
son" to "mother dear," — who has for climax the "fire
o' coals." Interesting by way of contrast to the old dramatic and choral group is the incremental repetition in
relative climax — like that of "Edward" — along with
a quite perfunctory ballad commonplace. When Hughie

[1] See Child, ii, 347.
[2] See Child, introduction to no. 4, *Lady Isabel and the Elf-Knight,*
for variants of these three cries, — for example, in the Bohemian,
i, 41.
[3] No. 11.
[4] No. 13, version A.

Grame [1] is awaiting a felon's death, he looks "over his
left shoulder," and spies his father lamenting sorely;
"peace, father; they can take life but not my hope of
heaven;" then "over his right shoulder," and sees his
mother tearing her hair; but now, for the third increment,
instead of a minatory message, our ballad breaks lamely
into anti-climax and makes Hughie wish merely to be
"remembered to Peggy my wife," who had brought
about his doom. Usually, however, like the "legacy"
conclusion, the "climax of relatives" is effective enough.
Thus when Lady Maisry's lover [2] arrives too late to save
her from the flames lighted by her next of kin, he cries, —

> "'O I'll gar burn for you, Maisry,
> Your father and your mother;
> An I'll gar burn for you, Maisry,
> Your sister an your brother.
>
> "'An I'll gar burn for you, Maisry,
> The chief of a' your kin;
> And the last bonfire that I come to,
> Mysel I will cast in.'"

Best of all, in this respect, is the ballad of "The Twa
Brothers" [3] with its wide contrast between two versions;
one of them, with motive and conclusion almost wholly
of the "Edward" type, goes back to the dramatic, choral
class, has no narrative whatever, and is a single situation
developed in the well-known way. It was [4] "sung after

[1] No. 191, A, stanzas 19–23.
[2] Child, no. 65, A.
[3] No. 49, A and I.
[4] See Child, v, 291. It is not necessary to assume direct borrowing
from *Edward*.

a St. George play regularly acted on All Souls' Day at a village a few miles from Chester. . . . The play was introduced by a song . . . and followed by two songs of which this is the last, *the whole dramatic company singing.*" The more familiar traditional version has an epic opening which tells the tragedy in a couple of stanzas; two brothers wrestle, presumably quarrel,[1] and one is stabbed by the other. As in the typical ballad of situation, this brief, straightforward bit of narrative is followed by dialogue and incremental repetition to the end. After vain attempts to stanch the flowing blood, Sir Willie carries Sir John to kirkyard, and the relative-climax follows in a most effective form: —

> "'But what will I say to my father dear,
>   Should he chance to say, Willie, whar 's John?'
> 'Oh say that he 's to England gone
>   To buy him a cask of wine.'
>
> "'And what shall I say to my mother dear,
>   Should she chance to say, Willie, whar 's John?'
> 'Oh say that he 's to England gone
>   To buy her a new silk gown.'
>
> "'And what will I say to my sister dear,
>   Should she chance to say, Willie, whar 's John?'
> 'Oh say that he 's to England gone
>   To buy her a wedding ring.'
>
> "'But what will I say to her you loe dear,
>   Should she cry, Why tarries my John?'

[1] Professor Child prefers this assumption as accenting the generosity of the victim. The absurdity of the brothers attending school, pointed out in B where they are "little," really applies to A; the corruption is in this detachable narrative explanation. See above, p. 92.

'Oh tell her I lie in fair Kirkland
And home will never come.' " [1]

This is art; but it is an unconscious art, due in the first
instance to the old choral conditions. Indeed, instead
of developing under epic treatment, this incremental
repetition in the climax of relatives tends, like other
forms and formulas, to disappear; in "Bonny Lizie
Baillie" and "Glasgow Peggie," [2] corrupted and disordered ballads, it is present in a very mangled state.
Still more significant is its progress into the mechanical
and the unmeaning, and even into burlesque. An inferior
but lively ballad, "Glenlogie," [3] makes father and mother
give their daughter quite profitless counsel, and then puts
"her father's chaplain" in the climax of consolation.[4] In
another ballad,[5] sister, brother, mother, and father come
successively in and call Janet a vile name; she defends
herself; then in comes her old nurse weeping, warning

[1] This "very pathetic passage," as Professor Child calls it, i, 436,
ranging it with a few similar cases, "is too truly a touch of nature to be
found only here." We are therefore relieved for once of the painful
necessity of deciding whether A copied B or B copied A. But on other
accounts the increments in this stanza are noteworthy throughout. A
somewhat similar Flemish use of the relative-climax is where in *Hale-
wijun* the girl says to father, brother, sister of the dead man that he is
dallying somewhere, but to the mother that he is dead.

[2] Nos. 227, 228.

[3] No. 238, A.

[4] He is like the Flemish shrift-father in *Roland*, who gives Louise
the permission refused by father, mother, and brother. See also no. 73,
I, Child, iv, 469.

[5] *Lady Maisry*, version B; compare I. The incremental repetition is
very effective. Artistic poetry has another way of managing such a
climax: compare Tennyson's *Home they Brought her Warrior Dead*.

Janet of her fate, and offering a messenger to run with news to the lover. A version of "Lord Thomas and Fair Annet," very disordered, it is true, makes the hero visit his father and get bad advice, while a sister's son ("sat on the nurse's knee") gives nobler counsel, which is communicated further and superfluously to mother, brother, and sister. This is confusion. Actual burlesque, always a proof of antecedent popularity, reaches this climax of relatives in a version of the "Mermaid,"[1] still beloved for its swing and its lively chorus. Captain, mate, and boatswain of the doomed ship cry incrementally that their wives will soon be widows; when

> " . . . next bespake the little cabbin-boy,
> And a well bespoke boy was he:
> 'I am as sorry for my mother dear
> As you are for your wives all three,'" —

pathetic enough; but in the burlesque it runs: —

> "Out and spoke the cook of our ship,
> And a rusty old dog was he;
> Says, 'I am as sorry for my pots and pans
> As you are for your wives all three.'"

So much for the use of incremental repetition in a commanding motive or typical, important formula.[2] Ballads

---

[1] No. 289. A is serious; E is the burlesque.

[2] If incremental repetition appeared only in these formulas of relative-climax, best of three, legacy, and what not, which themselves occur not only in ballads, but in folk tales and other forms of literature, then one could argue that borrowing could account for it and its origin need not be sought in choral conditions of the primitive ballad. The point is that incremental repetition is the fundamental fact in ballad structure,

clung to the art of it, and often the narrative halts to
admit a touch of the old device. In "Bewick and
Grahame," a father tells his son to choose: "fight your
sworn-brother or fight me." — "Fight a man that's faith
and troth to me? How can I do it?" —

> "'What's that thou sayst, thou limmer loon?
> Or how dare thou stand to speak to me?
> If thou do not end this quarrel soon,
> Here is my *glove*, thou shalt fight me.'
>
> "Christy stoop'd low unto the ground,
> Unto the ground, as you'll understand,[1]
> 'O father, put on your glove again;
> The wind hath blown it from your hand.'
>
> "'What's that thou sayst, thou limmer loon?
> Or how dare thou stand to speak to me?
> If thou do not end this quarrel soon,
> Here is my *hand*, thou shalt fight me.'"

This second class of survivals in incremental repetition
now nearly touches, as here, the old dramatic and dominant note, and now falls almost to commonplace; in these
cases it is permanence of structural form, and so far vital,
— not a mere unintelligent habit. "Lord Ingram and
Chiel Wyet," [2] a traditional ballad, shows this structural
permanence in its five opening stanzas; incremental
repetition leads up to the cause of tragedy, but in no

belongs not to ballads, but to the ballad, and occurs under all circumstances, great or trivial. Borrowing is an impossible theory in this case.

[1] Note the mixture of traditional and ballad-mongering styles; the
matter is distinctly good, with this pathetically urged excuse for the
father's brutality.

[2] No. 66, A.

dramatic situation, and with the relative-climax [1] subordinate. In other words, the ballad, bound to set forth certain facts, chooses the old structural method and holds it to the end. In shorter compass, incremental repetition gives an emphatic effect: [2] —

> " They had na been a week from her,
>   A week but barely ane,
>   When word came to the carline wife
>   That her three sons were gane.

> " They had na been a week from her,
>   A week but barely three,
>   When word came to the carline wife
>   That her sons she 'd never see." [3]

Frequently such a formula is reduced from stanzas to lines, but keeps the proportion: —

> ' She 's led him in thro ae dark door,
>   And sae has she thro nine;
>   She 's laid him on a dressing-table
>   And stickit him like a swine.

> " And first came out the thick, thick blood,
>   And syne came out the thin,
>   And syne came out the bonny heart's blood;
>   There was nae mair within." [4]

Here one approaches the third class, the commonplace, [5] the repetition without any reason save that it is remem-

[1] Here the "asking permission" with climax of the lady herself, as in *Katharine Jaffray*.

[2] *The Wife of Usher's Well*, no. 79.

[3] Compare the similar structure, pretty enough in its place, quoted above on p. 116, note 4.

[4] *Sir Hugh*, no. 155, A.

[5] For ballad commonplaces in general, see below, Chap. IV.

bered and applied appositely or grotesquely as the case
may be. It is hard to draw the line of division. Exigencies of the stanza, not mere remembrance, force an old
proverb into this form: —

> "And mony ane sings o' grass, o' grass,
>   And mony ane sings o' corn,
>   And mony ane sings o' Robin Hood
>   Kens little whare he was born," [1] —

which may be contrasted, for its nugatory pair of antecedent repetitions, with the famous stanza: —

> "Methinks I hear the thresel-cock,
>   Methinks I hear the jaye;
>   Methinks I hear my Lord Barnard,
>   And I would I were away." [2]

Repetition is so pervasive as to become inconsistent, but
not quite commonplace, in a traditional version of "Sir
Patrick Spens:" [3] —

> "Laith, laith were our Scottish lords
>   To weit their coal-black shoon;
>   But yet ere a' the play was play'd,
>   They wat their hats aboon.

> "Laith, laith were our Scottish lords
>   To weit their coal-black hair;
>   But yet ere a' the play was play'd,
>   They wat it every hair;" —

[1] No. 102, A, 17. See also the next stanza.
[2] No. 81, A; better perhaps in B: —

> "' Methinkes I heare Lord Barnett's horne;
>   Away, Musgreve, away!'"

[3] No. 58, B, 12 f.

while in another version,[1] one stanza puts the drowned Scots lords at Sir Patrick's head, and the corresponding stanza neatly groups them at his feet. On the other side of the account, a famous pair of stanzas from this ballad, with the same relation, are rightly praised by Professor Child: [2] —

> "O lang, lang may their ladies sit
>   Wi their fans into their hand
> Or eir they se Sir Patrick Spence
>   Cum sailing to the land.
>
> "O lang, lang may the ladies stand
>   Wi thair gold kems in their hair,
> Waiting for thair ain deir lords,
>   For they 'll see thame na mair." [3]

This is no commonplace. Commonplace is the unnecessarily repeated choice of three, — as with horses of different colors, inevitable at certain stages of certain ballads, and wearisome enough. This commonplace, however, may at any time become effective through the situation; so in "Mary Hamilton" the heroine is told to put on her robes [4] of black or else her robes of brown, but refuses, repeating the negative for each, and adds: —

[1] No. 58, F, 13 f.

[2] A, 9, 10. "It would be hard to point out in ballad poetry, or other, happier and more refined touches." — These touches are due entirely to the incremental repetition and its suggestion.

[3] This is completely spoiled in J, where the sequence of three stanzas puts the fan into Lady Spens's hand, the tear into her ee, and the *black shoon on her feet*, — probably for mourning purposes.

[4] Color repetition often becomes inconsistent, as in the Swedish ballad, above, p. 89.

"But I'll put on my robes of white,
To shine thro Edinbro town."

So, too, in the French "Renaud," companion piece to 'Clerk Colvill," where the widow asks what robe she shall wear, and the mother replies: —

"'Mettez le blanc, mettez le gris,
Mettez le noir pour mieux choisi'.'"

But these happy touches lie not in the structural plan; what concerns us now is incremental repetition as a formula of no æsthetic or dramatic value in its particular application. Such a formula as that of the page and the "broken briggs" often becomes superfluous; often, again, the singer is simply using traditional phrases for a traditional case. A list of "commonplaces" in both kinds is printed under that name in the last volume of Professor Child's collection;[1] it includes plenty of incremental repetition, — as where poison is put to cheek, chin, lips, or when one steps into water, once to knee, then to middle, then to neck,[2] or where bells are rung at the first kirk and Mass said at the next. But such commonplace, though often individually identical, must not be confused in kind with the capital tendency of ballad structure to run its material, whatever the origin, into this mould. In that ancient and sterling ballad of "Child Maurice," for example: —

"'And heere I send her a mantle of greene,
As greene as any grasse,

[1] Vol. v, 474 f.
[2] *Lady Isabel*, B, 4 ff.; *Child Waters*, B, 7 ff.

> And bidd her come to the silver wood
> To hunt with Child Maurice.

> " 'And there I send her a ring of gold,
> A ring of precious stone,
> And bidd her come to the silver wood,
> Let for no kind of man,' " —

one has the ballad structure not as a commonplace, but as a law of literary form, independent, *sui generis*, and found nowhere else. It is not a commonplace in the literal sense, but a case of structural law, a category, inflexible in its form, but perfectly amenable to change of material and contents, as may be seen by comparing the corresponding passage in the Scottish traditional version: —

> " 'Here is a glove, a glove,' he said,
> Lined with the silver grey;
> You may tell her to come to the merry greenwood,
> To speak to Child Nory.

> " 'Here is a ring, a ring,' he says,
> 'It 's all gold but the stane;
> You may tell her to come to the merry greenwood,
> And ask the leave o' nane.' "

It may vex the hurrying reader now and then, and offend by mere silliness, —

> "He lean'd him twofold o'er a staff,
> So did he threefold o'er a tree," [1] —

or by superfluity, as when an effective single stanza in the

---

[1] *Gude Wallace*, no. 157, A, 9.

song of "Waly, Waly" is ineffectively doubled in the later ballad: [1] —

"Whan we came through Glasgow toun,
    We was a comely sight to see;
My gude lord in velvet green,
    And I mysel in cramasie.

"Whan we cam to Douglas toun,
    We was a fine sight to behold;
My gude lord in cramasie,
    And I myself in shining gold."

Structure and situation have here nothing in common; the style does not fit the facts. On the other hand, a Kentish version of "Lamkin," [2] formed in this way throughout, although it has no literary interest, has its strong dramatic traditional interest, and justifies even the superfluity of daughters, Lady Betty, Lady Nelly, Lady Jenny, and the ominous "etc." which surrenders this ballad at discretion.

It is the fate of the popular muse that she is credited with nothing but the trivial, the commonplace, the harmlessly absurd; whatsoever is more than these, critics assign to one of her high-born sisters. But there can be no doubt that in the long reaches of tradition, and in the

---

[1] *Jamie Douglas*, no. 204, A, Child, iv, 93. This is from the recitation of one who had it from an old dairywoman. The traditional ballad turns instinctively to this repetition. Some of Buchan's copies are of this structure from end to end; noteworthy is *The Baron o' Leys*, no. 241, C. Changing dress at this, that, and yonder town is common: cf. *Le Capitaine et la Fille Prisonnière*, Puymaigre, no. xii (p. 44) — the first town blue satin, the second in diamonds, the third for the wedding.

[2] No. 93, K, Child, ii, 233.

wide sweep of choral song, æsthetic elements have been produced which the poet has only copied and perfected, and which still appeal in their own rude, unconscious art. One has but to think of the high poetic uses to which genius has put the communal refrain in a hymeneal of Catullus or Spenser, and of the refinement, often to artifice, which it has undergone in forms like the roundel and the ballade. These are rescues; despite the waning vogue of choral poetry, despite the epic processes, the literary invasion, repetition as the main mark of choral structure in verse retained some of its old power amid its old haunts. Unable to keep its larger vitality, incremental repetition still refused to disappear from the ballad; one may think of that pretty myth of the dew, burned away from field and lawn, but still glistening in the copses. It is the legacy of an early and a popular art, no invention of the poet in a library. It is the genius of the ballad itself, formally expressed, springing from quite intelligible conditions of a singing, dancing, dramatic festal throng; hence the unique and ancient appeal of this stretched metre at its best.

> " 'If the child be mine, Faire Ellen,' he sayd,
>   'Be mine, as you tell me,
>   Take you Cheshire and Lancashire both,
>   Take them your own to be.
>
> " 'If the child be mine, Faire Ellen,' he sayd,
>   'Be mine, as you doe sweare,
>   Take you Cheshire and Lancashire both
>   And make that child your heyre.'

" She saies, 'I had rather have one kisse,
     Child Waters, of thy mouth,
   Than I would have Cheshire and Lancashire both,
     That lyes by north and south.

" 'And I had rather have a twinkling,
     Child Waters, of your eye,
   Than I would have Cheshire and Lancashire both,
     To take them mine owne to bee.' " [1]

---

[1] As a matter of mere statistics, incremental repetition is found consistently, and mostly along with the refrain, in all the ballads which are grouped by Professor Child as oldest and nearest the primitive type; when exceptions occur, it is almost certain that the fault is with the record, — an impatient editor or collector, an economic publisher. Comparing the manuscript collections in the library of Harvard University with editions made from them, one notes short cuts and evasions of this kind, now trifling and now grave. For the rest of the ballads, a careful examination shows that more than one half of these retain the structural feature, reverting to it at the most important and the most unimportant moments, that is to say, for accenting a motive, a deed, a situation, and for rendering a commonplace. The long chronicle ballads, and the lowest types of the broadsides, ignore it altogether.

CHAPTER II

THE BALLADS

I. THE OLDEST GROUPS

NGLISH and Scottish ballads may be grouped according to their subject, their form, their relative age. The oldest ballads, apart from any question about the time when they were recorded or rescued from oral tradition, have mainly a stanza of two verses, a constant refrain, and the mark of verbal repetition in its most distinct shape; they are placed by Professor Child in the forefront of his collection; and first of all stands a ballad of riddles.

Along with gnomic poetry of varying kinds, the riddle is of quite immemorial age. Together they formed a counterpart to those great chorals of primitive verse which dealt with deeds and things; and this intellectual invasion of poetry can still be traced in low stages of culture. The Botocudos of South America sang, and are probably still singing, in chorus of almost endless repetition, short sentences which not only laid down the lines of epic, as "Good hunting to-day," but also embodied the result of scientific observation and blazed a path for later wisdom-literature and didactic: "Brandy is good!" This little gnomic song can be matched by a formal collection, a didactic poem, in Anglo-Saxon, where there are long sequences of statements not a whit more incisive or complicated than Botocudan lore, — "frost will freeze, and fire will burn," for an example. Between epic and didactic lie the *versus memoriales* which Anglo-Saxon preserves in its oldest recorded poem, the "Lay of Widsith," as a very ancient form of history:—

"Atla ruled Huns, Eormanric Goths;" —

but it is clear that the "sentence," the piece of pure wisdom, was an early favorite in choral verse. Lovers of the deep things in poetry, who are inclined to sneer at such commonplace, should analyze the wisdom of the moderns and reduce a metaphysical poet, old or new, to intelligible prose. Primitive verse put its abstractions simply; or else, by an easy change, posed a frank little problem for intellectual effort. Our riddle ballad is still a plain affair, in sharp contrast to the far older, yet far more intricate riddles of Anglo-Saxon record, which were translated from a Latin source, as well as to the half-scientific questions and answers in a compilation like "Solomon and Saturn." Whether or not all the "catechism" literature of that time, mainly about the sky and the seasons, is to be referred to Greek sources, there was a short, simple question, now in verse and now in prose, which the people always loved, and which men of later times, like Randle Holmes,[1] copied

[1] MS. Harl. 1960. See Tupper, *Publications Mod. Lang. Assoc.*, 1903, xviii, 211 ff. On the riddle chap-books see Petsch, *Palaestra*, iv, 6 ff.

into a commonplace book, precisely as they copied ballad and song. Even now, this sort of question has its vogue in rural districts and in the upper classes of the nursery; and for older days not only did a learned riddle, particularly if its learning were biblical, drift among the people, but literary collections were often recruited from the popular supply. In the "Demaundes Joyous," printed after the French in 1511, "Which," it is asked, "is the moost profytable beest and that man eteth least of? — This is Bees."

In ballads, one has to distinguish the riddles made or produced in the throng from those of the minstrel's stock in trade. Tragemund, — perhaps "interpreter," *dragoman*, — in the old German ballad,[1] is a "travelling man," the Widsith of riddles, who answers long lists of questions with consummate ease; some of them have found their way into English ballads. But it is a fact that the riddle belonged originally with the popular festal dance. To this day a riddle is put by preference in rime; in older days it was sung, and was answered by song; and there is plenty of evidence that all went once to choral measure. Radloff gives us a glimpse of primitive conditions among the Tartar tribes of Siberia, where a public assembly is amused by the improvised flyting of sundry singers or by a riddle-contest in song. A girl who takes part in such a contest first

---

[1] "*Wager and Wish-Songs*" is Uhland's division; and he says they are "sprung from social intercourse," — probably true for ultimate origins. See his *Abhandlungen über die deutschen Volkslieder*, pp. 181 ff.

flouts her opponent, then flatters, and finally falls into a series of riddles or questions: what was first created? who was so-and-so's father? why do the waters freeze? The other singer answers every riddle, so that the girl fairly resigns the game and presents him with a coat as prize of victory. In repetition, variation, interlaced stanza, these riddle and flyting verses from Siberia are amazingly like the Scottish and German ballads, although there is no possible link between them. Instead of rivalry at the dance, a little story frames the Scottish ballad contest:[1]—

> "There was a knicht riding from the east,
>   (*Sing the Cather banks, the bonnie brume*)
> Wha had been wooing at monie a place.
>   (*And ye may beguile a young thing sune*)."

This strange knight asks a widow for her three daughters; the youngest, who is of course brightest, is put to the test:—

> "'O what is heigher nor the tree?
> And what is deeper nor the sea?'"

he asks in a series of questions which end with a challenge to name something "worse than a woman;" and she answers all, affirming that "Clootie," the devil, is worse than woman. The fiend, named and revealed, goes off in fire.

One must sunder the good riddle, which is kept for its own sake, and either teaches by its truth or pleases

---

[1] No. 1, C, from recitation. — The riddle tales, of course, run on the same plan.

by its ingenuity, from the riddles which only serve to help the situation and fill out the story. A variant of the riddle flyting, very interesting in the present case, matches one question or demand not by its answer but by another question or demand. Usually these alternate; but in "The Elfin Knight" [1] a clever maid wins her victory, baffling the elf, by a torrent and cumulation of desire for impossible things in answer to his request for a sark without any cut or hem, made without knife, shears, needle and thread. "Plow," she says, "plow with your horn my land by the sea, sow it with your corn, build a cart of stone and lime and let Robin Redbreast draw it home, barn it in a mouse-hole, thresh it in the sole of your shoe, winnow it in the palm of your hand, and sack it in your glove!" Baring-Gould gives a version once "sung as a sort of game in farm-houses" of Cornwall "between a young man who went outside the room, and a girl who sat on the settle, . . . and a sort of chorus of farm lads and lasses," a most interesting survival.[2] Indeed, the earliest form of this type of ballad was made in actual dances; the strenuous "long dance" of Holstein still goes to such a song. Like the ballad of the *springeltanz*, and like the cumulative ballad sung at the dance

[1] No. 2. See, also, Child, iv, 439.

[2] The present writer remembers a sort of yokel flyting, where reciprocal challenges were given in prose to perform an impossible task. "Rub the sunshine off that wall!" — "You wheel all the smoke out of the smokehouse." — These "demands joyous" soon passed the bourn of propriety; but the "smoke house" request was evidently traditional.

of the Frisians, this song of the long dance is an affair of choosing partners, perhaps an old wedding measure.[1]

> " ' I know a pretty maiden,
>   I would that she were mine ;
>   I 'll marry her, if from oaten straw
>   She 'll spin me silk so fine.'
>
> " ' And must I out of oaten straw
>   Spin thee silk so fine,
>   Then make thou me some brave new clothes
>   Out of the leaves o' line.'
>
> " ' And must I make thee brave new clothes
>   Out of the leaves o' line,
>   Go now and fetch for me the shears
>   From out the midst of Rhine.' "

So it flies back and forth, with interlaced quatrains, as in the Siberian song ; but all in time to steps and movements of the dance, and in that form of incremental repetition which the situation demands.[2] There can be no

[1] Riddles are asked at weddings in Russia. — Child, i, 418.

[2] French songs of the dance have been studied in Jeanroy's admirable *Origines de la Poésie Lyrique en France*. There one sees how a dance, with its song of the leader and the refrain of the dancers, could lapse and leave the song itself by perfectly plain steps to proceed through stage after stage to such apparently artificial forms as the *rondeau* and its complications. The name, however, like "ballad," betrays its origin in a popular dance. When the entire throng of dancers sang and acted, say, a song of bride-chasing, then a ballad, not a folk song, would result and did result. J. Bédier, "Les plus anciennes danses françaises," in *Rev. d. d. Mondes*, Jan. 15, 1906, gives some interesting evidence of this sort. The refrains can be traced back into the thirteenth century. For German dance-songs combined with the riddle, see Uhland on the *Kranzlieder* in his *Abhand. z. d. Volksl.*, p. 208. For repeated and interlaced stanzas in old Portuguese lyric, and their origin in the chorus

doubt that our own riddle ballads go back to such a dance, but they were too popular not to fall into the epic procession. The mere flash of riddle and answer, the thrust and parry of alternate demand for impossible things, might well satisfy a festal and choral throng; but in the popular tale these demands were converted into the story of an actual quest with triumphant results, and in the narrative ballad they could be fused with a motive of courtship, an ordinary, every-day affair, or else blend with the supernatural. "Captain Wedderburn's Courtship," [1] for example, reverses the Elfin Knight's proceedings. The captain carries off his lass; she refuses to marry him until he has brought her sundry impossible things; but our ingenious officer reduces these to wares of any market. "Get me a chicken without a bone," she says; and "here's your egg," counters the captain. So it goes on until the maid resigns her game. "Now she's Mrs. Wedderburn," concludes the ballad, with a final change rung on its jingling and saucy refrain. Here is broad Scottish daylight. "King John and the Bishop," however, a far-come story, has its roots in oriental folklore; while "Proud Lady Margaret" is shadowed by unnatural dark. The knight who seeks this lady in her bower, and is told to guess certain riddles or die, turns out to be a brother come back from the grave "to humble her haughty heart." Question and

of a communal dance, see H. R. Lang, *Liederbuch d. königs Denis*, pp. xcv, cxxxviii ff.
    [1] No. 46; the next ballads named are 45 and 47.

answer are no longer in the foreground, and romance is dominant.

As with form, so with material. Like incremental repetition in structure, this old notion of impossible things becomes a ballad commonplace, an equivalent for the Greek kalends; not till crows are white, swans are black, stones float, "when cockle-shells grow siller bells," or "till salt and oatmeal grow both of a tree," this or that will be done.

> " 'Whan will ye come hame again, Willie?
> Now Willie, tell to me.'
> 'When the sun and moon dances on the green,
> And that will never be.' " [1]

More romantic, but of the same piece, is Scott's pretty verse about the rose in winter-snow. "Never," of course, is the word for all this; now and then, however, the impossible is assumed as possible through magic, and we have the companion piece to many popular tales. What Professor Child calls a "base-born" but lively little ballad, "The Twa Magicians," [2] describes the pursuit of a lady by a coal-black smith.

> "O bide, lady, bide,
> And aye he bade her bide;
> The rusty smith your leman shall be
> For a' your muckle pride," —

runs a lively chorus; and there is no difficulty in thinking of this ballad as an actual dance, with rapid changes

[1] No. 49, D; and note the long sequence in no. 299. Child's list, i, 437, includes foreign sources.
[2] No. 44. The French versions are more delicate. See Crane, no. xxx.

of figure to suit transformations of the lady from dove to eel, to duck, to hare, of the smith from "another dove" to trout, to drake, to greyhound, and so to less romantic conclusions. The blacksmith wins, and the piece has a defiant, half-scurrilous tone; it has strayed into evil courses, although it confesses a nobler origin. Another ballad, where by implication the maid wins her flyting and her case, has wandered very far from the old ways, and seems quite alien to popular tradition. Professor Child was right, however, in making room for "The Gardener." [1] "Can you fancy me," says a gardener to the leal maiden who goes by, "to be my bride? You'll get all my flowers for clothing, — the lily for smock, gillyflowers on your head, gown of the sweet-william, coat of 'camovine,' apron of salads, stockings of the broad kail-blade, and gloves of marygold." She answers with a farewell and a return offer of clothing from no summer flowers: —

> "'The new-fallen snow to be your smock,
>   Becomes your body neat;
> And your head shall be deck'd with the eastern wind,
>   And the cold rain on your breast.'"

Popular fancy, and the chances of tradition, varied this sort of thing at will. Dr. Thomas Davidson remembered a fragment of the Aberdeenshire version: —

> "'The steed that ye sall ride upon
>   Sall be o' the frost sae snell;
> And I'll saddle him wi' the norlan winds,
>   And some sharp showers o' hail.'"

[1] No. 219.

From these flyting-verses to outright imprecation is no long journey. The evil wish [1] was a dread weapon for antiquity, provided one knew his *gramarye;* and magic, with werewolves and whatever other transformations, was but a step or so into the dark. Elaborate imprecation, however, apart from stock phrases like " an ill death may you die," makes little figure in the ballads. We find the regular last will and testament of curses at the end of "Edward," of "Lord Randal," and of some other ballads; [2] but it forms no part of the story. Solemn, and to some extent effective, is the imprecation of the "Wife of Usher's Well :"—

> " 'I wish the wind may never cease,
>   Nor fashes in the flood,
> Till my three sons come hame to me
>   In earthly flesh and blood.' "

That old woman, again, who kneels on the plank over black water, and bans Robin Hood,[3] is impressive enough, and one laments the lost stanzas which told more of her; she and the women who weep for the outlaw's case are weird sisters indeed, heightening the sense of coming doom and playing almost as romantic a part as the old nobleman who curses Triboulet in "Le Roi S'Amuse." But there is very little of this in the bal-

---

[1] The late classical and sophisticated example, of course, is Ovid's *Ibis*. In Ireland the old bards were particularly dreaded.

[2] For a notable series of such wish-legacies to the culpable relatives, see the end of version I of *The Maid Freed from the Gallows*, no. 95.

[3] *Robin Hood's Death*, st. 8.

lads. The mother's malison, in a ballad of that title, is unnatural; and only wildest anguish can account for Fair Annie's cry: [1] —

> "'Gin my seven sons were seven young rats,
>   Running on the castle wa',
> And I were a gray cat mysell,
>   I soon would worry them a'.
>
> "'Gin my seven sons were seven young hares,
>   Running o'er yon lilly lee,
> And I were a grew-hound mysell,
>   Soon worried they a' should be!'" [2]

"Fair Annie" with her wild wish has brought us far from the riddles and the flytings; this ballad is within measurable distance of romance, and echoes withal the tragedy of domestic complications. Yet we have made no *détour*. Domestic complication, in the widest range of the term, furnishes a theme for the majority of English and Scottish ballads; and there will be no better way to approach our task of describing them in their narrative essence than by this well-trodden path of the stolen sweetheart or bride. Moreover, one begins thus with a general

---

[1] See nos. 216 and 62.

[2] The deserted or cruelly treated maid, in a stanza too effective to be called commonplace, wishes all the evil for herself, and all the good either for her false lover or for her unborn child. See the stanza from *Child Waters* (no. 63), quoted below, or this from the song which goes with *Jamie Douglas* (no. 204): —

> "'Oh, oh, if my young babe were born,
>   And set upon the nurse's knee,
> And I my sell were dead and gane!
>   For a maid again I'll never be.'"

and human fact; the theme of family woes, in its main outlines, needs as little to be borrowed from some other "source" as the basal idea of having a family needs to be borrowed from race to race. A few primary instincts are still conceded even by the comparative folk. "Fair Annie," to be sure, is found also in Danish and Swedish versions; it tells a story which Marie de France told seven centuries ago, from an old Breton tale, in her "Lai del Fresne;" and behind both ballad and tale lies a common source "too far back for us to find." Yet it must be said that the material, so far as situation and action are concerned, lay everywhere at hand in the life out of which tale and ballad sprang.[1] A knight from over sea, doing the grand tour of those days, steals Annie and takes her home. She bears him seven sons and rules his house, till he bethinks him to get a lawful wife with shiploads of dower. His choice falls unwittingly on Fair Annie's sister, whom he brings to his castle, and who hears the "imprecation," quoted above, just in time to adjust matters, give her "tocher" to the old love, and "gae maiden hame." The complication and adjustment, this recognition motive, so effective at a crisis and so dear to Euripides, is found in a few other ballads, in "Babylon," "Child Maurice," "Horn," and belongs

---

[1] So in the Scandinavian ballads : "Perhaps no set of incidents is repeated so often in northern ballads as the forcing of the bower on the strand, the giving of keepsakes," and so on, says Mr. Child of the *Gil Brenton* group. In the Faroes it is the robbing of a girl by Frisian pirates. *Quidquid agunt homines* is a good source, and borrowing is not necessary for original motives.

of course to an incipient romance; but the robbery of a bride or sweetheart was common stuff and found frequent dramatic, choral presentation in ballads of the primitive type like that Faroe song of the Frisian pirates and its English version of "The Maid Freed from the Gallows." This is fundamental; the later epic process falls into two general classes. Either it connects with legend of the countryside, and so simply echoes the life of its makers and transmitters, or else it attracts to itself a motive or a story of international interest, a touch of old myth, a complex of partly local and partly foreign supernatural lore. Thus we have a short but intense "local" ballad, — "Earl Brand," let us say, — with purely human interest; or else a "Lady Isabel and the Elf Knight," with store of uncanny associations. These have still the mark of choral origins, in their incremental structure, their brevity, their fondness for the dramatic situation. Farthest from choral origins, an affair for the reciter rather than the singer, is the long, leisurely, "elegant" ballad of the type of "King Estmere." It will be well to look more carefully at these three types.

For the choral foundation, much has been said already in the discussion of "The Maid Freed from the Gallows;" but that is not a ballad of bride-stealing, however the Faroe version seems to point out such an origin. Luckily the Ditmarsh folk in Holstein come again to the rescue with a genuine ballad which they used for their *trymmeken* dance, and doubtless once made in the dance itself;

it reflects a perfectly simple fact of those old days in a
dramatic form which has already absorbed sundry epic
elements, and, by the hazard and imperfections of record,
has dropped sundry choral and dramatic features, re-
ducing its incremental repetition, and evidently cutting
out many details.   What carried it as actual " ballad,"
held the swing of the dancers, and contributed in no
small degree to its vogue, was the refrain, which was
sung as a chorus alternating with the lines of the text,
not as a "burden" or undersong :—

> "Sir Henry and his brothers, brothers all three,
>   — With power —
> They built them a boatie, a boatie for the sea,
>   — All for the noble roseflower.
>
> "And when the boatie, the boatie ready was,
>   — With power —
> They sat them all within it, they sailed far away,
>   — All for the noble roseflower.
>
> "When they westward, westward well had come,
>   — With power —
> There stood at his threshold a goldsmith's son,
>   — All with the noble roseflower.
>
> " 'Be ye now welcome, ye gentles all three,
>   — So fine and so fair —
> And will ye now mead, or will ye now wine?'
>   — Said the noble roseflower.
>
> " 'We will not have the mead, we will not have the wine,
>   — With power —
> But we will have the goldsmith's daughter so fine
>   — The noble roseflower.'

"'The goldsmith's daughter, 't is she ye shall not get,
 — So fine and so fair —
For all to Little Loikë her trothword is set,
 — The noble roseflower.'

"'Little Loikë, his bride he never shall get,
 — With power —
On that we three men will wager our necks
 — For the noble roseflower.'

" Little Loikë he drew out his shining brand
 — With power —
Henry's little finger he's hewed from the hand
 — For the noble roseflower.

"Sir Henry, he drew out his shining brand
 — So fine and so fair —
Little Loikë's head he has hewed sheer away,
 — For the noble roseflower.

"'Lie there, thou ancient, thou curly poll,
 — With power —
My heart with a thousand joys it is full
 — For the noble roseflower.'

" Little Loikë's children they wept so sore
 — With power —
'Tomorrow we must bury our father dear
 —For the noble roseflower.'"

This old ballad was thought by Müllenhoff to have been
in its original form a kind of sword-dance; [1] but as it
stands, it was used for a very strenuous and very dramatic dance, full of adventurous steps and gestures, in which
all the festal throng took part. In its long career, as we

[1] See Chambers, *Mediæval Stage*, chap. ix, for the popular origins
and the survivals in England.

have said, it has surely suffered both abbreviation and corruption of the text; for the original "ballad" we must restore the activity and purpose of Henry's brothers, here inactive, silent, and apparently superfluous. Their parts have been cut. So, in many French ballads, three girls, three young fellows, three cavaliers, three barons, three drummers, and so on, appear in due introduction; but only one of the three does or says anything. The others must be restored by analogy with longer, fuller ballads, — say "Guenillon." Here three cavaliers pass by the wood; the oldest cries, "I see a girl," the next, "She sleeps," but the youngest, "She shall be my love," — each in a stanza interlaced with the next, and with refrain and constant incremental repetition. Some ballads, of course, refuse to be cut; what would "Babylon" be without the two sisters, and their fate, as foil to the third? But in the main it was as obvious to cut the repetitions as it was to insert new details; and one may thus conjecture that the original "Sir Henry" had little of the narrative introduction, but a great deal more spinning out of the situation, more of the fight, and a succession of speeches by the three brothers, with the same insistent and incremental repetition that one finds in the Faroe ballad, itself a dramatic presentation, at the dance, of a maid stolen by Frisian pirates.

Cut loose from the dance, such a ballad could linger, like "Babylon," in the middle way of tradition, holding the ancient structure by reason of the central situation and its needs, and appealing to epic interest by tragic complication and climax. It could fall, as we have said, into one of two classes; it would tend to the local and domestic sort, or to the general and the romantic, the ballad of international type. In the first case, mainly tragic, the story grows out of a simple dramatic situation, is localized, and while not necessarily "true," needs no alien elements to explain it. It may acquire some romantic details in its course; but it remains a simple tale of love and obstacles, flight, fight, and death. This, at least, is the course of "Earl Brand," known also by Scott's version of "The Douglas Tragedy," localized near Yarrow banks, and by Percy's artificial "Child of Ell;" it is the story, found in many European ballads, notably in the Scandinavian "Ribold and Guldborg" and "Hildebrand and Hilde," and perhaps based on the old Hilde saga, of a girl who elopes, is intercepted by her father and her seven bold brethren, or simply by the brothers, and sees them all slain by her lover, who then rides home with her to his mother's bower, a mortally wounded man. In some of the Hilde versions, however, the elopement is happily achieved; and these have a parallel, if not a descendant, in "Erlinton," closely related to "Earl Brand," where the outlaw has killed the fifteen knights but spared the "auld, grey-headed" leader, and says to his bride: —

> "'Now ye'r my ain, I have ye win,
> And we will walk the green woods within.'"

In ballads of this first or purely domestic class, one invokes no metaphysical aid; no unnatural or supernatural element intervenes. " She is an honest woman," says dying Earl Brand as he rides up to his mother and defends the runaway bride from a hasty charge of wantonness; "marry her to my brother." All the characters are fair flesh and blood; the ballad is a piece of the wild old life in primitive days, and originally nothing more. To the simple dramatic foundation, indeed, have come epic features, derived from whatever immediate source, but common to many European versions, such as Carl Hood the informer, who may be Woden himself if one will, and the dying man's ride home. The name Brand may be from Hildebrand. Certain phrases of the Danish are repeated almost word for word in the English; though the latter has failed to appropriate the important climax of the fight where the maiden names her lover's name and so, by the old belief, robs him of his supernatural or unwonted power. But whether this main situation, the fact of flight, interception, and fight, repeated as it is by the nature of the case in every story of the kind, needs to be an importation from abroad or even a descent from older tales, is questionable. It was certainly no new thing.

Supernatural forces, on the other hand, along with a distinctly novel and striking fact, are at work from the outset in ballads of the "Lady Isabel" type. "Lady Isabel and the Elf Knight," which has "perhaps . . . the widest circulation" in all balladry, and claims over thirty pages of Professor Child's masterly introduction, owes its importance to its story and its story to widely related narrative elements. A woman, charmed by mystic horn or harp, by haunting echo of song, rides off to uncanny places, to lone nook of the forest, to Wearie's Well, to a "rank river," a sea, with the elfin knight, or with his counterpart, whom she has failed to detect, as her wiser sister did, and dismiss with a posing riddle. Whatever we do with that irrelevant bird in an English version, the elf is no ordinary lover, and the elopement is from no healthy impulse as in "Earl Brand." Birds, again, reveal the fate of Isabel's predecessors in sundry continental ballads; in one case these are turned to doves, and coo a timely warning. The severed head of the baffled betrayer speaks, and cunningly suggests magic which shall restore him to life. In most of the versions the girl escapes; but in "Young Andrew" [1] there is a different tale. She asks her merely mortal lover to marry her. "Bring your father's gold, then," he says. This done, he leads her to a hill and strips her of her fine clothes, as in the Isabel group; she goes home only to die at the door, while Andrew is properly but mysteriously devoured by a wolf, — maudlin tragedy, harrowing but alien stuff fitted awkwardly into the ballad of tradition. The best and oldest of the Isabel versions in English are very brief; only by combination of all, good and bad, can one make out the story as a whole. Two theories account for it. According to Professor Bugge, it is Judith and Holofernes retold and retouched. Professor Child, with some concession to Judith, prefers "an inde-

[1] No. 48, from the Percy MS.

pendent European tradition . . . of a half-human, half-
demonic being, who possessed an irresistible power of
decoying away young maids and was wont to kill them
. . . but who at last found one who was more than his
match." Modified, this story appears also in the Blue-
beard tales. That it is a good story, whatever its origin,
no candid reader will deny; but it is not necessary to find
its trail in every ballad of elopement. The "Fair Flower
of Northumberland,"[1] for example, where an English
lady frees a Scot from prison and flies with him, but is
cruelly used and deserted on Scottish soil, needs no elfin
explanation of the man's brutality, nor yet a source
in the Halewijn ballads of Flanders, particularly in
Halewijn's offer of a choice between gallows and sword.
Both in the very small group where supernatural elements occur, and in the large "domestic" group, the
hero, by modern ways of thinking, is more or less brutal;
indeed Child Waters himself, by his main treatment of
Fair Ellen, could give points even to Bill Sykes. But
that was the medieval way.

A third class of these ballads, freed from all choral
and dramatic constraint, without even a refrain, and yet
encumbered by no supernatural elements, could tread
a romantic path that was broad and easy and long. At
the extreme from all the leaping and throbbing of the
Holstein song about Sir Henry and the winning of his
bride is the ambling gait of "King Estmere." Here is

[1] No. 9. The epic element is pronounced, but version C has ample
traces of the choral form, and Deloney's copy (A) has its refrain.

a gentlemanly monarch, no protagonist, who takes counsel and help of his wise brother,[1] Adler Young, and seeks as wife the daughter of King Adland. Together the brothers ride; together they woo; and the betrothal duly takes place, not without features which suggest Siegfried's longer courting in the "Nibelungen." Then comes romantic danger in the shape of a "paynim," — surely Percy's own word. The King of Spain intervenes; but by the "gramarye" of Adler Young, who returns disguised as boy to Estmere, now in the familiar lendings of a harper, this foul "sowdan" is ignominiously baffled, with all his fighting men looking helplessly on, and is killed out of hand.

Of elopement ballads which belong to the older period, and show elements of romance or myth linking them to versions current throughout Europe, "Fair Annie" has been already described. "Gil Brenton"[2] has the same romantic interest, and the same averting of tragedy, in a closely allied plot; the long Scottish version, taken down from recitation in 1783, holds many primitive ballad traits, dwells on the dramatic situation, and is filled with incremental repetition almost from end to

[1] *Will Stewart and John*, no. 107, seems to be a degenerate *Estmere*. It is ridiculous in parts, for the hero takes to his bed at every rebuff; but it has interesting "allusions to manners and customs." The superfluous "Adlatts Parke" of the first stanza can hardly be a recollection of King Adland's demesne; but the brothers are understudies, conscious or not, of King Estmere and Adler Young; as we are told, —

"William he is the elder brother,
But John he is the wiser man."

[2] No. 5.

end. Refrains, too, are preserved with the majority of the versions. In the story, Gil Brenton brings home his bride, and sevenscore ships with her; but as she comes near the house, she weeps, and her page puts a good old triad of questions: —

> " ' O is there water i' your shee?
> Or does the win' blaw in your glee?
>
> " ' Or are you mourning i' your meed
> That eer you left your mither gueede?
>
> " ' Or are you mourning i' your tide
> That ever ye was Gil Brenton's bride.' " [1]

In corresponding stanzas of repetition, she denies questions one and two, but admits the truth of the third. Willie the page — the bride appears with no name — tells her that Gil Brenton has sent home already seven king's daughters, badly damaged, because they were not leal maids. Frightened, for good reasons, she tries the expedient of Ysoude and Brangwain, substituting her bower-woman; but miraculously speaking blankets, sheets, and pillows tell Gil Brenton the truth. His angry mother now puts questions, and finds out from the bride that once she met a knight in greenwood, who left tokens with her, easily recognized by the auld queen as belonging to Gil Brenton. So all is well, and a son is soon born; and for superfluity of confirmation —

> ". . . it was well written on his breast-bane,
> 'Gil Brenton is my father's name.' "

[1] Shee = shoe; glee = glove; meed = mood; gueede = good.

Ballads of this kind have the double value, first, of fidelity to the old way in their almost choral structure, their dramatic style, their descent by purely oral tradition, and, secondly, of the new epic and romantic interest which they share with the Scandinavian and other versions. The new interest gets full justice in an absorbing story and a good climax; the old interest remains not only in structure and style, but in details, in the importance attached to mere changes of the situation: —

> " The auld queen she was stark and strang;
> She gar'd the door flee aff the ban'.
>
> " The auld queen she was stark and steer;
> She gar'd the door lye i' the fleer." [1]

Robustious as she is, the auld queen plays a serviceable part here and smooths a rough path for the bride; in "Willie's Lady," close to "Gil Brenton" in form and derived from the same traditional source, the mother-in-law is evil-disposed and long prevents by her witchcraft the birth of Willie's son.

From these fine ballads we pass all too rapidly down a steep path to the common tales of runaways fair or foul, most of them localized in Scotland and many of them dropping to very low levels of verse. One or two of them, however, belong to the kingdom of romance. Brown Robin,[2] disguised as one of his love's thirty-

---

[1] A similar pair of couplets in the Danish ballad *Valdemar og Tove* (Olrik, B), 37, 38, which dates from MSS. of the sixteenth century.

[2] The ballads now cited are nos. 97, 102, 103, 106, 109, 108.

three Maries, or bower-women, escapes with her to the
wood: —

> "O she went out in a May morning,
>   In a May morning so gay;
> But she came never back again,
>   Her auld father to see."

"Willie and Earl Richard's Daughter" purports to
account, by like love and a later elopement, for the birth
of Robin Hood "in the gude green wood, amang the
lily flower;" but it has nothing to do with the Robin
Hood cycle. Rose the Red and White Lily, ill-treated
by their stepmother, take to the woods of their own
motion, and get into fine complications; but their forest
is of pasteboard and the ballad has no good greenwood
sights or sounds. Even less value attaches to "The Famous Flower of Serving-Men," where fair Elise plays
Cesario to a king and marries him, and to the doggerel
"Thomas of Potte," or "Tom Potts," a real serving-man,
who, in ninety-six stanzas, once thrilled a humble audience, and even got a sneer from Swift, over adventures
that end in his bridals with the daughter of Lord Arundel.
"False to Potts I'll never be," was her word from the
start, like Mrs. Micawber's; but it is interesting to see
the old ballad commonplaces floundering through the
mire of a minstrel broadside. The "little foot-page"
must run with a letter to the lover for a tip of forty
shillings; and the seventeenth-century serving-man's
point of view is made even more conspicuous by the fact
that good news in the answer raises our messenger's

gratuity to a gorgeous ten pound. Another poor ballad, also from the Percy manuscript, "Christopher White," in verses equally deject, tells how the wife of a merchant, as she "sate in a deske," sent money to her old lover, a banished man; he comes back in the merchant's absence, and proceeds to bolt not only with the wife but with "spoone and plate," silver and gold. The merchant is philosophical, if not emotional or even logical: —

> "All young men a warning take,
> A warning, looke, you take by me ;
> Looke that you love your old loves best,
> For in faith they are best companye."

"George Barnwell" looms close upon us here, and it is a far call from "Gil Brenton" and the rest; we are dealing with the degenerate remnant of that journalism noted on an earlier page, although a very faint touch of tradition gives it a claim to ballad honors. As we shall have little to do hereafter with the broadside style, it may be well now to point out that it never occurs, however humble the environment and the transmitters, in genuine ballads of tradition. The people to whom these stall-copies were recited or sung [1] or sold were, to be sure, no more ignorant or humble than the country folk who themselves sang and recited the simple but always dignified and competent verses of "Babylon" or "Gil Brenton;" the difference lies in the ballads, one living in

[1] Singing, however, was often a good antiseptic. Who wants to quarrel with the doggerel inclinations of *The Bailiff's Daughter of Islington*? Once hear it (no. 105) sung, and one forgives the drone of the words.

its native tradition, another getting into the hands of minstrel or printer and losing all but the faintest reminiscence and echo of its origin. Only such reminiscence, such echo, or the possibility of them, justified Professor Child, as he expressly declares, in "suppressing disgust" and admitting worthless or nearly worthless ballads, — the worthless because it might be "a debased representative of something genuine and better," and the others because something better, however little, clung to them.[1] In the first of these classes may be ranged three inferior ballads [2] which deal with international love-affairs. Johnie Scot goes to the English court, loves the king's daughter, and hies back to Scotland; her disgrace is discovered and she is put in prison to starve. Johnie returns with five hundred men, fights "an Italian" whom the king keeps, slays him, and wins the daughter. Willie o' Winsbury, in like predicament, is so blindingly and blushingly blond, clad in silk and scarlet, —

> "His hair was like to threeds o' gold,
> And his skin was as white as milk," —

that the king yields at once. "Take Janet," he says; and Willie, like his countryman Johnie Scot, insists that there shall be no dower, — a daring fiction. "Lang Johnny More" is a mere imitation, almost a parody, as Mr. Child says, of "Johnie Scot;" and is unconscionably long.

[1] See the Introduction to *Young Ronald*, no. 304, v, 182. Cf. *The Knight's Ghost*, no. 265; Mr. Child says that it "has not a globule of old blood."

[2] Nos. 99, 100, 251.

A larger group of ballads [1] deal with local elopement and bride-stealing; some of these Scottish verses are based on fact. The best of them, "Katharine Jaffray," whether itself the work of Scott or compiled from tradition, was certainly the model for his "Young Lochinvar;" it tells of bride-stealing in two senses. A Scots laird snatches his former Scots sweetheart from his English rival on the very day of the wedding, and rides off with her safe from pursuit. Mr. Child notes that "the attitude of the young woman to her first lover is not distinctly brought out in several copies;" perhaps it did not matter. In "Lord William," — or "Lord Lundy," — valuable chiefly because it comes from recitation, the bride is forced into marriage, but is rescued by her old lover. "Bonny Baby Livingston," in another traditional ballad, borne off to the Highlands for a forced marriage, gets word to her lover, Johny Hay, and is rescued with all the honors. Eppie Morrie, again, is the Scottish Brunhild; though carried to a castle and left with her would-be husband, she defends herself stoutly until morning, when the Lowland lover brings her help. Even more intrepid is the unnamed heroine of a late but jolly little piece, "Walter Lesly," with an effective refrain; tied on horseback and taken to an alehouse on the way to "Conland," she slips off while Walter indulges in a very intempestive nap.

[1] Printed by Child in his fourth volume. The numbers are from 221 on, and need not be further noted. — *Walter Lesly* is no. 296.

> "Then over moss and over muir sae cleverly she ran,
>   And over hill and over dale, without stockings or shoon;
>   The men pursued her full fast, wi' mony shout and cry,
>   Says, 'Will ye go to Conland, the winter-time to lye?'

> "'I'd rather be in Duffus land, dragging at the ware,
>   Before I was wi' Lesly, for a' his yellow hair,
>   For a' his yellow hair, and sae well's he can it tye;
>   I'll go no more to Conland, this winter-time to lye.'"

Another heroine, in "Broughty Wa's," swims her way
to freedom. There can be no doubt that these random
ballads were often "founded on fact;" the case is clear
for a fragment called "The Lady of Arngosk." Isobell
Dow, in 1823, remembered this bit of song and the facts
that gave rise to it; the rest of the verses she had forgotten. Her own mother was waiting-maid, about 1736,
to the Lady of Arngosk, a Miss Margaret Gibb, and
often told the daughter how Mr. Graham, a Highlander,
carried off mistress and maid to Braco Castle, and se-
cured them in an upper room till morning, when Mr.
Jamieson, the favored lover, appeared with hue and cry
and forced Graham to surrender his prisoners unharmed.
Whereupon, of course, the countryside rang with a ballad, which C. K. Sharpe, the well-known collector, had
heard in his youth, but of which he could remember
only one stanza. Helped a trifle more by Isobell Dow,
whose memory also failed her, Sharpe, in 1823, could
print only these opening verses: —

> "The Highlandmen hae a' come down,
>   They've a' come down almost,
>   They've stowen away the bonny lass,
>   The Lady of Arngosk.

"They hae put on her petticoat,
Likewise her silken gown;
The Highland man he drew his sword,
Said, 'Follow me ye's come.'

"Behind her back they've tied her hands,
And then they set her on;
'I winna gang wi' you,' she said,
'Nor ony Highland loon.'"

So local history found its way into ballads.

But the lady in the case did not always fare so well, as the ballad of "Rob Roy" can testify.[1] Jean Key, a widow of two months, was carried off by Rob Oig, younger son of Scott's hero, and forcibly married to him, dying within a year, while the MacGregor himself was tried and executed for his crime. Less tragic is "John o' Hazelgreen," where Scott found the refrain of his song; a gentleman abducts a girl who is moaning for John, and rides off with her, despite her tears, only to take her to his own house and be welcomed by his own son, — who turns out to be John of Hazelgreen.

There are ballads, again, where the lass is willing, but the parents are opposed. Duncan Grahame, a Highlander, persuades Bonny Lizie Bailie to marry him, —

"And she's up to Gillecrankie
To go among the heather.

"And she's cast off her high-heel'd shoes
And put on a pair of laigh ones,
And she's away with Duncan Grahame
To go among the brachans."

[1] See Scott's Introduction to his *Rob Roy*. The date of the occurrence was 1750.

Lizie Lindsay flies from Edinburgh with a young fellow who says his father is an old shepherd, takes her through rough ways till she wishes herself home, and finally reveals himself as Sir Donald. Glasgow Peggie goes through the same experiences to find herself Countess of Skye.[1] In these ballads, disordered though they seem to be, and favorites as they were in the stalls, there are glimpses of the old choral beginnings. One comes now and again on the trail of really dramatic versions, but does not find them; although it is known that ballads like "Andrew Lammie" were actually presented as a kind of rural play. Dugald Quin,[2] who courts Lizzie Menzies, wins her despite her father, and turns out to be a well-conditioned man, — the Old Lady's Manuscript notes that he was Marquis of Huntly, — carries on his wooing in a jolly dialogue full of repetition and lilt of the dance; there is hardly narrative enough for a ballad, comments Professor Child, and it is all the nearer to choral song. There is the same lilt, the same lively dialogue, in "The Beggar Laddie," as well as in "The Duke of Gordon's Daughter;" this young person elopes with her captain, who falls heir, in the nick of time, to an earldom. Young Peggy runs away in unexciting style; but Lady Elspat is intercepted in her flight and the lover is haled before a justice who turns out to be his uncle: all, in fact, ends well except the ballad,

[1] Different uses of this well-worn motive are found in *The Broom of the Cowdenknowes* and in *The Jolly Beggar*.
[2] No. 294.

which, as Mr. Child remarks, is "not impressive." In
"Glenlogie," where, again, the ancient structure is well
maintained, an impetuous girl falls in love with a man
already engaged, and her parents will do nothing; but
the good chaplain, in a travesty of the relative-climax,
writes so eloquently to Glenlogie that the laird yields at
once: —

"'Cheer up, bonnie Jeannie, ye are flow'r o' them a';
I have laid my love on you, altho I was promised awa'.'"

Reminiscent of "Tom Potts" in subject but not in
manner are two ballads which tell how a lady elopes with
her inferior: "Richie Story," founded on fact, where
repetition and refrain partly cloak poor stuff, and "The
Kitchie Boy," a very bad reminder of "Hind Horn." [1]

So much, barring a brace of quite negligible attempts,
for the ballads of bride-stealing and elopement. At their
best they echo the new call of romance with the old voice
and phrase of tradition; at their worst they are nevertheless fairly representative of their times, reflecting the life
of rural and isolated Scottish communities, even if Willie
of Douglas Dale,[2] who made a wife of his highborn sweetheart, took her to the wood as day dawned "and lions
gaed to their dens!" This glimpse of perilous and fearsome
adventure, however, was not all. Tradition laid hold of a
theme well known in European tales, and sang in two
sterling ballads [3] the trials and triumph of lovers who

[1] Compare *Lady Diamond*, no. 269, a poor echo of Boccaccio's
Guiscardo and Ghismonda, with the lover a "kitchen-boy."
[2] No. 101.
[3] Nos. 25, 96.

baffle the opposition of kinsfolk, outwit the vigilance of brothers and parents, and meet happily at last. "Willie's Lyke-Wake," an old, two-line, traditional ballad, with refrain and constant repetition, tells how the hero feigns death, and his love comes to the wake. The corresponding Swedish version, immensely popular, is "often represented as a drama by young people in country-places." The other of our ballads reverses the rôles of man and maid. In the "Gay Goshawk," a bird brings an English girl her Scottish lover's letter to the effect that he cannot wait her love longer. "Bid him bake his bridal bread and brew his bridal ale," she answers, "and I'll meet him." She goes to her father and asks one boon: "if I die, bury me in Scotland." She takes a "sleepy draught," — the device is familiar in romance, — seems dead, and is carried, as she directed in the usual incremental stanzas, repeated at the fulfillment of them, from kirk to kirk, until her lover meets her on safe ground. The seven brothers, amazed at cherry cheeks and ruby lips, are sent home "to sound the horn," outwitted by one more clever lass in the long epic series.

II. BALLADS OF KINSHIP

The mention of sister and brothers carries us to the large group of ballads that deal with complications of household and kin. Tragedy hovers over these, and, as in the case of their highborn rivals from the Oresteia to "Hamlet," seldom fails to fall upon them. Doggerel itself cannot hide in them the dignity of tragic passion; but when that old simplicity of repetition is allowed to do the

work alone, to carry the hopeless struggle of personality
against fate, and when the traditional note is untroubled,
then the ballad achieves those results which make the
critic claim it as art. We may, for the first of these cases,
regret the contamination of broadside style, but we cannot help admiring the genuine pathos of a "Bewick and
Graham" in the dilemma where choice halts between two
duties, both of them sacred yet mutually destructive, the
flaming sword over each path, and no God to intervene.
We know how a Greek chorus swells the agony of this
choice, and how soliloquy after soliloquy of Hamlet,
speech after speech of Rodrigue, rebel against it; our
ballad, already far gone in broadside ways, can still
sustain the old note in however deplorable style. Bewick
and Graham [1] are two young men living near Carlisle
who have "sworn brotherhood," perhaps, as Scott says,
"the very latest allusion" to this ancient rite; but their
fathers quarrel over the wine, and old Graham goes
home half drunk and whole angry to tell his son that
there must be a fight to the finish for the brothers-in-
arms. Most significant is the difference in style between
the original dialogue, which carries the two main situations as well as the preliminary quarrel, and the doggerel
minstrel verse which completes and fills out the "story."
Force, dignity, delicacy, little marred in the transfer to a
stall-copy, are set over against helplessness of expression
and dragging verse. Take the part where Graham tells
his son that the fight must be fought.

[1] No. 211. Contrast stanza 7 with the dialogue quoted!

"'Oh, pray forbear, my father dear;
    That ever such a thing should be!
Shall I venture my body in field to fight
    With a man that's faith and troth to me?'

"'What's that thou sayst, thou limmer loon?
    Or how dare thou stand to speak to me?
If thou do not end this quarrel soon,
    Here is my glove, thou shalt fight me.'

"Christy stoop'd low unto the ground,
    Unto the ground, as you'll understand!
'O father, put on your glove again,
    The wind hath blown it from your hand.'

"'What's that thou sayst, thou limmer loon?
    Or how dare thou stand to speak to me?
If thou do not end this quarrel soon,
    Here is my hand, thou shalt fight me.'

"Christy Grahame is to his chamber gone,
    And for to study, as well might be,
Whether to fight with his father dear,
    Or with his bully Bewick he.

"'If it be my fortune my bully to kill,
    As you shall boldly understand,
In every town that I ride through,
    They'll say, There rides a brotherless man!

"'Nay, for to kill my bully dear,
    I think it will be a deadly sin;
And for to kill my father dear,
    The blessing of heaven I ne'er shall win.

"'O give me my blessing, father,' he said,
    'And pray well for me for to thrive;
If it be my fortune my bully to kill,
    I swear I'll neer come home alive.'"

Protesting their love, the young men fight; Graham wounds Bewick mortally, but, true to his vow, falls on his own sword and dies. Bewick is still living when his father comes up: —

> "'Arise, arise, O son,' he said,
> 'For I see thou's won the victory.'
> 'Father, could ye not drunk your wine at home,
> And letten me and my brother be?'"

With a request to dig a grave wide and deep, and to bury them both in it, — "but bury my bully[1] Grahame on the sun-side, for I'm sure he's won the victory," —young Bewick has done, and the real ballad ends; although five stanzas are added to tell of the contrition of the two fathers. It is sterling stuff; "infectious" Mr. Child well calls it.

Nearly every family relation is involved in these canticles of love and woe which come from the very heart of traditional song; and they pass by obvious transition into the other group, also tragic in the main, of stolen or lawless love. But even here is no tragedy of what we now call romance; it is not a private grief, given in a kind of confidence to the reader; it is the tale of love and death as a community would voice it, square to the facts and going not a handbreadth beyond them. Even in the ballads of lovers, interest lies outside, as it were, of their private fate. While it cannot be said of balladry, as a recent writer has said of early Greek dramatic literature, that there is "perfect freedom from those pairs of lovers

[1] Billy, comrade.

who have been our tyrants since modern drama began,"
it is true that ballad-lovers are free from our curse of
sentiment. There is approach to it in a Scottish ballad
already cited as a favorite for dramatic presentation
among the Aberdeenshire folk; this piece may now be
described as a story where unequal station, the united
opposition of the maid's immediate kin, and more homely
but effective blows of fate, bring love to a swift and tragic
end. "Andrew Lammie" [1] is in the modern conventional style, but it has touches of the old way. A recurring
stanza: —

> "Love pines away, love dwines away,
> Love, love decays the body;
> For love o' thee, oh, I must die:
> Adieu my bonnie Annie ! " —

ought to be artificial, but does not so affect us. The
figure of the trumpeter, Andrew, blowing his last farewell — "I come, my bonnie Annie " — from the tower
of Fyvie castle to the mill of Tiftie where Annie lies beaten
to death by the blows of father, mother, and brother,
is a picture that is helped neither by similar scenes in
modern sentimental literature nor by the portrayal of it
in an actual image of the lover, set up on one of the castle turrets; still, it is pathetic enough and "justifies the

---

[1] No. 233. In no. 239, another tragic ballad, Jeanie is forced by her
parents to marry Lord Saltoun, though she loves Auchanachie Gordon. Brought home from the wedding, she dies just as Gordon returns
and asks to see her: —

> "He kissed her cold lips, which were colder than stone,
> And he died in the chamber that Jeanie died in."

remarkable popularity which the ballad has enjoyed in the north of Scotland."

Sentiment of this kind, however, has no part in the old breed of ballads which tell the tragedy of kin. The naked rock is covered by no vines of comment or suggestion; it is all hard fact, mainly brought out by a dialogue and in a dramatic situation. Some of these ballads are too familiar to describe. The false wife and wicked mother is revealed only by the very last line of "Edward," dialogue throughout: —

> "'Sic counseils ye gave to me.'"

"Edward," which the latest editor of the "Minstrelsy" calls a "doctored" ballad, with its hint to Heinrich Heine for one of the finest verses in the "Two Grenadiers," with its slow, strong movement, its effective repetition, its alternating refrain of simple vocatives, may be "doctored;" but would that its physician could be found!

After all, it is rather the cruel wife of which "Edward" tells than the cruel mother; but a traditional ballad[1] of the old two-line pattern with a refrain, and related to certain Danish versions, justifies its title. The young mother kills and buries her babe or babes, and goes back to her father's hall as leal maiden, only to see children playing there, who reproach her with her crime: —

> "'O cursed mother, heaven's high,
>   And that's where thou will ne'er win nigh.
>
> "'O cursed mother, hell is deep,
>   And there thou'll enter step by step.'"

[1] *The Cruel Mother*, no. 20.

Another cruel mother, who also has a brief chance to play the cruel mother-in-law, gives poison to her son because he marries against her will.[1] Cruelty in these cases, however, was felt to be the sin against nature; and ballads, though by no means so frequently in our English versions as elsewhere, turn for material to the stepmother and to the mother-in-law. A German scholar and historian of ancient things, Professor Schrader, has recently written a little monograph [2] on the mother-in-law which deserves to be widely known. Referring to the hackneyed stories, allusions, jokes, of modern days, Schrader follows the tradition through popular and classic literature back to its source in the evolution of the family. The fundamental fact is the relation of the husband's mother to his young wife; what can be and has been a helpful, pleasant alliance, appears at certain stages of culture, particularly represented by the Russian and even the modern Greek ballads, as unimagined woe. The worst stories come directly from life, and ballad or tale simply follows fact, — a hint for the too eager discoverer of a literary origin for every narrative in verse. A few English pieces reflect, however faintly, these Greek and Russian horrors; but in no case does one find old tragedy warmed over and served as a proper new jest. Often the man's mother, however suspicious of the bride, gladly takes

[1] *Prince Robert*, no. 87.

[2] *Die Schwiegermutter und der Hagestolz*, Braunschweig, 1904. For a few cases of the bad mother-in-law in continental ballads, see Professor Child's account of the "Testament" formula, i, 143 f.

charge of his child, as in "Earl Brand" and in the mawkish "White Fisher;" in the finest version of "Fair Janet," Willie goes with the new-born babe to his mother and is bidden to return and comfort his "fair lady," while the "young son" shall have nurses three. In "Gil Brenton" we saw the mother-in-law jealous of her son's rights, but helpful to disentangle a bad knot and prevent tragedy. In "Willie's Lady," however, a two-line piece from Scottish tradition, our *böse Schwiegermutter* stands out plain enough, working, by foul magic, to prevent the son's wife from bringing forth her child; the Billie Blin, "a serviceable household demon," who appears in three other Scottish ballads, reveals the remedy for this witchcraft. It may be said that the shadow of that aversion felt by the man's mother for his wife is a kind of compensation for the close relation of mother and son. Matriarchy in the background or not, the ballads give vast preference to the maternal as compared with the paternal relation. It is a justified suspicion of her son's sweetheart which makes the mother put those swift and throbbing queries in "Lord Randal." Mother, wife, and brother give the last consolations to Clerk Colvill; no father appears, and a tendency to neglect that important personage may be remarked in the ballads throughout. Advice comes chiefly from the mother, as one notes in the best version of "Lord Thomas and Fair Annet;" the addition of the father in some other versions is perfunctory; while in "Edward," the part of Orestes is reversed. Tradition, to be sure, would always set the matter right, if facts permitted, and the nearest way was to make the mother and her counsels as odious as might be. The hard-hearted mother-in-law personates her son, and ruthlessly turns his true-love from Gregory's door, in a familiar and pretty ballad known in several versions and by different titles, — "The Lass of Roch Royal." Poor Isabel, or Annie, goes baffled to her death, and Love Gregory wakes: —

> "'O wo be to you, ill woman,
>   And ane ill death mott you die !
> For you might have come to my bedside,
>   And then have wakened me.'"

The same complication, only that the mother's pains and benefits here concern her daughter and baffle the lover, has wandered into a tragic ballad, "The Mother's Malison, or Clyde Water." In fact, both motives appear. The man's mother begs him not to tempt his fate. Like the mother of Johnie Cock, who, however, spares malison and only expresses fears, Willie's mother offers him in incremental stanzas, with corresponding stanzas for his rejections, the best bed in the house, the best hen on the roost, and then, since he will not bide, the curse of drowning in Clyde. His appeal to the river, as Mr. Child points out, has a classical parallel: —

> "'O spair me, Claid's water,
>   Spare me as I gaa !
> Make me yer wrak as I come back,
>   But spare me as I gaa !'"

The girl finds him drowned in the stream, and says that the two mothers will be sorry: —

> "'For we's bath slipe soun in Clide's water.'"

To match the close relation of mother and son, we get a glimpse of the daughter who can dare everything for love of her sire. In a vigorous old ballad,[1] which has a parallel tradition to support its facts, but fails to maintain them in the light of history, Sir John Butler's hall is laid about and taken by his "Uncle Stanley" and other merry men. Ellen, the daughter, comes down "laced in pall," faces the invaders, and, *splendide mendax*, declares that her father is abroad. In vain. A faithful retainer makes a desperate stand at Butler's room: —

> "Ffaire him ffall, litle Holcrofft!
>   Soe merrilye he kept the dore,
> Till that his head ffrom his shoulders
>   Came tumbling down upon the ffloore."

Tangled as this story seems to be, truth lies somewhere behind it; the devoted daughter and the faithful servant — contemporary, almost, with that Paston family whose letters tell so much of domestic relations in the fifteenth century — are no fable, whatever their exact date and place.

The figure of the stepmother flits very dimly across the ballad. She gets short shrift in "The Laily Worm." She appears in "Rose the Red and White Lily," wicked of course, but subordinate and baffled; "Lady Isabel," [2] however, who this time has no elf-knight, but a lover beyond the sea and a weak father at home, is bidden by her angry and abusive stepmother to drink poisoned wine. She asks first to go to Marykirk, where she sees

[1] *Sir John Butler*, no. 165, from the Percy MS.   [2] No. 261.

her own mother sitting in a golden chair. "Shall I fly, mother, or drink?"—"Drink," is the answer; "your bed is made in a better place than ever hers will be." Isabel drinks and dies; the stepmother goes mad "in the fields."

Fickle husbands and false wives play no great part. In the group of comparatively modern ballads, a certain Earl of Aboyne,[1] who is courteous and kind to every woman, nevertheless has the fault that "he stays ouer lang in London." At last he comes; his lady marshals all the grooms, minstrels, cooks, chambermaids, a stanza for each degree; stately she steps to meet him: "Welcome, thrice welcome from London." "Kiss me," says the earl lightly; "for the morn should hae been my bonny wedding-day had I stayed the night in London!"—"Go kiss your ladies in London!" answers the offended wife. —"An unworthy welcome," cries he; "men, we'll go back." She begs to be taken with him, but in vain; lives a scant year, and dies of broken heart. The earl absurdly enough puts fifteen lords in black, and weeps up to the very gates of Aboyne. Another wife, the Lady of Leys,[2] is more medieval in her point of view; when she learns of the baron's escapade, —

> "That the laird he had a bairn,
> The warst word she said to that was
> 'I wish I had it in my arms,'"

[1] No. 235. Version J removes the absurdities by making Peggy Irvine his truelove, to whom he is pledged, and not his wife. In no. 240, *The Rantin Laddie*, an Earl of Aboyne fathers the bairn of a sweetheart and brings her home in due form.

[2] *The Baron o Leys*, no. 241.

offering to sell her jointure-lands and so release her "rantin laddie" from his alternative of death or ten thousand crowns. A foolish husband is Earl Crawford,[1] whose ballad is based on facts that happened in the sixteenth century and was traditionally recited or sung late in the nineteenth. Lady Crawford, a trifle jealous of her lord's devotion to their child, jests about its paternity; and the angry man sends her home. She dies of a broken heart just as Crawford has determined to take her back. There is no death in the ballad of "Jamie Douglas,"[2] but there is a very sad wife, who speaks throughout in the first person, takes into the ballad some stanzas of the fine song of "Waly, Waly," and blames Lockwood, a retainer of the Marquis, for bringing about their separation. This separation is historical fact, and took place in 1681. Another Douglas ballad exists only in a single stanza: —

> "The Countesse of Douglas, out of her boure she came,
>   And loudly there that she did call:
> It is for the Lord of Liddesdale
>   That I let all these teares downe fall," —

but this more serious case of marital troubles seems not to be true.

With the actual breach of marriage vows, balladry has little concern. There is a small group of serious ballads which belong here, two of them excellent; and these are matched by a single but successful humorous ballad well known in many lands. "Our Goodman"[3] comes unexpectedly home and sees a horse at the door.

[1] No. 229.   [2] No. 204.   [3] No. 274.

> " 'What's this now, good wife,
>   What's this I see?
>   How came this horse here
>   Without the leave o' me?'
> 'A horse?' quo she. — 'Ay, a horse,' quo he.
>   'Shame fa' your cuckold face,
>   Ill mat ye see!
>   'T is naething but a broad sow
>   My minnie sent to me.'
> 'A broad sow?' quo he. — 'Ay, a sow,' quo she. —
>   'Far hae I ridden,
>   And farer hae I gane,
>   But a sadle on a sow's back
>   I never saw nane.' "

All the rest is incremental repetition on the frame of these
stanzas, — jack-boots are explained as water-stoups,
sword as porridge-spurtle, or stirring-stick, and so on to
a climax which the hearer can continue as he pleases. It
has been noted above [1] that this ballad, a situation full
of repetition and capable of unlimited insertions, is sung
in several parts of France "as a little drama." In rare
cases, it has a serious ending; but that is against the
spirit of the piece, and we need not be alarmed at the
threat: —

> " Je t'y mènerai z'en Flandre
>   Et puis t'y ferai pendre . . ."

which the woman parries with "Keep that terrible fate
for French robbers!" [2]

[1] See p. 103, and Child, v. 90.

[2] Two young girls "play" this ballad, one made up as angry shepherd,
the other as timid shepherdess, singing it from house to house, accompanied by the young folk of the village. — Puymaigre, *Chants Populaires*, 1865, pp. 215 ff.

Serious enough are the other English ballads which deal with this theme. "Child Owlet" and the "Queen of Scotland,"[1] one tragic, the other not, are negligible; but "The Bonny Birdy," with its "admirably effective" refrain, where an ill-treated bird reveals to a husband the treachery of his wife, and two ballads from the Percy Folio, "Old Robin of Portingale" and "Little Musgrave and Lady Barnard,"[2] deserve the highest praise. The story, naturally enough, is the same in both of these pieces, but they differ in details. Old Robin, after he has slain, with surprising agility for his years, not only Sir Gyles the lover, but four and twenty of Gyles's "next cousins," knights, who came to help ding the husband down, and has then cruelly, but by good right, mutilated the offending bride, is seized with generous remorse, laments in conventional but effective stanzas his violence to a woman and his slaughter of a good knight, burns the cross into his own flesh, — "shope the cross in his right sholder, of the white flesh and the red," — and fares on a crusade.

> "God let never soe old a man
> Marry soe yonge a wife . . ."

is the opening word of the ballad, which reminds one here of Heine's "Es war ein alter König." Lord Barnard, however, in the companion piece, is not said to be old, and his lady was not married against her will; she is pure wanton. Barnard's wild ride for vengeance, and the song of warning when his horn blew, — "Away, Musgrave, away!" — half heard and understood by the lover, un-

[1] Nos. 291, 301.   [2] Nos. 82, 80, 81.

heard by the lady, are as effective as may be, and were popular long ago. Percy noted the quotations from this ballad by Beaumont and Fletcher.[1] Passions jostled each other rudely in the old time. Barnard rides for vengeance, but will not "kill a naked man," and of his two swords gives Musgrave the better; wounded at the first stroke, a conventional situation, he slays his man at the second. Lady Barnard will pray for Musgrave's soul, she says defiantly, "but not for thee, Barnard!" He cuts her cruelly in the old act of mutilation for adultery, and her heart's blood runs trickling down. Then, as with Robin of Portingale, the sudden repentance: —

> "'Woe worth me, woe worth, my mery men all,
>   You were neer borne for my good;
> Why did you not offer to stay my hand
>   When you see me wox so wood?[2]

> "'For I have slaine the bravest sir knight,
>   That euer rode on steed;
> So have I done the fairest lady
>   That ever did woman's deed.'"[3]

[1] *Knight of the Burning Pestle*, v, 3; *Bonduca*, v, 2; *Monsieur Thomas*, iv, 11.

[2] Wood = mad.

[3] B, the Percy MS. version, has the better reading:—

> " That ever wore woman's weed," —

and adds an interesting line: —

> " So have I done a heathen child," —

that is, an unbaptized, unchristened child. — A very curious marital complication, not the sort, one would think, for ballads or any other literature, is recorded in the *Earl of Errol*, no. 231, a saucy, dashing ballad on the Earl's part.

It will be noted that "Child Maurice" ends somewhat
in this way and with such an imprecation. But " Child
Maurice" is not a simple tale of lawless love and revenge;
like "Babylon," it belongs to the tales of mistake and
tragic "recognition." The wife is at least true to her
vows; the supposed lover whom she was to meet in the
Silver Wood, and whose message was overheard by the
husband, is her son; and the swift, unexpected climax
of discovery and death is a far better foil for these words
of despair from the husband. He has tossed Child
Maurice's head to her: "lap it soft and kiss it oft, for thou
lovedst him better than me!" And she: " I never had
child but one, and you have slaine him." Not only is
the husband's outburst better phrased: —

> "Sayes, 'Wicked be my merrymen all,
> I gave meate, drinke, and clothe !
> But cold they not have holden me
> When I was in all that wrath !
>
> "'For I have slain one of the curtiousest knights
> That ever bestrode a stede,
> So have I done one of the fairest ladyes
> That ever ware woman's weede,'"—

but it is thus that we know of her breaking heart and
death. No wonder that Gray, as sensitive a critic, as
scholarly a poet, as ever lived, almost lost his balance over
a version of this ballad, and wrote in words that cannot
be quoted too often: "It is divine. . . . Aristotle's best
rules are observed in it in a manner which shews that the
author never had heard of Aristotle. It begins in the fifth

act of the play. You may read it two-thirds through without guessing what it is about; and yet, when you come to the end, it is impossible not to understand the whole story." [1]

Supernatural complications in the crime against wedlock will be noted in "James Harris," one of that small group of ballads which deals with the other world. [2] True wives and leal maidens also find words of commendation. Brown Adam, [3] the outlaw, comes back from greenwood to find his wife sturdily but despairingly resisting not only a gallant's purse of gold, but a drawn sword; and Brown Adam has

> ". . . gard him leave his bow, his bow,
> He's gard him leave his bran';
> He's gard him leave a better pledge,
> Four fingers o' his right han'."

A poor ballad, "Redesdale and Wise William," is interesting not only for the "Cymbeline" motive, a wager between two men about a woman's virtue, but because in this case it is Wise William's sister, not his wife, whose chastity is put to proof. Redesdale loses his lands and goes over sea. Brother and sister, it would seem, are an older combination for these instances of close confidence and affection than husband and wife or lover and sweetheart; and it has been suggested [4] that the various tales

---

[1] Gray to Mason, *Works*, ed. Gosse, ii, 316. The "play" is Home's *Douglas*.

[2] See below, p. 216.

[3] No. 98.

[4] By the late Gaston Paris, as reported by one of his students. The present writer has sketched the case for the sister's son in a paper of that

should be so ordered in their final chronology. The ballads have preserved some remarkable traces of the precedence of a sister's son over a man's own son, a condition which was noted by Tacitus among the ancient Germans, and is the subject of considerable comment by ethnologists who find it still surviving among barbarous nations and savage tribes. There is no English ballad, however, which brings out this whole complex of relationship so well as the Danish "Nilus og Hillelille," reminding one not only of the scene in the old "Waltharius," where Hagen refuses to fight his brother-in-arms until the latter kills Hagen's own sister's son, but also of the vague tradition that on the Danish throne itself it was the custom for the king to be succeeded not by his own issue, but by his sister's son. Sir Nilus marries Hillelille the fair; riding homeward with his bridal train, which includes his two sister's sons, they are overtaken on the heath by wind and rain and cold. Nilus would take shelter with his bride's mother's brother, Sir Peter, but there is feud between them. Nilus has killed Sir Peter's brother. "I will reconcile you," says the bride. They ride to Peter's house; and Peter reproaches his niece for her marriage. He had a better match for her; moreover, — Sir Nilus knows whom he has slain! The bride goes to her room; the men drink mead and wine. Peter goes out and brings in his brother's sword, throwing it down on the table: "You know you killed him?" Nevertheless, Nilus shall go in

title in *An English Miscellany*, the Furnivall Memorial Volume, Oxford, 1901.

peace and all his men, "save only thy two sister's sons!"
These are ready to fight. Sir Nilus looks on and at last
sees them felled dead to the earth. In spite of a pious vow,
Nilus draws his sword and plays the man, getting at last
a mortal wound. "Come, Hillelille; it is time to ride!"
They ride home; his sister meets him, and asks for her
two sons. "Be a mother to my wife," cries the dying
man, after he has told the fate of his dearest kin. But the
sister cannot do that. "How can I be fain with her who
has made me lose my two sons and my brother?" Nilus
dies in his sister's arms; and the bride falls dead of grief.
The grouping of relatives here is extraordinarily interesting; brother and sister, the sister's sons, the mother's
brother — such are the nearest and dearest of kin. No
one English ballad shows this concentration; but the
cumulative details of a score of ballads come to the same
thing. The substitution of wife for sister is evident, along
with some well-worn details, in Buchan's contribution
from the north of Scotland, "The Twa Knights."[1]

On the whole, ballad ideals of true wifehood, while
including loyalty to the marriage vows in a narrower
sense, would undoubtedly make it cover more positive
virtues. We may remember that our old epic, the Beowulf, sets up two types of womanhood, or of queenhood,
one very good and one very bad; if we sought for a
similar pair in the ballads, we could find the good wife
and mother sharply outlined in the heroine of the ballad
of "Captain Car," an English version of which is practi-

[1] No. 268.

cally contemporary with the event that it narrates, — the burning, in 1571, of a castle not far from Aberdeen, along with the mistress and twenty-seven inmates; while the more shadowy figure of the bad wife is revealed in the "Baron of Brackley." [1] Even those fierce times could not away with the brutality of Car, or, as some versions have it, of Adam Gordon; and the answer of the Lady Hamilton, who, it seems, should be a Forbes, awoke an admiring response in the ballad world. Leaning on her castle wall, she sees a troop coming, and thinks it to be her "wed lord," but it turns out to be traitor Captain Car. "Give over thy house, thou lady gay," he bids; and adds insult to the demand.

> " ' I will not give over my hous,' she saithe,
>   ' Not for feare of my lyffe ;
>   It shall be talked throughout the land,[2]
>   The slaughter of a wyffe.' "

She fires shots that miss Car but kill "other three." Hard pressed, she demands safety for her eldest son; the captain bids her let the boy down in a sheet, and assures a good reception. This is done; he cuts out the child's tongue and heart, and casts them over the wall to the mother. Owing to a traitor within her castle, the place is now fired.

> " But then bespake the little child,
>   That sate on the nurses knee;
>   Saies, 'Mother deere, give ore this house,
>   For the smoke it smoothers me.'

[1] Nos. 178, 203.
[2] See similar phrase below, p. 210, from a widow.

> " ' I would give all my gold, my childe,
>   So would I doe all my fee,
>   For one blast of the westerne wind
>   To blow the smoke from thee.' " [1]

But there is no thought of surrender and dishonor; she dies with her children; and she was indeed "talked throughout the land," a wife such as wives should be. Types are generally taken from folk in high place. A lowlier but vivid ideal of wifehood is in "Adam Bell;" while the wife of Geordie, who saves that hero from the very block, by offering all she holds dear,[2] mills, uncles, her own children, is at least of gentle blood. But in the "Baron of Brackley," a ballad fairly Homeric for simplicity,[3] for the effective use of name and place, and more than Homeric in its intense clannish sentiment, there is another kind of wife. Barring the question of dates, and the probable confusion of two Brackleys, one killed by a Farquharson, in 1666, another — very likely the husband of our heroine — in 1592, there is no doubt of the type and reputation of the wife as portrayed by the ballad. Inverey with his caterans comes down Deeside "whistlin' and playin'," knocks at Brackley's gates, and demands his blood. The baron naturally hesitates to go out. His lady taunts him with cowardice; and he summons his fighting kin for a hopeless struggle.

> " At the head o the Etnach the battel began,
>   At little Auchoilyie thei killd the first man.

[1] Text of the Percy MS.

[2] In B, no. 209.

[3] Professor Child is surely not quite just to its qualities in bracketing it with *The Fire of Frendraught* (196) as "fairly good."

"First they killed ane, and soon they killed twa,
Thei killed gallant Brackley, the flour o them a'.

"Thei killd William Gordon and James o the Knock,[1]
And brave Alexander, the flour o' Glenmuick.

"What sichin and moaning was heard i the glen,
For the Baronne o Braikley, who basely was slayn!

"'Cam ye bi the castell, and was ye in there?
Saw ye pretty Peggy tearing her hair?'

"'Yes, I cam by Braikley, and I gaed in there,
And there saw his ladie braiding her hair.

"'She was rantin, and dancin, and singin for joy,
And vowin that nicht she would feest Inverey.

"'She eat wi him, drank wi him, welcomd him in,
Was kind to the man that had slayn her baronne.'

"Up spake the son on the nourice's knee,
'Gin I live to be a man, revenged I'll be.'

"Ther's dool i the kitchin and mirth i the ha',
The Baronne o Braikley is dead and awa'."

Such are the ballad's typical wives, good and bad,[2] drawn by the hand of tradition on a background of actual experience. We turn again to the tragedy of kin, and those ballads which derive not so much from actual persons and events as from the general store of human passions and the general experience of fate. "The Cruel Brother," already noted, is "one of the most popular of

[1] Text: "Knox."
[2] See, also, the *Three Ravens*, and *Bonny Bee Hom*, below, p. 198, for constancy.

Scottish ballads," according to Aytoun the most popular; it holds to the primitive form and has a varying stock of refrains. A knight, or "gentleman," chooses and wins the youngest of three sisters:—

> " One o' them was clad in red:
> He asked if she wad be his bride.

> "One o' them was clad in green:
> He asked if she wad be his queen.

> " The last o' them was clad in white:
> He asked if she wad be his heart's delight."

This is strongly suggestive of the old partner verses in genuine ballads of the dance; and it is followed by similar repetitions which express the "asking-permission" formula, also choral in its source. Our wooer asks all the bride's kin for consent, forgetting only her brother John. The tragedy has slipped from its old levels, where a brother was really his sister's keeper and found a husband for her as Sir Peter had vainly done in the Danish ballad cited on a preceding page; here is mere ferocity of resentment for a slight, when, on the wedding-day, John sets the bride upon her horse for the ride to church, and stabs her to the heart. She makes the usual legacies, interesting in this case for the glimpse of a bad sister-in-law who may have inspired brother John's crime.

> "O what will you leave to your father dear?
> 'The silver-shod steed that brought me here.'

> " What will you leave to your mother dear?
> 'My velvet pall and my silken gear.'

"What will you leave to your sister Anne?
'My silken scarf and my gowden fan.'

"What will you leave to your sister Grace?
'My bloody cloaths to wash and dress.'

"What will you leave to your brother John?
'The gallows-tree to hang him on.'

"What will you leave to your brother John's wife?
'The wilderness to end her life.'"

As in the Danish ballad quoted above, brother and sister represent a relation of ancient sanctity, and there are traces of the brother's almost paternal position. Another brother, in "Lady Maisry," bids his sister give up her lover across the border, or be burned alive; seven brothers avenge a like stolen love in "Clerk Saunders;" while in a far poorer piece, Earl Rothes betrays a young lad's sister, and the boy swears that when he is grown he will thrust his sword through the betrayer's body.[1] Not only slighted authority is in play; there is the modern motive of rivalry. Spread over the British Isles, not even now quite extinct as tradition, and popular to the point of parody, "The Twa Sisters"[2] is a good match for "The Cruel Brother," is equally primitive in form and as rich in the old repetition. Best known in the version of the "Minstrelsy," with a refrain "Binnorie, O Binnorie," this ballad is palpably compounded of the dramatic "relative" situation with epic and romantic elements which may be reduced to the idea that a dead girl's lover, or else a great harper, strings his harp with three locks

[1] See nos. 65, 69, 297.   [2] No. 10.

of her yellow hair with strange results in the playing. The younger of two sisters, chosen as usual by the wooing knight, who, however, has also courted the elder with sundry gifts, is pushed into the water by her rival and is drowned. The miller finds her body in his dam, and wonders; but the harper, who comes by, strings his harp with her hair and plays to the king at dine:—

> "The first tune he did play and sing,
>   Was, 'Farewell to my father, the king.'

> "The nextin tune that he playd syne,
>   Was, 'Farewell to my mother, the queen.'

> "The lasten tune that he playd then,
>   Was 'Wae to my sister, fair [1] Ellen.' "

Here the harp, with its farewell, represents the usual conclusion in a series of legacies. So, in the ballad noticed twice before, when accident or jealousy brings two brothers to blows, and then, with fatal conclusion, to forgiveness and love, the affecting messages for home take the place of the legacy formula. More complicated, and of course without this legacy conclusion, is the rivalry of two brothers in the best versions of "Lord Ingram and Chiel Wyat,"[2] — in one case they are uncle and nephew, — where both lay their hearts on one lady. Ingram courts her openly, and gets consent of kin; Wyat has secretly gained her love. The wedding is set; she sends the usual bonny boy with a message to Wyat; and immediately after the marriage tells her unwelcome husband that she

---

[1] C reads "false."   [2] No. 66.

had warned him in every detail. He will father the bairn,
he says; she refuses with contempt. Then up starts Chiel
Wyat, out of space it would seem; and the brothers kill
each other. Lady Maisry goes mad.

Still another form of brotherly vengeance, like Hamlet's, spares the woman and seeks out the man. A brother
could love well as Wise William did, and he could hate
well, — if not, as just now, the sister, then the sister's
spouse. Here is another brother John, who harbors nobler
ideas of vengeance for a sister's ill-placed love.

> " ' O true-love mine,[1] stay still and dine,
>   As ye ha' done before, O !'
> 'O I 'll be hame by hours nine,
>   And frae the braes of Yarrow.'
>
> " ' O are ye going to hawke,' she says,
>   'As ye ha done before, O ?
> Or are ye going to weild your brand
>   Upon the braes of Yarrow ?'
>
> " ' O I am not going to hawke,' he says,
>   'As I have done before, O.
> But for to meet your brother Jhon
>   Upon the braes of Yarrow.' "

An unequal fight, a blow from men at his back, and the
lover or husband is "sleeping sound on Yarrow," whither
the lady goes to find him, and to die. Landscape and ballad hold together; it is superfluous to dwell on the charm
of these haunting lines, which, in nearly all versions, keep

---

[1] *The Braes o Yarrow*, no. 214, A. In all versions "the family of the
woman are at variance with the man." In group A–I hero and heroine
are married; in J–P lovers (Child).

the melodious name of the river sounding from verse to verse, and are echoed by the masters of English poetry.[1]

A tragic complication of kinship which literature is wont to avoid, but which was not unknown in wilder times, is the lawless love of brother and sister. The mere possibility of it gives superfluous horror to the tragedy of "Babylon." In "Sheath and Knife," in "Lizie Wan," [2] the relation is known and nakedly horrible; in "'The Bonny Hind" and "The King's Dochter Lady Jean," [3] it is ignorance on the man's part and ignorance as well as helplessness on the woman's part. Despite their subject, all these ballads are of the old and sincere kind, particularly "Sheath and Knife." Mother and child die in the forest; Willie comes back forlorn to his father's court, where are minstrels and music and dancing: —

> "'O Willie, O Willie, what makes thee in pain?'
> (*The brume blooms bonnie and says it is fair.*)
> 'I have lost a sheath and knife that I'll never see again.'
> (*And we'll never gang doun to the broom onie mair.*)"

Lizie Wan confesses to her father and is killed by the brother, Geordie; in remorse he tells his mother what he has done, and will sail in a bottomless boat, coming back

---

[1] No. 215, *Rare Willie Drowned in Yarrow*, pretty enough, but little more than a lament of a girl for her lover, with no story, has more details when transferred in other versions from Yarrow to the "waters of Gamry."

[2] Nos. 16, 51. The assumption that 51, *Lizie Wan*, and 52, *The King's Dochter*, are the same ballad, asserted positively by Mr. Henderson in his edition of the *Minstrelsy*, iii, 376, seems unnecessary in view of this vital difference between ignorance and knowledge.

[3] Nos. 50, 52.

when "the sun and the moon shall dance on the green."
In "The Bonny Hind," Lord Randal's daughter asks her
sudden lover who he is; he is Jock Randal, come o'er the
sea; and she kills herself at once. Lady Jean, king's
daughter, has the same experience, the same fate, — but
this ballad, while traditional, is not well told.[1]

Complications of the family might also follow the
treachery of a servant. Most audacious, and most tragic
in its results, is the faithlessness of the churl servant in
"Glasgerion,"[2] or, as the Scottish traditional version has
it, "Glenkindie." The hero, who may be, along with
Chaucer's Glascurion, a historical Welsh bard, is the
harper who can harp ladies mad; and a king's daughter
bids him to her bower. He tells his boy, Jacke, who promises to waken him in time for the tryst; but the servant
forestalls his master. " Have you left bracelet or glove?"
asks the lady, when Glasgerion arrives. He swears by
oak and ash and thorn, a fine old heathen oath, he had
never been in her chamber. " No churl's blood shall
spring in me," she says, and draws her knife. Glasgerion

---

[1] *Leesome Brand*, no. 15, should be named in connection with births
in the forest. Tristram, however, or the false Robin Hood, is less likely
to result than the babe or babes that are slain either purposely or by
neglect. The frankness of the ballads about this matter is only matched
by their convention of necessary absence on the part of the man, even
if death be caused by his absence when no one else can help. Note also a
remarkable ballad, which tells of a maid who marries, full of foreboding,
after five of her six sisters have died in childbirth. Her own fears come
true. See *Fair Mary of Wallington*, no. 91. There is a corresponding
Breton ballad.

[2] No. 67, from the Percy MS.

goes home a woe man. "Come hither, thou Jacke, my boy; if I had killed a man to-night, I would tell thee; but if I have not killed a man to-night, Jacke, thou hast killed three!"

Not so poignant, so swift and grim, are the other ballads of trust betrayed by servants. In "Captain Car" we saw that a steward, or the like, betrayed his lady and "kindled in the fire." Also subordinate to the main story is the treachery of the nurse in "Lamkin,"[1] where the lady of the house and her child are likewise done to death, but here by one man, the mason, who has built the castle, has had no pay for it, and in the lord's absence takes fiendish revenge. An old Kentish version of this ballad, which is mainly from Scotland, and very widespread there, ends in a cumulative relative-list[2] which can be indefinitely drawn out: Lady Betty is bidden to come down and see her mother's heart's blood run; down she comes and begs to die for her mother; but again the call sounds, this time for Lady Nelly to come and see her sister's blood, then Lady Jenny, and so on. The Scottish versions, however, simply make the nurse, a false limmer, let Lamkin in at a little shot-window while men and women of the castle are away. Lamkin kills the baby, and so brings down its mother, who is killed despite her appeal for mercy. The rhythm of most of the versions — Child prints twenty-six — is peculiar: —

> "'O still my bairn, nourice,
>   O still him wi' the wand!'

[1] No. 93.   [2] See p. 103, above.

'He winna still, lady,
    For a' his father's land.'
'O still my bairn, nourice,
    O still him wi' the bell!'
'He winna still, lady,
    Till ye come down yoursel.'" [1]

More epic than "Lamkin," which is of the older "situation" type of ballad, is "Fause Foodrage;" [2] here the faithless retainer slays his king, but lets the queen live till she bears her child. If it prove a lass, it shall be well nursed; a lad-bairn must die at once. The queen, escaping from her guards, bears a boy; but exchanges it with the baby girl of Wise William and wife. When he grows up, the lad kills the usurper and marries Wise William's lass. The style is not good; king and queen need not be taken seriously. In "Sir Aldingar," [3] however, already mentioned as the probable theme in one of William of Malmesbury's anecdotes, we have an old widespread tale, with trial by combat, and with variations of incident which can be traced to the stores of romance.

[1] The nursery, where this ballad, so full of repetition and so insistent in tune, was most at home, varied Lamkin's name. One Northumberland nurse sang: —

" Said my lord to his ladye,
    As he mounted his horse (bis)
Take care of Long Lankyn
    That lies in the moss. (bis)
Said my lord to his ladye,
    As he rode away,
Take care of Long Lankyn
    Who lies in the clay."

He was Longkyn, Lammikin, Balcanqual, and so on.

[2] No. 89.

[3] No. 59. See above, p. 53.

It is told in the straightforward ballad way, and is at the other extreme from the story by allusion and suggestion, — say "Count Gismond," where Browning gives a glimpse of the same material. Sir Aldingar, false steward, would have seduced our comely queen; but "our queen she was a good woman, and evermore said him nay." He puts a leper into the queen's bed; "a loathsome cripple," says Harry King, "for our dame Queen Elinor." Accused, she remembers her dream; a griffin has stript her of crown and kirtle, and would have borne her away to its nest, but for "a little hawk flying out of the east," which strikes down the griffin. Forty days are given the queen to find a champion, else she is to be burned. A messenger rides south, in vain; the second, riding far east, speeds better, finding "a little child," who sends word to the queen that when bale is highest boot is nighest, and that her dream — repeated in detail — will come true. It does; and Aldingar, mortally wounded by the child, confesses all: "thy wife, King Harry, —

> "Thy wiffe she is as true to thee
> As stone that lies on the castle wall."

The "lazar," made whole, is steward in Aldingar's stead. This is from the Percy Folio. Another version, "Sir Hugh le Blond," with a steward called Rodingham, comes from the recitation of an old woman in Scotland. A poor ballad, "James Hatley," [1] makes Sir Fenwick, aged thirty-three, steal the king's jewels and lay the blame on Hatley, who is but fifteen. The youth gives Fenwick three

[1] No. 244.

wounds, forces confession, and marries the king's daughter, who has got for him this favor of trial by battle. An ambitious false steward to the Lord of Lorn[1] is sent with his master's only son, a youth of prodigious learning, on the grand tour, beginning with France, and undertakes to drown the heir; he has a kind of mercy on the boy, however, strips him of his finery, clothes him in leather, and makes him take another name and tend sheep. The recognition comes, after tedious stanzas, at the French court; the ballad derives very superfluously from a romance. There are, of course, other ballad persons who betray their trust of service or hospitality; and for the most part they get a good curse for their pains. That old palmer who tells the foresters of Johnie Cock, old Carl Hood in "Earl Brand," the old wife in "Adam Bell," and the imitated "Auld Matrons" in her own ballad,[2] — it is not clear why all informers should be old,—match the "great-headed monk" who betrays Robin Hood to the sheriff of Nottingham.

The truelove also can be false or fickle, — and still a truelove; the adjective having lost in most cases its qualifying force. True love at its best, stronger than death, is beautifully sung in the ballad of "The Three Ravens,"[3] which is unfortunately not so well known as its cynical pendant, "The Twa Corbies." Instead of hawk and hound and lady fair, all false to the new-slain knight, —

> "Down in yonder greene field
> There lies a knight slain under his shield.

[1] No. 271, from Percy MS. [2] No. 249. [3] No. 26.

> "His hounds they lie downe at his feete,
> So well they can their master keepe.

> "His haukes they flie so eagerly
> There's no fowle dare him come nie."

His love comes, kisses his wounds, and carries him to the shroud:—

> "She buried him before the prime,
> She was dead herself ere even-song time." [1]

Another true truelove is the lady of "Bonny Bee Hom," whose fidelity is better brought out by the widow's song [2] which the ballad partly repeats:—

> "There shall neither coif come on my head, nor comb come in my hair;
> There shall neither coal nor candle-light come in my bower mair;
> Nor will I love another one until the day I die,
> For I never lov'd a love but one, and he's drowned in the sea."

The lover was not expected to show such devotion after his sweetheart's death, nor was he always a model of constancy before; but in this case he could often look for swift revenge. Young Hunting and Clerk Colvill, in their fine ballads, [3] desert first loves at the cost of life itself. The clerk belongs with the supernatural class; but Young Hunting gets his death at a mortal woman's hands. "Rock your young son never an hour longer for

---

[1] That thief in Heine's poem is the real counterpart to our knight: "Hanged he was at six in the morning, and buried by seven;" but the sweetheart, tender and true, —
> "Sie aber, schon um Achte,
> Trank rothen Wein, und lachte!"

[2] *Lowlands of Holland*, see no. 92, and Child's note. — The Widow of Ephesus is too cynical for traditional ballads.

[3] Nos. 68 and 42; see, also, 86 and 12.

me," [1] he says, in no gentle fashion; "I have found another love, and the very soles of her feet are whiter than thy face." She coaxes him to bide a while, plies him with the good ale and the beer, plies him with the good ale and the wine, and stabs him with the inevitable "little penknife." A bird bids her keep her clothes from the blood; reminded of the witness, she tries to lure the bird and kill it, but in vain. She boots and spurs Young Hunting, and throws him into the wan water of Clyde, "a green turf upon his breast" to hold him down. The king misses his son; the lady swears incrementally, "by the corn," that she has not seen him since yesterday morning, and "by the moon" that yesterday noon was her last sight of him. Probably he was drowned in Clyde. Divers dive for him to no purpose; but the bird comes in now, tells how to find the body by the candle test, and reveals the murder. Desperate, the lady accuses another woman; but the trial by fire clears May Catheren and burns the guilty one to death. The tables are turned in "Young Benjie," who is told by his Marjorie that she would choose another love. He persuades her to walk with him by wan moonlight, and throws her into the linn. During the lykewake the dead woman tells her brothers of the murder, and prescribes Young Benjie's punishment. Spare his life, but blind him; "and ay, at every seven year's end, ye'll take him to the linn for penance." Jellon Grame, [2] for no apparent reason, — in another

---

[1] Brutal betrayal and desertion, unrelieved by romance, is very rare; see *Trooper and Maid*, a late and negligible ballad, no. 299.

[2] No. 90.

version he is called Hind Henry, and is jealous of Brown Robin, — slays his sweetheart in the mysterious Silver Wood, but spares the child she bears him, bringing it up as his "sister's son." On a day, Jellon Grame somewhat absurdly confesses, and the boy kills him. Young Johnstone stabs his bride, and repents too late; his motive is not clear. Two Scottish ballads, "The Duke of Athole's Nurse" and "Sir James the Rose," [1] tell of revenge by a slighted leman. The beautiful ballad of "Lord Randal" does not say what motive the sweetheart had to poison him; she may have feared desertion, or she may have tired of him. The fickle lover certainly plays his part in three fine ballads, "Lord Lovel," "Lord Thomas and Fair Annet," "Fair Margaret and Sweet William," [2] — the latter being provided with that rare character of English balladry, a ghost, — and in some indifferent local ballads, like "The Coble of Cargill," "Burd Isabel and Earl Patrick," "Lord Thomas and Lady Margaret," [3] where the injured woman respectively "bores" her love's boat and sinks him on his visit to another mistress, puts a curse and death on him, and poisons him, a vagrant and wretched outcast, at her door. "Lord Lovel" every one knows; [4] every one should know how Lord Thomas quarrels with Fair Annet, and, by advice of mother and brother, marries the nut-brown bride with

---

[1] Nos. 212, 213.

[2] Nos. 75, 73, 74.

[3] Nos. 242, 257, 260.

[4] For the rose and briar which grow from the tombs of the lovers and unite in a true-lover's knot, see Child, i, 96.

her gold and gear, and how at church the jealous bride
stabs the old love, and Lord Thomas then kills the bride
and himself. A stanza of "Fair Margaret and Sweet
William," where Margaret's "grimly ghost" comes into
the bridal chamber, is quoted in "The Knight of the
Burning Pestle," as well as William's word: —

> "'You are no love for me, Margaret,
> I am no love for you.'"

"Bonny Barbara Allan" is double fickleness, tragic
where Robert Henryson's old pastoral of "Robyn and
Makyn" and Burns's "Duncan Gray" take a lighter
view of the same situation. "Lady Alice" is a pretty
little echo of Barbara, and still, says Mr. Child, "in
the regular stock of the stalls." "The Brown Girl,"
printed near the end of the collection,[1] while not an old
or traditional ballad, is a lively summing-up of the whole
case for this rejected brunette. Brown as brown can be,
her eyes black as sloe, she is cast off by a fastidious love
simply because she is "so brown." In half a year he is
love-sick indeed, sends first for "the doctor-man" and
then for the brown girl "who once his wife should be."
Come to his bedside, she can scarce stand for laughing,
but strokes him back his troth,[2] and promises "*to dance
and sing*" — not weep — on his grave "a whole twelve-
month and a day."

In another group of ballads, most of them purely traditional, it is not fickle or false lover, not quarrel, not the

---

[1] No. 295.

[2] Taken from *Sweet William's Ghost*, no. 77; so the next from *The
Unquiet Grave*, no. 78.

cooling of affection, but the hand of fate, that brings dule and sorrow out of stolen love. "The Bent Sae Brown" [1] ends well, but should not do so. "Fair Janet," however, "Lady Maisry," "Clerk Saunders," "Willie and Lady Maisry," and the "Clerk's Twa Sons" [2] have tragedy and to spare. Janet bears her babe; but Sweet Willie has hardly carried it off to his mother's bower, when her father comes and bids her dress for her wedding to an auld French lord. Janet puts on the scarlet robes, and rides the milk-white steed to her marriage; but will not dance with her auld French lord after dinner. Sweet Willie comes along to dance with the bride's maidens. Then Janet speaks:—

> "'I've seen ither days wi' you, Willie,
> And so has mony mae,
> Ye would hae danced wi' me mysel,
> Let a' my maidens gae.'"

But thrice she turns in the dance, when she falls at Willie's feet never to rise again. He sends home the key of his coffer:—

> "'Gae hame and tell my mother dear
> My horse he has me slain;
> Bid her be kind to my young son,
> For father he has nane.'"

Lady Maisry's English lover is far away when she refuses to give him up, and her brother condemns her to the fire. The effective conclusion has been quoted already.[3] When the seven brothers surprise Clerk Saunders and May Margaret asleep, six are for sparing him. "Lovers dear,"

---

[1] No. 71.   [2] Nos. 64, 65, 69, 70, 72.   [3] Above, p. 122.

says one in excuse; "this many a year," says the second, and "sin to part them," the third; "or to kill a sleeping man," the fourth; "I'll not twin them," cries the fifth, and the sixth is for all hands going softly away. But the seventh stands by his grim idea of duty to kin and name, and runs his sword through the lover. Willie and Lady Maisry are in the same plight, but the deed is done by her father. In the "Clerk's Twa Sons of Owsenford," two youths, abroad for learning, die in Paris, by process of law, as penalty for stolen love; their father tries in vain to save them, and comes home to tell his distracted wife that he has "put them to deeper lore."

To be sure, balladry knows that stolen love is sweet, and romances know that a happy ending of it is most desired. A far and faint echo of the old daybreak song of Provence may be heard in "The Gray Cock,"[1]—a modern affair. Careless lovers now make amends, now jest off the matter, in what Mr. Child calls "pernicious" ballads, however popular, like "The Broom o' Cowdenknowes" and "The Wylie Wife of the Hie Toun Hie."[2] Better is "The Knight and Shepherd's Daughter," suggestive of the Wife of Bath's tale.

One of the pearls of English balladry, by judgment of such lovers of the ballad as Child and Grundtvig, belongs to a little group where a peremptory and half-heartless, if free-handed, lover puts his devoted sweetheart to a series of ignoble tests in order to get rid of her. True, in a dramatic poem like "The Nut-Brown Maid," these tests are

[1] No. 248.　　　　[2] Nos. 217, 290. See, also, no. 110.

hypothetical and meant only to try feminine love and devotion to the uttermost; and in the Patient Griselda stories, actual trials lead to the same triumph of woman's constancy. It has been suggested that the man in this latter case is under a spell, and can be released only by the almost supernatural endurance of his wife. In "Child Waters," however, the tests are real enough, and the motive is surely what it seems to be, — the wish of a wealthy and careless lover to rid himself of an encumbrance. Something else may shimmer in the epic background; but in the ballad there are simply a loving and long-suffering woman, a man harsh to the verge of brutality, and circumstances which in their climax of trial make the ballad's closest friends cry out with pain.[1] The best version makes the hero send poor Ellen to the town to fetch, and actually to carry, a woman for his pleasure; in "The Nut-Brown Maid" an equally revolting rivalry is proposed; in an understudy in low life of "The Nut-Brown Maid" (called "A Jigge," Percy Folio, ii, 334) Margaret proffers a like service to her soldier. How and where, then, is one to find characteristics which so far outweigh these defects as to gain from the two great masters of balladry unqualified praise? "Child Waters" "has perhaps no superior in English, and if not in English, perhaps nowhere."[2] Grundtvig gives a reason. In no ballads is

---

[1] It has been noted that the *Erec* of Chrestien de Troyes shows a much more consistent and likely type of woman's constancy. But the ordinary medieval reader and hearer liked a stronger dose of endurance; and Chaucer's Griselda falls into line with the main procession.

[2] Child, ii, 84.

there such richness of feeling, of lyric expression, as in the English; and "Child Waters," he says, shows this supreme quality in all its versions. We have already quoted exquisite stanzas from its opening; but there is even finer and nobler matter left. Other ballads tell a story of women who follow an unwilling lover and force his hard heart to take pity on them. Not to speak of continental ballads, with which we have here no concern, "Prince Heathen," [1] fragment as it is, points that way, although in very corrupted shape. In "The Fause Lover Won Back," [2] a maid, sitting in her bower-door, sees Young John hurry by. "You seem bent on a long journey," she says; "Whither away?" With "a surly look" he tells her that is not her concern: "I'm ga'en to seek a maid far fairer than ye." After an interpolated stanza or so, she kilts up her fine clothing and goes after him. Then the choral stanza comes in by way of answer to his command that she turn back, and continues in alternation with some helpless but progressive incremental verse:—

> "'But again, dear love, and again, dear love,
>   Will ye never love me again?
> Alas for loving you sae well,
>   And you nae me again!'

> "The first an town that they came till,
>   He bought her brooch and ring;
> And aye he bade her turn again
>   And gang nae furder wi him."

Seeing the effect of her stanza, she very properly repeats it and gets this time at the next town "muff and gloves,"

[1] No. 104.   [2] No. 218.

while he again, but more feebly, bids her go back "and choose some other loves." A third time the stanza, and at the third town "his heart it grew more fain," though his agitation permitted of no purchases. The last town, presumably, is Berwick, where he buys her a wedding-gown and makes her lady of halls and bowers.[1] So much for the vagrom song. Its increments and repetitions are matched in "Child Waters;" but all hint of the trivial is gone from this noble ballad, however unsophisticated the style. The unmeaning increment, even, is here,[2] but it is carried by the dignity and force of the situation: —

> "There were four and twenty ladyes,
>   Were playing att the ball;
> And Ellen, was the ffairest ladye,
>   Must bring his steed to the stall.
>
> "There were four and twenty faire ladyes
>   Was playing at the chesse;
> And Ellen, she was the ffairest ladye,
>   Must bring his horse to grasse."

And *exitus acta probat*. Nothing could be more dignified and pathetic than the close. The man's mother, here again serviceable and yet authoritative, as in "Gil Brenton," hears Ellen groaning by the manger side. "Rise up," she says to her son; "I think thou art a cursed man, for yonder is either a ghost or a woman in her pangs." And Child Waters goes to the stable and listens to Ellen, who sings: —

---

[1] Version B, from a woman's recitation, ends more prettily.
[2] As well as the tremendously effective increment: see above, p. 133.

"Lullabye, my owne deere child!
Lullabye, deere child, deere!
I wold thy father were a king,
Thy mother layd on a beere!"

The "tests" are done, if one will; rather it is the callous hero who cannot resist this final appeal. "Peace, good, fair Ellen," he says, and the adjectives are a kind of apology; " bridal and churching shall be on one day." [1]

III. THE CORONACH AND BALLADS OF THE SUPERNATURAL

Ballads of superstition, as modern arrogance chooses to call them, are as rare in English as they are abundant in Scandinavian collections. Nevertheless, the quality of the English and Scottish versions in this class is often supremely good. The dead man was mourned in song; his fate was followed into the other world; and when he returned to visit the glimpses of our moon, he rarely failed to be impressive. Originally, he was doubtless mourned by solemn dance as well as song, and the coronach seems to point to such origins, however ancient and remote we are fain to suppose them on Scottish and English soil. [2] Unfortunately, there is no ballad of the parting soul, only that very effective "Lykewake Dirge," which Aubrey reported as sung at rustic funerals, early in

[1] Dr. Furnivall makes no allowance for the Child, and reviles his "cursedness" utterly: see Hales and Furnivall, *Percy Folio*, ii, 278.

[2] The actual dance at funerals — like the *caracolu* of Corsica, noted above, p. 95 — seems, however, to have been common in modern Scotland: see Pennant's *Tour*, 1774, p. 99. "The nearest of kin," he says, "opens a melancholy ball, dancing and greeting" — weeping; and this goes on all night. Here are both *caracolu* and *vocero*.

the seventeenth century, by a woman like a *praefica*.
"When any dieth," says an old account of it, " certaine
women sing a song to the dead bodie, recyting the journey
that the partye deceased must goe." The refrain, or
chorus, is very insistent and plainly of popular origin.
But this is not a ballad. The few ballads which seem to
belong to the coronach order "recite the journey" which
led to death, but not the way beyond. Every one knows
the pretty verses of "Bessy Bell and Mary Gray." "The
Death of Queen Jane," while it is effective enough, echoes
rather the gossip of the people than their grief. "The
Bonny Earl of Murray" has been already quoted.[1]
"Young Waters,"[2] too, though not "the queen's love," is
suspected by the king; and a glimpse of the *vocero* or
lament may possibly be found in his good-night words:—

> "'Aft I have ridden thro Stirling town
> In the wind bot and the weit;
> Bot I neir rade thro Stirling town
> Wi' fetters at my feet.
>
> "'Aft I have ridden thro Stirling town,
> In the wind bot and the rain;
> Bot I neir rade thro Stirling town
> Neir to return again.'"

A genuine bit of *vocero* is surely imbedded in the fragments of "Bonnie James Campbell,"[3] when the widow
sings:—

[1] See pp. 95 f.

[2] Dr. W. W. Comfort has pointed out the resemblance of the motive
in this ballad — the queen, by calling Young Waters fairest of all the
company, excites the wrath and vengeance of the king — to a passage
in *Charlemagne's Journey to Jerusalem*.

[3] No. 210.

> "'My meadow lies green,
>   And my corn is unshorn,
>   My barn is to build,
>   And my babe is unborn.'"

Another widow is more heroic and, while less melodious in her lyric, far more picturesque and definite. The laird of Mellerstain [1] was slain in feud; a fragmentary ballad from the Abbotsford texts hears "a lady lamenting sair."

> "'Cowdenknows,[2] had ye nae lack?
>   And Earlstoun, had ye nae shame?
>   Ye took him away behind my back,
>   But ye never saw to bring him hame.'"

She looks about her to see the body brought back: —

> "And she has lookit to Fieldiesha,
>   So has she through Yirdandstane;
>   She lookit to Earlstoun, and she saw the Fans,
>   But he's coming hame by West Gordon."

She sees at last the corpse. "How can I keep my wits when I look on my husband's blood?" Then for a strong close: —

> "'Had we been men as we are women,
>   And been at his back when he was slain,
>   It should a been tauld for mony a long year
>   The slaughter o' the laird of Mellerstain.'"

[1] No. 230. The murder took place in 1603.

[2] A place is still used in Scotland to denote not only its laird, but its inhabitants as a body. "Ettrick has been here," or "Teviotdale," said the borderer coming back to a plundered home and noting the "signs." Compare the Bible phrase, "Reuben had great searchings of heart," — for the tribe. The names of places are very effective in this fragment; compare also the final stanza with that from *Captain Car*, quoted above, p. 185.

The wider grief of the clan coronach is echoed by the dialogue with Willie Macintosh,[1] who, perhaps in the year 1550, burned Auchindown, a Gordon castle, and is confused in the ballad with another Willie whose clansmen were killed by Huntly himself:—

> "'Bonny Willie Macintosh,
>   Whare left ye your men?'
> 'I left them in the Stapler
>   But they'll never come hame.'
>
> "'Bonny Willie Macintosh,
>   Whare now is your men?'
> 'I left them in the Stapler,
>   Sleeping in their sheen.'"[2]

The noblest coronach of all has made a far journey from its original form. Who does not think of those other faithful followers, the Scots lords that sleep by their leader, half owre to Aberdour, fifty fathom under sea? The short version of Percy's "Reliques" "remains, poetically, the best," as Mr. Child declares, who cannot regard the ballad as historical; here is the heart of the story; and precisely such an admirable situation and sequel would attract all manner of additional details in later copies.[3] The eleven stanzas of this version, however, need no explanation or comment; it is from those

[1] No. 183.

[2] Shoes.

[3] Thus, besides the well-known "new moon late yestreen," the fatal mermaiden rises "with coral and glass:"—

> "'Here's a health to you, my merrie young men,
>   For you never will see dry land.'"

This apparition, without the warning, occurs in another ballad of shipwreck, *The Mermaid*, no. 289, which is still sung.

exquisite lines already quoted,[1] where ladies of the court
and wives of the absent lords wait in vain, and from the
fine, impersonal conclusion, that one infers the old lament.[2] It has been noted, too, that something of this
clan-grief is audible in the concluding stanzas of the
"Baron of Brackley." But it is only an echo of old
choral cries; the voice of epic and tradition drowns it
almost to extinction.

Like the coronach, and yet the reverse of it, is the Good-
Night. Strictly taken, this should be the supposed last
words of a criminal before execution, written by some
humble pen and sold under the gallows. In balladry,[3]
however, a Good-Night tells the hero's story. This hero
may be really condemned to death and executed, like
Lord Derwentwater, or expecting execution, like Jock
o' the Side in Newcastle prison, or captured in arms and
killed without judicial process, like Johnie Armstrong,
hanged, with his followers, "upon growing trees," or
else may fly the country and escape trial, — for a time, —
like Lord Maxwell, whose "Last Good Night" suggested
the phrase and mood of Childe Harold's song. Of

---

[1] See above, p. 129.

[2] Some of the details in longer versions of *Spens* are repeated in
Young Allan, no. 245, when forty-five ships (or any number that one
will) went to sea, and only Young Allan comes back safe with his craft,
saved by the skill of a "bonny boy" who takes the helm, orders feather-
beds and canvas laid round the boat, and gets Young Allan's daughter.
The interesting feature is that the ship obeys the boy, and at his voice
springs as spark from fire, as leaf from tree.

[3] See nos. 208, 187, A, 169, 195. 305, a long ballad, tells how Outlaw Murray escaped punishment and was made sheriff of Ettrick forest.

course there are farewells that approach the Good-Night, as that pretty stanza in which a captive far from home, Young Beichan or another, bewails his fate: —

> "'My hounds they all go masterless,
>   My hawks they flee frae tree to tree,
>   My youngest brother will heir my lands,
>   My native land I'll never see.'"

But the singer of this stanza is not under the shadow of death, as Maxwell is, when he flies from home and kin, with, —

> "'Adieu, Lochmaben's gates so fair,
>   The Langholm shank, where birks they be,
>   Adieu, my lady and only joy,
>   And trust me, I maunna stay with thee.'"

Maxwell escaped for a time, but Lord Derwentwater goes to the block; the omens of ill, as he sets out for London at the king's command, the "old gray-headed man" who starts up "with a pole-axe in his hand," and the last words: —

> "'The velvet coat that I hae on,
>   Ye may tak it for your fee;
>   And a' ye lords o' merry Scotland
>   Be kind to my ladie!'"—

these and other elements of the ballad are of the essence of traditional song. Peasants of Northumberland told, as late as a century ago, how the river ran red with blood by Derwentwater's hall, and the aurora, brilliant on the night of his execution, was long called by his name. In "Johnie Armstrong" the wrath of a clan is heard. Johnie, decoyed to Edinburgh to meet his king, is told that the morrow he and eightscore men shall hang. "Asking grace of a graceless face!" he cries in a line that we meet again; and he is close upon smiting off the monarch's head. But "all Edinburgh" rises, and Armstrong plays the man in vain, a "cowardly Scot" at his back running him through the body, while he heartens his men: —

> " '. . . Fight on, my merry men all,
>   I am a little hurt, but I am not slain;
>   I will lay me down for to bleed a while,
>   And then I'le rise and fight with you again.' "

In another version, he speaks his Good-Night on hearing his doom from the king; then —

> " 'God be wi' thee, Kirsty, my brither,
>   Lang live thou Laird of Mangertoun!
>   Lang mayst thou live on the border-syde
>   Or thou see thy brother ryde up and down.
>
> " 'And God be wi' thee, Kirsty, my son,
>   Whair thou sits on thy nurse's knee!
>   But and thou live this hundred yeir,
>   Thy father's better thou'lt never be.' "

A fine Good-Night, of course, can be made of the concluding stanzas of "Mary Hamilton," [1] as well as of random stanzas in other and inferior ballads. It is blended with the familiar legacy-formula. A dying man, murdered by exceptionally foul means, sends farewell to his wife, his brother, who has "a heart as black as any stone," his daughter and five young sons, his followers and good neighbors, and asks that two lairds will have his fate

---

[1] See below, p. 243.

always in mind as they ride the border, and revenge
him.[1] A covenanter,[2] marching to fight, bids farewell, in
presentiment of death, to kin and home: —

> "'Now farewell, father, and farewell, mother,
> And fare ye weel, my sisters three,
> And fare ye well, my Earlstoun,
> For thee again I'll never see.'"

Closer to the other world than those faint funeral cries,
than these reminiscent good-nights, are the actual relics
of superstition. In two ballads of the sea, "Bonnie Annie"
and "Brown Robyn's Confession,"[3] "fey folk" are in the
ship, and lots are cast to see what victim must be sacri-
ficed. Jonah in the first case proves quite unreasonably
to be Bonnie Annie; it should be the captain who has
betrayed her, and who, fairly enough, refuses to throw
her overboard; but at last: —

> "He has tane her in his arms twa, lo, lifted her cannie,
> He has thrown her out owre board, his ain dear Annie."

She floats to Ireland, and he buries her in a gold coffin.
Brown Robyn only gets his deserts, when, upon his own
confession of monstrous crimes, his sailors tie him to a
plank and throw him into the sea. But his "fair confession" brings along the Blessed Virgin and her Son; she
asks, will Robyn go back to his men, or to heaven with
her? He chooses and gets the second alternative. These
pretty ballads of the sea are matched by more gruesome

[1] *Death of Parcy Reed*, no. 193, B.
[2] *Bothwell Bridge*, no. 206.
[3] Nos. 24, 57.

stuff. "James Harris," or the "Dæmon Lover" by Scott's title, would have made a fine tale, and has been "improved" into some elegance; its traditional guise is homely to a degree, being best preserved in a broadside formidably called "A Warning for Married Women, being an example of Mrs. Jane Reynolds . . . born near Plymouth, who, having plighted her troth to a Seaman, was afterwards married to a Carpenter, and at last carried away by a Spirit, the manner how shall presently be recited." Set to "a West-Country tune," this ballad tells how James Harris, the seaman, returns as a spirit, and tempts our wife away from the carpenter-husband and their three children: —

> "And so together away they went
> From off the English shore,
> And since that time the woman-kind
> Was never seen no more."

The recited Scottish copies draw no such decent veil over the wife's fate. When she sails two leagues, in version D, which Child thinks the best of all, she begins to remember those whom she has left. The demon lover consoles: he will show her "where the white lilies grow on the banks of Italy." At three leagues, "gurly grew the sea," and grim his face. He will now show her where the lilies grow "in the bottom of the sea."

Commerce of mortal with creatures of the other world is among the oldest themes in story. "Thomas Rymer," [1] one of the ballads recited by that very useful person, Mrs.

[1] The ballads which follow are nos. 37, 39, 42, 113, 40, 41.

Brown of Falkland, and also told as a romance in the poem "Thomas of Erceldoune," there mingled with prophecy and politics, is based on the tale of a man who is favored with a fairy's love and with an excursion to the fairy world. To kiss a fairy or a ghost, as we learn from other ballads, puts a mortal within the jurisdiction of the dark powers; if he eats food in fairyland, moreover, he will never come back to earth. In our ballad the "queen of Elfland" very considerately takes with her a mortal loaf and "claret wine" as Thomas's refreshment; for True Thomas must come back, and be the prophet of Tweedside, after seven years in the lower world. As may be supposed, the theme of this ballad has almost endless connections with romance, tale, and myth; enough for our purposes that it tells simply and prettily the story of True Thomas's meeting with the elf-queen, whom he takes at first for the Holy Virgin, his kisses, the long journey in darkness near the roar of the sea, and talk by the way. In "Tam Lin," considerably touched by Burns, another old theme gets ballad treatment. Janet has a tryst at Carterhaugh, a place where Ettrick and Yarrow join, with no earthly knight, but with an elfin grey. "Who are you?" she asks him, against the ancient law; but Tam is a mortal, carried off by the Queen of Fairies. To rescue him, Janet must pull him down at midnight from horseback in the fairy ride. He turns to various shapes in her arms, esk, adder, bear, lion, red-hot iron, burning brand; then, as he has directed, she throws him into "well water," a kind of baptism, and he is once again "a naked

knight." Jenny, blithe as a bird, covers him with her green
mantle; and the Queen of the Fairies vents her vain rage
from a bush of broom. Less potent by title, but here more
dangerous, is the mermaid who is beloved and then deserted by Clerk Colvill, or Colvin; she has many relatives
in European tales, and many ancestors in legend and
myth. The Scottish ballad, another of Mrs. Brown's reci-
tations, is effective if imperfect. The clerk promises his
new-wed wife not to go near the Wall o' Stream and visit
the mermaiden again. He does it, of course, and finds
the mermaid washing a sark of silk, bides with her, and
feels cruel pains in his head. "Cut a strip from my sark,
and bind it about your head; you will be cured," says she;
but he is killed. At first he seeks to slay her, but she
changes merrily to her fish-form and disappears in the
stream. He rides sadly back to die near mother, brother,
and wife. The tables, however, are turned in a pretty
little ballad [1] from Shetland, with an ending suggestive
of Heine in his favorite sudden close. A woman is rocking
her child, and sings to it that she would fain know its
father. Up starts one who claims that honor, however
grimly he may look.

> " 'I am a man upo the lan,
>   An I am a silkie in the sea.' . . .

> " 'It was na weel,' quo the maiden fair,
>   'It was na weel, indeed,' quo she,
>   'That the great Silkie of Sule Skerrie
>   Suld hae come and aught a bairn to me.'

[1] *The Great Silkie* (seal) *of Sule Skerry*, dictated in 1852 by an old
lady of Shetland.

"Now he has taen a purse of goud,
  And he has put it upo her knee,
Sayin, 'Gie to me my little young son,
  An tak thee up thy nourris-fee.

"'An it sall come to pass on a simmer's day,
  When the sun shines het on evera stane,
That I will tak my little young son,
  An teach him for to swim the faem.

"'An thu sall marry a proud gunner,
  An a proud gunner I'm sure he'll be ;
An the very first schot that ere he schoots,
  He'll schoot baith my young son and me.'"

Finally, in a ballad which tells how closely the singing of
it is knit in with its very being, but which is only a fragment, we have the mortal woman yearning for her mortal
baby from the exile of Elfland, whither she has been
taken to nurse the elf-queen's bairn. The repetitions lead
up to the queen's promise that when the bairn stands,
the nurse may go back home. The musical opening
stanzas have been already quoted above.[1] "Hind Etin,"
another ballad of the union of mortal and elf, has suffered severely in tradition; in Scandinavian versions it is
effective enough.

Another group [2] deals simply with transformation by
magic and the happy solution, if such is to be. Three of
these are alike in essential features. "Kemp Owyne,"
where incremental repetition is admirably used in the dis-
enchanting process, tells how the kemp frees Dove Isabel

---

[1] See p. 35.
[2] Nos. 34, 35, 36, 270, 32, 33.

from a mysterious Craigie's sea, where she lies enchanted into a most repulsive beast with her hair twisted about a tree-trunk. At each of the kisses which he gives her, the hair loosens by a fold, and he gets first a belt, then a ring, then a "royal brand," all of great virtue. She steps out "as fair a woman as fair could be." In "Allison Gross," a witch of that name turns a girl into an ugly worm; but the Queen of Fairies releases her. The Laily Worm (or loathsome serpent) and the Machrel of the Sea are brother and sister, so transformed by a bad step-mother; the "worm" is about to kill the eighth knight that has come along, but it is his own father. The step-mother is forced to restore son and daughter to human shape, and then is burned to death.[1] In "The Earl of Mar's Daughter," this young woman sees a dove on a tower, calls it, and brings it to her bower; but Cow-me-doo turns at evening tide into a handsome youth, whom his mother, skilled in magic spells, thus transforms to pleasure himself with fair maids. She bears him children, whom he carries off to his mother; and she will marry nobody for three and twenty years, when a lord comes to woo her. "I'm content to live with my bird, Cow-me-doo." "That bird," says the father, "shall be killed." Cow-me-doo goes to his mother for help; she sends four and twenty sturdy men, disguised as storks, while the seven sons fly along as swans, and their father as a gay goshawk. They arrive in time to stop the marriage; and

---

[1] This ballad in the Old Lady's Manuscript is "pure tradition, and has never been touched by a pen."

"ancient men," who have been at weddings these sixty years, aver they never saw "such a curious wedding-day." Behind the homely phrases, however, lies a pretty tale. "King Henry" is a variant of the story told by the wife of Bath: a hideous creature begs shelter, food, and lodging of the king, and in the morning is revealed as a beautiful woman. "Kempy Kay" is mere foulness in describing a repulsive creature whom the kemp seeks for bride; but, in compensation, "The Wee Wee Man" offers a charming study in miniature.

This is all magic, white or black; it meddles with no world beyond, save the vague realm of faery, and it calls no spirits from their haunt. Three ballads, one of them supremely good, deal with the spirit world and the doings of the parted soul: and a fourth, poorer than the usual poor ballad, nevertheless echoes the best-known of all modern ghost-poems.[1] "The Unquiet Grave," a slight but pretty thing, has features in common with the second lay of Helgi in the Norse Edda, and was taken down from recitation in Sussex. A youth mourns at his sweetheart's grave for a year; then she speaks and complains that he disturbs her rest. "I crave a kiss of your clay-cold lips." "It would be your death," is the answer.

> " ' 'T is down in yonder garden green,
>   Love, where we used to walk,
>   The finest flower that e'er was seen
>   Is withered to a stalk,' " —

perhaps as much too neat as the final stanza is too feebly

[1] Nos. 78, 77, 272, 79.

pious for ballad style. "Sweet William's Ghost," [1] to use the critical word-of-all-work, is far more convincing. To get the meaning of ballad-treatment in a case like this, the reader should compare not so much the obvious parallels in tradition as poems like Wordsworth's "Laodamia" or Goethe's "Braut von Corinth," poems, noble as they are, which have that second intention never found in a sound ballad of tradition. William comes back from the grave and asks Margaret for his "faith and troth." She desires a kiss, and he gives her the usual warning. She stretches out her hand, or, in another version, a stick on which she has "stroked her troth," and returns him his plighted faith. He thanks her, and vanishes; but she follows him far to his grave, only to be told that there is no room there for her, — or that there is room. In one version, before she will give back her troth, she asks her lover a question about the other world, a question perhaps not without significance: What becomes of women who die in travail ? Their beds, he replies, are made in heaven by our Lord's knee, well set about with gillyflowers. Spirits often demand back or give back plighted faith; in the "Child of Bristowe," [2] a dead father makes the effort twice. Rubbing the stick may be a precaution in transfer, to avoid direct touch, as savages rub an afflicted part upon

[1] On comparison with the Helgi lay, see Bugge, *Heltedigtene*, i, 206 ff. (1896).

[2] Ed. Hazlitt, v, 373 ff.

> "Therefor, sone, y pray the,
> Gef me my trouthe y left with the,
> And let me wynde my way."

a tree to get rid of the disease.[1] But the lover sometimes came back to claim not his troth, but the bride herself. "If ever the dead come for the quick, be sure, Margaret, I'll come again for thee," promises the hero of this ballad; and if "The Suffolk Miracle," even more than "James Harris," is "blurred, enfeebled, and disfigured" in broadside shape, it tells, after its silly and imperfect fashion, the tale found everywhere in Europe, often in ballad form, the basis of Bürger's famous "Lenore," — which was at one time thought to have been taken from "The Suffolk Miracle" itself.[2] This, however, Bürger never saw; nor could it inspire anybody or anything. Fortunately we do not leave the matter here. If the clumsy broadside marks as low a fall as decent materials can ever reach, traditional verse of any land seldom rises to the height of our best "supernatural" ballad, "The Wife of Usher's Well." "Nothing that we have," says Mr. Child, "is more profoundly affecting." And it is quite sufficient as it stands in the Minstrelsy version from the recitation of an old woman in Lothian. Even so good a poet as Allingham has gained little by combination, and has lost pitiably by invention where he supplies a stanza of his own "to complete the sense." There is a background of old legends, of old myth: the mother will have ocean storms never cease till her three sons come back, and in

[1] Interesting is Uhland's note on the loss of color in trees, or the like, accounting for paleness and what not, *Kl. Schrift.* iii, 405, and note to *Volkslieder*, no. 99, p. 488.

[2] Child, v, 60, note.

the mirk November night they do come, with signs of the other world upon them; she welcomes them with all she has, makes their bed wide, and sits down by them, till the crowing of the cocks, here faintly reminiscent of Scandinavian mythology, calls them to their place. What marks our ballad, however, is its singular dignity, its reticence. The repetitions, while of the traditional ballad form, are impressive and not loquacious; and the concluding stanza, spoken by the youngest son, would be hard to surpass: —

> " 'Fare ye weel, my mother dear,
>   Fareweel to barn and byre ;
>   And fare ye weel, the bonny lass
>   That kindles my mother's fire.' " [1]

IV. LEGENDARY BALLADS

Many of the ballads named in the preceding section could be transferred to this, and some now to be described, if regarded from another point of view, might well take their places elsewhere; on the whole, however, the general idea of transition through local and historical pieces to the deliberate epic of the chronicle class will justify the arrangement which has been made.

Classical traditions, which probably gave Hero and

[1] A version from Shropshire, and one from North Carolina, in the United States, make the widow pray to Christ, or to God ; in the former, Jesus sends the three sons back, and they escort their mother to the door of heaven, where Jesus bids her return to repent for nine days, then takes her in. In the second version, the oldest "baby" wakes up his brothers and bids farewell to the mother. — Child, iii, 513; v, 294.

Leander as a theme to so many ballads of the continent, have sent a fragment to the far coast of Shetland.
"King Orfeo," of course, comes directly from medieval
romance; but the old story of Orpheus and Eurydice is
here, changed in name and place, but still more changed
by its genuine and traditional ballad setting. It may be
quoted in part, omitting the almost unintelligible Scandinavian refrain. A king lives in the east, a lady in the west.
Presumably she is wooed and won, but tradition, or the
singer's memory, is silent about that. The king goes
hunting, leaving his "Lady Isabel" alone, and at last
learns her fate: the king of Faery has pierced her bosom
with his dart. Some verses are lost, in which he sees her
among fairy folk, follows, and comes to a gray stone.

> "Dan he took oot his pipes ta play,
>   Bit sair his hert wi' döl an wae.
>
> "And first he played da notes o' noy,
>   An dan he played da notes o' joy.
>
> "An dan he played da göd gabber reel,
>   Dat meicht ha' made a sick hert hale.
>
> .   .   .   .
>
> "'Noo come ye in inta wir ha',[1]
>   And come ye in among wis a'.'
>
> "Now he's gaen in inta dar ha',
>   An he's gaen in among dem a'.
>
> "Dan he took out his pipes to play,
>   Bit sair his hert wi' döl an wae.

[1] A messenger has come from behind the gray stone, and asked him
into the hillside.

"An first he played da notes o' noy,
An dan he played da notes o' joy.

"An dan he played da göd gabber reel,
Dat meicht ha' made a sick hert hale.

"'Noo tell to us what ye will hae :
What sall we gie you for your play?'

"'What I will hae I will you tell,
An dat 's me lady Isabel.'

"'Yees tak your lady, an yees gaeng hame,
An' yees be king ower a' your ain.'

"He's taen his lady, an' he 's gaen hame,
An' noo he's king ower a' his ain."

Our interest here is aroused in the concentration upon a
single situation, with thin strips of narrative at beginning
and end, and in the inevitable structure of the piece. The
refrain must not be forgotten; and one would feel no
surprise upon hearing that the ballad was a real ballad,
danced and acted as well as sung. In any case, there is the
story of Orpheus, — or half of it, — in Shetland; and
it is a purely traditional, oral ballad. When, however, a
sacred legend grew popular in verse and traditional, it
was pretty sure to be written down. The oldest recorded
English ballad is of this class,[1] and was preserved until
lately in a thirteenth-century manuscript at Trinity College, Cambridge. As in the old riddle ballad of the fifteenth century, "Inter Diabolus et Virgo," the repetitions
are here in part neglected, but the ballad structure, the
simple conception, the dialogue, are maintained, not to

[1] See for these legends and carols, nos. 23, 22, 21, 54, 55, 56, 155.

mention absurd details like the collusion of Judas's sister in the theft of his money, and the trivial motive for his betrayal of Christ. In smoother but similar seven-beat verses, two to the stanza, is told the charming little legend of St. Stephen, "clerk in King Herod's hall," who is bringing the boar's head, the right Christmas dish, when he sees the star bright over Bethlehem: —

> "He kyst adoun the boris hed and went into the halle:
> 'I forsak the, Kyng Herowdes, and thi werkes alle.
>
> "'I forsak the, Kyng Herowdes, and thi werkes alle;
> Ther is a chyld in Bedlem born is beter than we alle.'"

Is Stephen mad? The thing is as true, quoth Herod, as that yon capon in the dish shall crow; whereupon the capon crows "Christus natus est!" Stephen, very illogically, is sent out to be stoned to death; "and therefore is his even on Christ's own day." [1] In "The Maid and the Palmer," a woman is washing at the well; a palmer asks her for drink and is told she has neither cup nor can. "If your lover came back, you'd find cups and cans." She says she has no lover. "Peace! You have borne nine children!" She asks if he is "the good old man that all the world believes upon," and demands penance. In Scandinavian ballads, he is called Jesus outright. He tells her she is to be a stepping-stone for seven years, seven more a clapper in a bell, still seven again she must "lead an ape in hell," and may then come maiden home. The ultimate source is the Samaritan woman blended with Mary Magdalen

[1] S. Stephen's "own day" is of course 26th December.

and even with Martha;[1] but the English version from
the Percy Folio betrays nothing of this. Moreover it is in
the usual four-beat ballad measure of two verses and
refrain. The other three ballads of this group are really
carols. In the "Cherry-Tree Carol," Joseph refuses to
pluck Mary one cherry from the orchard; whereupon the
unborn babe commands the highest tree to bend down
and give fruit to his mother. In "The Carnal and the
Crane," a crow wishes to know many things about the
birth of Christ, and the wise crane answers him. The most
interesting legend which is woven in here is that of the
husbandman, sowing his seed, by whom Joseph, Mary,
and Jesus passed in their flight. Jesus bids him God-
speed; he shall fetch ox and wain to carry home this day
the corn he has sown. The farmer falls on his knees;
"thou art the redeemer of mankind." He is told to say,
should any inquire, that Jesus passed by him as he was
sowing his grain; Herod comes along as he is gathering
the crop, and is furious at the inference of a captain that
"full three quarters of a year" have elapsed since it
was sown. "Dives and Lazarus," telling the familiar
story, is remarkable for its pervasive incremental repetition; it is in the four-line ballad measure. Besides
these legendary pieces in Child's collection, a fresh can-
didate for ballad honors has recently appeared in "The
Bitter Withy," or "The Withies;" and it is hard to see
why it should not be ranged with the rest. It has fallen
into homely courses of style and phrase, and the ex-

[1] Child, i, 229.

planatory stanza with which it closes is very rare in balladry, "St. Stephen and Herod" furnishing perhaps the
only parallel. Professor Gerould, in a paper read before
the Modern Language Association, shows that tales
about the childhood of Christ, taken from the apocryphal
gospels, were current in both the north and the south
of Britain. The ball-playing is conventional; the sun-
beam-bridge and the catastrophe are, of course, the main
affair; and the chastisement, along with the reason for
the withy's nature, is not unskilfully added.

THE BITTER WITHY [1]

As it fell out on a Holy day
    The drops of rain did fall, did fall,
Our Saviour asked leave of His mother Mary
    If He might go play at ball.

"To play at ball my own dear Son,
    It's time You was going or gone,
But be sure let me hear no complaint of You
    At night when You do come home."

It was upling scorn and downling scorn,
    Oh, there He met three jolly jerdins: [2]
Oh, there He asked the three jolly jerdins
    If they would go play at ball.

[1] Communicated by Mr. F. Sidgwick to *Notes and Queries*, Series 10,
no. 83, with information in regard to the ballad's provenience and
traditional character. See also *The Journal of the Folk-Song Society*,
ii, 205, 300 ff., for other versions.

[2] In the Sussex version, "jolly dons;" Herefordshire, "jolly jor-
rans;" Manchester, merely "children;" and in a carol, which tells
the first part of the story, "virgins."

"Oh, we are lords' and ladies' sons,
   Born in bower or in hall,
And You are but some poor maid's child
   Born'd in an ox's stall."

"If you are lords' and ladies' sons,
   Born'd in bower or in hall,
Then at the very last I'll make it appear
   That I am above you all."

Our Saviour built a bridge with the beams of the sun,
   And over He gone, He gone He.
And after followed the three jolly jerdins,
   And drownded they were all three.

It was upling scorn and downling scorn,
   The mothers of them did whoop and call,
Crying out, "Mary mild, call back your Child,
   For ours are drownded all."

Mary mild, Mary mild, called home her Child,
   And laid our Saviour across her knee,
And with a whole handful of bitter withy
   She gave Him slashes three.

Then He says to His mother, "Oh! the withy, oh! the
      withy,
   The bitter withy that causes me to smart, to smart,
Oh! the withy it shall be the very first tree
   That perishes at the heart."

Best known of all the legends, and a widespread ballad,
is "Sir Hugh," which should also be read in the exquisite
Prioress's Tale of Chaucer for the difference between
artless and artistic narrative. The two stories are distinct;
nothing in the ballad corresponds to the devotion of the
little "clergeoun" and his reward; but one mother is as

pathetic as the other, and a feature of Chaucer's tale has crept into the traditional Scottish version of the ballad. "Gin ye be there, my sweet Sir Hugh, I pray you to me speak," and again, "Where'er ye be, my sweet Sir Hugh," may be compared with the description of the other searcher "with mother's pity in her breast enclosed."

Legend clung to old ballad ways. But romance, specially as it is retold by the minstrels, works into the chronicle and longer epic style. "Hind Horn,"[1] to be sure, is still situation with a mere touch of explanatory narrative; it gives "little more than the catastrophe of the famous Gest of King Horn," adding the silver wand with larks on it — birds to tell Horn of events? — and the ring whose stone pales at approach of misfortune, as romantic features. But the situation is everything, and it is treated in thorough ballad wise: repetition, refrain, and a local, mainly Scottish, setting. "Young Beichan,"[2] however, a favorite both in Scottish tradition and in English broadside, — it is one with "The Loving Ballad of Lord Bateman," which Cruikshank illustrated, — runs well to the romantic plan. Beichan, whose adventures agree in part with those in the legend of Gilbert Beket, father of St. Thomas, is taken prisoner by a Moor, released by the daughter on promise of marriage, goes home, and is about to wed another woman, when Susie Pye, the Moor's daughter, appears at his gates, is recognized, baptized as "Lady Jane," and married to Beichan. Dialogue is retained, but there is abundant explanation as well as

[1] No. 17.   [2] No. 53.

narrative. In one amusing case the reciter or minstrel reveals himself : —

"An' I hop' this day she sal be his bride," —

he says of Susie, at her love's gate, just as the complication is to be announced. With "Sir Cawline," [1] as with "King Estmere," already noticed, we are fairly in the romantic ballads; it "may possibly be formed upon a romance in stanzas, which itself was composed from earlier ballads," says Professor Child. "Events" crowd this ballad mightily. Sir Cawline, sick with love for the king's daughter, meets an elritch knight, a giant who is also a soldan, and finally a false steward, who lets loose a lion upon the unarmed Cawline at his prayers; but he wins his love at last, and they have "fifteen sons." Another ballad of adventure in the Percy Manuscript, "Sir Lionel," [2] has kept the older way, and may show the sort of ballad out of which a romance like "Sir Cawline" was made; there are also traditional versions, likewise in two-line stanzas with refrain. These ballads keep their dignity; absurdity and helplessness, however, beset such a poor affair as "John Thomson and the Turk," [3] which belongs in the negligible list.

Minstrel ballads,[4] so called, either treat a romantic old theme with a kind of impudent ease, or else treat an easy theme with success. "The Boy and the Mantle" is "a good piece of minstrelsy," as Professor Child calls it, but

[1] No. 61; see Child, ii, 61. [2] No. 18.
[3] No. 266. [4] See nos. 29, 30, 31, 267, 273.

it "would not go to the spinning-wheel at all." "King
Arthur and King Cornwall" and "The Marriage of Sir
Gawain," one in eight, the other in seven fragments, from
the mutilated Percy Manuscript, are of the same minstrel
source, and treat matters well known in romance. These
are long poems.[1] Shorter and more familiar, meant for
less critical audiences, are edifying stories like the "Heir
of Linn," and that prime favorite with humble folk, the
discomfiture of royalty at the hands of a yokel; for the
style and the faint waft of tradition about it, "King Edward and the Tanner" is included with ballads, while
"Rauf Coilyear" and others go with "metrical tales." So
we pass through the jocose to the slightly improper, and
through the slightly improper to the merry narratives
which are both "broad" and "gross." The list of these
is not long;[2] and one of them, " The Baffled Knight," is
harmless enough. The cynical "Crow and Pie," conceded
to minstrel-making, is very close to the rout of such things
as Tom D'Urfey selected for his "Pills to Purge Melancholy" and modern collectors gather in privately printed
and privately perused editions. Of the "Broomfield
Hill," which the freedom of a couple of centuries ago
allowed women to quote as they pleased, versions differ; one, says Mr. Child very happily, one smells of

[1] They are ballads because, as Professor Kittredge says, in his Introduction to the Cambridge edition of the *Ballads*, p. xxvii, they are
'composed in the popular style and perpetuated for a time by oral
tradition."

[2] The editors of the Cambridge edition were forced to leave out but
five of the three hundred and five ballads printed in the large collection.

the broom and another of the groom. The lady makes
tryst with a knight at the Broomfield Hill, but is told by
a witch-woman how she can come maiden home. The
knight sleeps until too late; and in the better version
there is a good dialogue between him and his steed or
hawk.

> " ' I stamped wi' my foot, master,
>   And gar'd my bridle ring,
> But na kin' thing wald waken ye
>   Till she was past and gane,' "

says the horse; and the hawk: —

> " ' I clapped wi' my wings, master,
>   And aye my bells I rang,
> And aye cried, Waken, waken, master,
>   Before the ladye gang.' "

There is all the difference in the world between this, or a
jolly bit of fun like "Our Goodman" already cited, and
a thoroughly debased and dingy affair like "The Keach in
the Creel." "The Jolly Beggar," especially in the Old
Lady's Manuscript, makes a kind of amends at the close,
and has a dash and jingle in it that half redeem it. And
the Old Lady did take it into her manuscript! "The
Friar in the Well" is an ancient story; and four other
ballads of this merry kind are harmless enough: the
"Crafty Farmer," who baffles a highwayman, riding off
on the thief's horse with the thief's plunder, besides sav-
ing his own saddle-bags; two matrimonial jests, "The
Wife Wrapt in Wether's Skin," a drastic taming of the
shrew, and "The Farmer's Curst Wife," who is returned
by Satan as impossible in a well-ordered Inferno, — a

ballad sung in Sussex with a "Chorus of whistlers" to
the two-line stanza; and finally the never-tiring verses
of "Get Up and Bar the Door," which even a Goethe
condescended to translate from this or whatever other
version.

Still mainly in the ballad style and formed by the ballad
structure are sundry popular and traditional perversions
of historical fact. These vary both from actual tradition
and thoroughly popular conception to the manufactured
broadside which holds a few shreds of communal stuff,
and from important events to mere local tradition. For
the tragic account, a little threnody "current throughout
Scotland," as well as in England, records the popular but
erroneous belief that Jane Seymour died from the Cæsa-
rean section at the birth of Prince Edward.[1] It is brief, of
course, lyrical, with a bit of dialogue, and a commonplace
for close: —

> "They mourned in the kitchen, and they mourned in the ha',
>   But royal King Henry mourn'd langest of a'."

A fragment in the Percy Folio reflects popular notions
about Thomas Cromwell's disgrace and death; he seems
to be playing John the Baptist to Katharine Howard's
daughter of Herodias and bluff King Hal's Herod. Even
more popular in tone is "Queen Eleanor's Confession,"
still sung in rural England; the old jest of a husband who
disguises himself as a friar in order to shrive his wife and
hear of her sins against him, is made even more grim by
the association, also in friar's garb, of the queen's lover.

[1] *The Death of Queen Jane*, no. 170.

The king, when all was heard, "looked over his left shoulder . . .

> "And said, 'Earl Martial, but for my oath,
>   Then hanged shouldst thou be.'"

Grundtvig says that this ballad, very poorly translated, is recited about Denmark with a Norwegian queen in the main part.[1]

At the other extreme from such popular and traditional verse are the ballads made to order, as it were, after a stirring event. Journalism triumphs in "Lord Delamere," one version of which was taken down from recitation in Derbyshire, but must have been learned originally from some broadside such as Professor Child prints as second choice. We miss the lilt and swing of the throng, even at third or fourth hand, in this caterwauling rime. It is helpless jog-trot, not the spinster's or the knitter's tune, but the butterwoman's rank to market; compared with the rhythm of a traditional ballad, with its style and form generally, with the spirit of really popular verse, these pieces of the "Delamere" sort sink out of sight, as if they fell from "Sweet William's Ghost" to the level of "James Harris." It is not only their speech that bewrays them. So far as facts go, however, there is as much perversion in one set as in the other. Like "Lord Delamere" in style, though better in execution, are sundry ballads based on international events real or supposed. "Hugh Spencer's Feats in France," prodigiously patriotic in the good old "frog-eater" vein with a touch of Dr. Johnson's opinion

[1] Nos. 171, 156; for the following, see 207, 158, 164, 284.

that "foreigners are fools," has plenty of repetition and uses the ballad commonplaces. Here is the familiar choice of three steeds, though with a difference and an extraordinary climax. Hugh, intending to joust for England's honor, finds no mere French horse that can bear him, white, brown, or black; so he calls for his old hackney from England.[1] The French spear breaks, of course; Spencer cannot get an English substitute, and several spears have to be bound together for his use. His remark to the French queen, which brings about this tourney, must have surprised the court, unaccustomed as it was to good, bluff English: —

> "'You have not wiped your mouth, madam,
> Since I heard you tell a lye.'"

Finally he runs amuck, killing all sorts of warriors; and the frightened monarch of France agrees to peace with England on any terms.[2] "King Henry the Fifth's Conquest of France" gives the story of the tennis-balls in dialogue, then briefly sums the triumphant battles and the march, by our balladist's account, "to Paris gates." "John Dory" was popular enough in the seventeenth century; it has the rollicking manner in more attractive guise. John Dory, perhaps Doria, goes to Paris: —

[1] These ballads are straightforward, at least, and unsophisticated. *The Rose of England*, no. 166, has neither quality, but is an elaborate allegory of the white and red. The red rose of Lancaster is rooted up by a boar (Richard III), and so on.

[2] In B and C, the coal-black steed is chosen; C, from Aberdeen, transfers its patriotism north of the Tweed, and makes "Sir Hugh" a Scot. This recited version is full of incremental repetition.

"The first man that John Dory did meet
Was good King John of France-a;
John Dory could well of his courtesie,
But fell down in a trance-a,"

offering, nevertheless, to bring "all the churles in Merry
England," bound, before the king.   A Cornishman
named Nicholl meets John Dory's ship, and the boaster,
after a hot fight, is clapt fast under hatches.   Not so good
are four ballads of the sea,[1] broadsides, but probably
enjoyed by their humble singers; only one need be named.
"The Sweet Trinity," a ship built by Sir Walter Raleigh
in the Netherlands, was not worthy of her little ship-boy,
who swam off with an auger, and sank the "false gallaly,"
but failed to get the reward promised him.   Our best
naval piece, of course, is "Sir Andrew Barton;"[2] it is of
the chronicle order, long, awkward in diction, but has the
genuine ballad manner in treating its main situation, and
tells the story of the sea-fight in lively, hearty style.   The
helpless note, of course, is there.   "Henery" Hunt, the
victim, informer, and word-breaker, —

"With a pure heart and a penitent mind," —

is ridiculous; but an older version may have done him
justice.   There are several puzzles in naval architecture
which all the study of ships in Henry VIII's time has not
yet solved; and an old superstition survives when Lord

[1] Nos. 285, 286, 287, 288. Raleigh is left out of 286, B; the ship is
built in the Lowlands, but is called *The Golden Vanity*.
[2] No. 167. *Henry Martyn*, no. 250, is an offshoot of the longer and
older ballad.

Howard throws the pirate's headless body overboard,
with three hundred crowns about the middle: —

"Whersoeuer thou lands, itt will bury thee."

King Hal, too, is chivalrous; he would give a hundred
pound if Sir Andrew were alive.

These are English ballads, bad and good. It is worthy
of note that Scots ballads of the same class, excepting here
and there an "Earl Bothwell" with its "I shall you tell
how it befell," seldom drop into the doggerel style, but
tend to keep a firm grasp of the situation, to maintain the
old structure and repetition, and to observe a kind of
dramatic brevity. "The Laird o' Logie" presents crisply
an adventure at the Scottish court under James VI, a
gentlewoman freeing her lover from prison and the gallows; while "King James and Brown," from the Percy
Folio, tells loosely and drearily a story of the same sover-
eign in his younger days. Brown, the hero, is an Englishman, and the ballad is plainly from an English source.
That it is a ballad, however, and that traditional verse,
even when sunk to the broadside, is quite a different
thing from journalism, may be readily seen by comparing
it with a poem on another of Brown's adventures written
by the much-ridiculed Elderton. Scottish versions con-
trive to keep a better traditional tone, even in such
slight and unmeritable pieces as "The Laird of Waris-
ton," where the laird is killed by a servant at the insti-
gation of the wife. She had some excuse.

"He spak a word in jest,
Her answer wasna good;

> He threw a plate at her face,
> Made it a' gush out blood. . . .

> "The Foul Thief knotted the tether,
> She lifted his head on hie,
> The nourice drew the knot
> That gard lord Wariston die."

Higher verse for higher themes.[1] An incident of feud or raid, a burnt castle and slain inmates, make up "Captain Car," already cited, and "The Fire of Frendraught," where the lady of the castle sets it on fire that she may destroy a hated guest, and "The Bonny House o' Airlie," where Argyll burns down Lady Margaret's house, but spares her life. She is properly defiant, and would give not only her house, but all her sons for Prince Charlie. "James Grant" makes a clever escape. But the best of all is that ballad of crime in high life, "Mary Hamilton." It is evidently founded on fact, and the fact, as Scott pointed out, seems to have been a case of child-murder at the court of Mary Queen of Scots, in 1563, for which the mother and the father — Queen's apothecary, but in the ballad "highest Stewart of all" — were hanged. By a curious coincidence, one Mary Hamilton, a maid of honor at Peter the Great's court in 1718, was executed for the same offense; and this affair, of which all the details are known, was at first thought by Mr. Child to be the foundation of our ballad. Later[2] he gave up Peter's Mary

---

[1] Nos. 178, 196, 199, 197, 173.

[2] See v, 298 f. The fear that sailors may tell her father and mother of her disgrace and death (iii, 383) seemed to make positively for the Russian theory. But see Mr. A. Lang in *Blackwood's Magazine*, Sept., 1895.

Hamilton as less probable than the Queen's Mary; and so all the evidence would now seem to point. But the ballad is the main thing. Twenty-eight versions of it are extant, — a few fragmentary, but most of them giving the story in full; and in all of these the hand of tradition, not of the maker or copyist or improver, has been at work. No ballad could offer better proof of the tendency of traditional material to vary in all its details, but to remain steadfast in its structural form. The famous concluding stanza of the version printed below is final in only five cases; three versions open with it, and it occurs incidentally in eleven. The color triad is fairly constant; but the variations of the seventeenth stanza are worthy of note. It makes the conclusion of one version:—

> "Yestreen I made Queen Mary's bed,
>   Kembed down her yellow hair;
>   Is this the reward I am to get,
>   To tread this gallows-stair?"

This is expanded or varied; seven years she has done these things, or else a stanza is very properly assigned to each industry, bed-making and hair-dressing, while one of Scott's copies more significantly ends thus:—

> "Aft hae I wash'd the king's bonnie face,
>   Kaim'd down his yellow hair;
>   And this is a' the reward he's geen me,
>   The gallows to be my share."

It is no part of the popular ballad to create or describe a character; seldom is there even external description, and then it is only of the conventional kind. One of the signs of dominant epic interest, and of the transfer from tradition to edition, is the incipient characterization which one notes in the "Gest of Robin Hood." Robin has sundry little ways of his own. He will not dine until some guest turns up, just as Arthur, on festal days, would not break his fast until an adventure occurred. In the higher mood of character, Robin harms no woman, takes from no poor man, is devoted to Our Lady. Even a heroic ballad like "Otterburn" tells something of its hero besides his feats; but the ballad of situation, in its primitive shape and in its best survivals, essays nothing of the kind. It is the deed, a swift back-and-forth of dialogue, a series of stanzas to accent its phase of the situation, which flash before us. There is no room for presenting character. In "Mary Hamilton," however, or in that part of it which most struck popular fancy, tradition developed something very like a "character," an individuality, which means more than a mere person filling the mould of an event. True, the phrases which express this character are themselves traditional, and have drifted in on the four winds of balladry; nothing is fixed; no effort at description is made, and even the modern reporter's inevitable adjective of beauty is absent. But the girl's loud defiance, her reckless flouting of a weak king, her wild pledge melting into tenderness at thought of home, her reproach for the hard queen's ingratitude, and the famous closing stanza with its admirable reticence in pathos, — these things make Mary Hamilton sufficiently individual. She has borne a child, as the ballad thinks, to Darnley, "highest Stewart

of a',", and has thrown it into the sea to sink or swim [1]—
"bonnie wee babe" she calls it, with faint memory of the
old exposure rite and a mother's hope for rescue; she
has been detected by the auld queen, and bidden to ride to
Edinburgh attired in black or brown. She rides in white;
laughs her loud laughters three as she goes up for trial;
and comes down the Canongate condemned, while
many a lady from window on window weeps for Mary's
fate.

> "'Make never meen [2] for me,' she says,
> 'Make never meen for me;
> Seek never grace frae a graceless face,
> For that ye 'll never see.

> "'Bring me a bottle of wine,' she says,
> 'The best that e'er ye hae,
> That I may drink to my weil-wishers
> And they may drink to me.

> "'Here 's a health to the jolly sailors
> That sail upon the main ;
> Let them never let on to my father and mother
> But what I 'm coming hame.

> "'Here 's a health to the jolly sailors
> That sail upon the sea;
> Let them never let on to my father and mother
> That I cam here to dee.

[1] So Y, 5 : —

> "' I put it in a bottomless boat
> And bade it sail the sea.'"

[2] "Moan." This stanza is E, 13; the rest is A. That the "king's
face gives grace" is an old saying: see Hill's *Boswell*, iii, 121, note.
For riding along the "Cannogate," see a very interesting sketch of
Edinburgh in 1544, in Mr. A. Lang's *Mystery of Mary Stuart*.

> "'O little did my mother think,
> The day she cradled me,
> What lands I was to travel through,
> What death I was to dee.
>
> "'O little did my father think,
> The day he held up me,
> What lands I was to travel through,
> What death I was to dee.
>
> "'Last night I wash'd the queen's feet,
> And gently laid her down;
> And a' the thanks I 've gotten the nicht
> To be hang'd in Edinbro town!
>
> "'Last nicht there was four Maries,
> The nicht there 'l be but three;
> There was Marie Seton, and Marie Beton,
> And Marie Carmichael, and me.'"

We could not part more appropriately from the genuine ballad of tradition, still undeveloped into epic breadth, than with this fine version on our lips.

V. THE BORDER BALLADS

The longer chronicle ballads are mainly traditional, but they have made good progress on the epic road. Some of them may come down to us as they were composed by the border folk whose feats they celebrate; but narrative art, of whatever origin, has laid hold of them as a class. Their faces are set away from the old lingering and dramatic fashion; if repetition and increment now and then intrude, the intrusion is marked. They are not, like "Mary Hamilton" and "Captain Car," sung and transmitted along with a lyric brevity, a lyric intensity; but they are told at epic will and in ample detail. To some extent they answer the call for history, like old Germanic ballads; people listened to them, — by invitation of the reciter in his opening lines, and not without a kind of acknowledgment of good audience and due pious civilities at the close. The feigned Canterbury raconteur and the actual reciter of a long ballad observed the same sort of etiquette, even to the prayer:—

> "Jhesue Crist our balys bete,[1]
> And to the blys us brynge!
> Thus was the hountynge of the Chivyat:
> God send us alle good endyng!"

The nun's priest ends his tale with a similar prayer; but Sir Knight is more terse:—

> "Thus endith Palamon and Emelye;
> And God save al this faire compaignye."

"God save al the rowte," blurts out the miller. It would be interesting to know how Chaucer fancied the actual recitation of his Canterbury Tales. His flexible couplets and his smooth stanzas called for something better than the chanting of a blind crowder; but it would be wide of the mark if one should assume for them the "easy, conversational tone" enjoined upon public readers and orators of our day. They were recited, doubtless, as very distinct verse. The "drasty riming," however, was suppressed, and metre was not commended to the ear as sing-song. Long chronicle ballads, too, must have tried for something of the same epic freedom in recitation;

---

[1] "Mend our ills."

while they were bound to the familiar rhythm, and associated with traditional tunes, in the majority of cases we
are not to think of them as actually sung. The old
antithesis of "sing or say" may guide us in the matter;
originally both danced and sung, then sung to a traditional tune as narrative lyrics, ballads that had passed
beyond such singable brevity and had struck into the long
epic road were doubtless recited in a kind of chant that
was rhythmic, harmonious, but without notes.

> "He sayed a lay, a maner song,
> Withoute noote, withoute song," [1]

writes Chaucer of the knight who, with a "deadly, sor-
rowful sound," is composing a complaint; but this is
lyric. To "sing and say," a hendiadys for telling a story
in song, is a very frequent formula, but the antithetical
phrase is quite as old. [2] Ballads of the chronicle type, we
may be sure, had dropped their lyric quality along with
the repetitions and the refrain; they were not "sung,"
but "said." True, certain of the border songs were sung
lustily enough, and at prodigious length. Sidney speaks
of his blind crowder as singing, however rude the voice;
and, above all, we are told that long ballads, even of the
Robin Hood order, were used directly for the dance. But
versions change, and our text of the "Cheviot," if that

[1] Identical rime indicates a difference in meaning.
[2] Interesting in this particular is Malmesbury's account of Aldhelm's
amiable vagaries, *Gesta Pontificum*, c. 190: "poesim Anglicam posse
facere, eadem apposite *vel canere vel dicere*. . . ." In Spenser's *Epitha-
lamium:* "You that say or sing," and in G. Herbert's *Posie:* "Whether I
sing or say or dictate," lies the same antithesis. Examples are endless.

ballad is what Sidney heard, is almost certainly not the text of Sidney's day. One feels that older forms of a chronicle ballad must have had twice the repetition and half the details which mark it now. Moreover, when a ballad is named with its dance, one cannot be sure that it is the ballad which we happen to know under that title. "The Complaynt of Scotland," [1] in a famous passage, mentions a group of shepherds who first tell tales, then sing songs and ballads, — including the "Hunttis of Chevet," — and finally fall to dancing, with "Robene hude" and "Ihonne Ermistrangis dance" among the measures named. The group and sequence have a slightly artificial and literary look, like the naval episode in the same work; but apart from this, apart even from the suggestion that the "Robene hude" was only a "Chanson de Robin," a "merrie and extemporall song," and conceding that quite long and lugubrious poems, like Mannington's "Lamentation," were used for the dance, it is clear that "Robin Hood and the Monk" and other extant ballads of the sort had no such office. They appeal too directly to epic interest. Dances were common at medieval funerals, naturally to a slow measure; the Lityerses song in Greece was a very mournful affair; but the steady pace of epic, with accumulating interest for its hearers, with lyric elements reduced to a mini-

[1] Edited by Murray for the Early English Text Soc., 1872, pp. lxxii, 63. In the play of *The Four Elements*, Hazlitt-Dodsley, i, 47, there is good fooling with description of a dance where folk sing the measure for it. The "Robin Hood in Barnsdale stood" is probably a genuine first line.

mum and all dramatic activity, even the chorus, suppressed, had long parted company with the dance.

Many difficulties, however, will be removed from this thorny subject, if one assumes that the paths of reciter and singer, though separate, were not very far apart. Perhaps "chanting" would best describe the way in which a ballad-singer or minstrel fared who minded his poetic scheme, and gave his hearers their honest measure of verse; it is likely that the reading and the singing were kept fairly close together by an exact insistence upon the rhythmic plan. Time or rhythm is the main factor in early verse; that is what the communal dance both begets and requires. An abominable cheerfulness or naturalness enjoined by modern elocution, and a total neglect of all distinction between verse and prose, have put this old rhythmic rendering of poetry out of date; but Tennyson used to read aloud his own verses in the despised singsong, while Carlyle swung a rapturous leg in time with the words, and muttered "Alfred's got it!" So with Tennyson's peers of earlier date. Hazlitt, in "Winterslow," says that there is "a chaunt in the recitation both of Coleridge and of Wordsworth which acts as a spell upon the hearer." Who, above all, would not have heard Scott himself, quickening his tired heart in the evil days, as he "chanted rather than repeated" his favorite version of "Otterburn?"[1] Making prose out of verse, we may be sure, is a modern accomplishment; and rhythm was once an inviolable fact in poetry, whether recited or sung. Mr.

[1] See the details in Lockhart's *Life* under July, 1831.

Thomas Hardy is good authority for the ways of the Wessex peasant; and the aged Wessex peasant of forty years ago, when he sang a ballad, had four centuries of the habit behind him. There is much to be learned from Grandfer Cantle's eccentric performance on Blackbarrow; [1] the "sing," the "say," and something of choral reminiscence are all there. "With his stick in his hand, he began to jig a private minuet . . . also began to sing, in the voice of a bee up a flue: —

> "The king' call'd down' his no'-bles all',
>   By one', by two', by three';
>   Earl Mar'-shal, I'll' go shrive' the queen',
>   And thou' shalt wend' with me'."

When old folk tried to recite a ballad to the collectors without this stay in a monotonous rhythmic chant, they often made sad work of it, and much disorder resulted in the copy. For example, a version of "The Wife of Usher's Well," taken down from the dictation of an aged fisherman in 1883, is badly damaged as verse. On the other hand, it is to that chanting vigor of recitation, in a style very close to singing, that we owe the almost uniform perfection of rhythm in our old ballads, short or long.

We may begin our study of the longer pieces [2] with

---

[1] See *The Return of the Native*, chap. iii.

[2] See, for the following, nos. 184, 185, 192, 186, 187, 188, 189; also 190, 191, 193. In studying the border ballads, we must remember the equality of all members of a Scottish clan, homogeneous conditions beyond dispute, and bear in mind, as Mr. Lang says, that "fidelity to a chief was more important than fidelity to king, country, and the fundamental laws of morality."

"The Lads of Wamphray," an old ballad based on the hanging of a freebooter about the year 1593, and the vengeance taken by his nephew. It is in the two-line stanza, — Scott's "Minstrelsy" prints it wrongly, — was surely sung though we have no refrain with it, and is full of repetitions and lively quotation: —

> "O Simmy, Simmy, now let me gang,
> And I vow I 'll neer do a Crichton wrang.
>
> "O Simmy, Simmy, now let me be,
> And a peck o' goud I 'll gie to thee.
>
> "O Simmy, Simmy, let me gang,
> And my wife shall heap it wi' her hand."

It differs, however, from the mass of ballads which were founded on deeds of the border, on feud, murder, burnings, in its fresh and immediate tone. It seems to spring straight from the fact; and one is tempted here, if anywhere, to apply Bishop Leslie's *ipsi confingunt*, and to charge the making of the ballad to the very doers of its deed of revenge. It is certainly not made at long range. There is no epic detail, and even the opening eight stanzas may be an afterthought. One takes seriously enough the story of Cnut's improvisation on the waters by Ely, the chorus of nobles and attendants, and the resulting song of battle and conquest, — or, rather, one accepts the picture as true while doubting the authenticity of the fragment; change these persons and conditions to the chief of some lawless house, surrounded by his retainers, singing a humbler theme with ampler traditional store of word and phrase, and the making of border ballads by men-at-arms in improvisation and choral becomes a quite intelligible fact. Between this first rude song and the recorded ballad, as some collector took it from the last of a long series of traditional versions, there are innumerable chances of popular and local variation, and of the "improvements" due to some vagrom bard.

Another border ballad, popular in England and cited by Tom Nashe himself, is "Dick o' the Cow." [1] Here is far more detail; it is a good story told in high spirits throughout. Dick is a fool, a Cumberland yokel; but for his stolen cattle and his wife's stolen coverlets he gets fine return, and withal fells an Armstrong in fair fight. No wonder that lusty folk everywhere liked this ballad. "The Lochmaben Harper," to be sure, may make a stronger bid for patriotism; but the stealing of English King Henry's horse by a silly, blind Scots harper has a calculated jocosity which leaves it far behind "Dick o' the Cow." The latter, as its burden shows, was sung; and if it is over long for lyric purposes, its sometime singers would doubtless remark that there can never be too much of a good thing. Incremental repetition has left plain traces here and there; but one notes the far more prominent characteristic of repeating two concluding lines of a stanza as beginning of the next, — a common feature in ballads of the epic sort. Other narrative traits

[1] *Cow* "may possibly mean the hut in which he lived; or brush, or broom." — Child.

abound. Quotation is indicated, and not, as in "The Lads
of Wamphray," sprung without notice: —

> "Then Johne Armstrang to Willie can say,
> 'Billie, a-rideing then will we.'" [1]

In "Kinmont Willie," of which a very generous portion
must be placed to the credit of Scott, so much, indeed, as
to make it almost an imitated ballad, the first-person
plural imparts a confidential tone, but fails to achieve
the immediate effect of the other pieces; one seems to be
reading something like a dramatic lyric of Browning,
with mosstroopers instead of the old cavalier and without
"my boy George," but all done to the life. Next, "in de-
ference to history," comes what may be a free version of
Kinmont Willie's story, "Jock o' the Side," which Professor Child calls one of the best ballads in the world, and
"enough to make a mosstrooper of any young borderer,
had he lacked the impulse." Jock is set free from Newcastle, Hobby Noble leading the small party of rescue, just
as Willie was set free from Carlisle; the ballad stirs one's
pulses with its opening line, and all is life and movement
to the end. "Archie o' Cawfield," almost a repetition of
"Jock," tells the same tale of rescue, two brothers here
risking life and limb for a third; the device of reversing the
horses' shoes is mentioned, and the recurring verses: —

> "There was horsing, horsing of haste,
> And cracking o' whips out o'er the lee,"

put a fine breeze about one's ears as one reads. One of

---

[1] *Can* = gan, — simply "did."

the brothers says the night's work has cost him his land;
the answer is prompt: —

> " 'Now wae light o' thee and thy lands baith, Jock,
> And even so baith the land and thee!
> For gear will come and gear will gang,
> But three brothers again we were never to be!' "

In "Hobie Noble," finally, we learn how that hero of the
rescue in "Jock o' the Side" is betrayed into the hands
of the English and taken to Carlisle. Two stanzas give
his Good-Night and his loathing of betrayal; while the
singer concludes, —

> " 'I'd rather be ca'd Hobie Noble
> In Carlisle, where he suffers for his faut,
> Before I were ca'd traitor Mains
> That eats and drinks of meal and maut.' "

"Jamie Telfer of the Fair Dodhead," [1] as printed in the
" Minstrelsy," was "improved" by Scott; it is a story
of cattle-lifting, revenge, and reprisal, and is somewhat
inferior to the preceding ballads. "Hughie Grame,"
accused of stealing the lord bishop's mare, is hanged
for the theft — unjustly, the ballad thinks, and the
ballad may be right. It has no other claim upon the
reader. "The Death of Parcy Reed" tells of the laird's

---

[1] It should be "in" the Dodhead, as Jamie was only tenant; "of"
would make him proprietor. — Child, v, 249. The version lately
recovered by Mr. Macmath shows that Scott is responsible, as was
guessed, for the simile —

> "The Dinlay snaw was neer mair white
> Nor the lyart locks of Harden's hair,"

and other additions in describing the fight.

treacherous murder; it is full of incremental repetition, has a "farewell" already cited, and in one version was "taken down from the chanting of an old woman" in Northumberland. The story, to be dated perhaps in the sixteenth century, still lives in local tradition. When his three supposed friends leave him practically defenseless to meet the troop that besets him, he offers the first his good steed, the second a yoke of oxen, the third his daughter Jean, if they will stay and back him: and all in vain.

Passing to the ballads of battle,[1] we find in most of them the traces of a minstrel and even the shadow of a printed book. We should feel more surprise that no great ballad came from the long and glorious struggle of the covenanters, if we did not remember a dozen other disappointments of this sort, including the late civil war in America and the futility of nearly all its verse. One is tempted to say that it has always been the small fights which made great poetry. Moreover, tradition herself is sometimes unable to preserve her children from indignities and absurdities; and parody, burlesque, incompetence, have spoiled many a fine original in the process of oral transmission. "The Battle of Harlaw" is a ballad mentioned as far back as "The Complaynt of Scotland;" it celebrated the victory won in 1411 by Lowlanders against an invading Lord of the Isles. This seems to have been lost; but a ballad on the same fight was "obtained from the country people" near Aberdeen. In spite of some obvious corruptions, it rings well, especially in the

---

[1] See nos. 163, 206, 205, 202, 198.

last stanza; the tune, moreover, is said to be "wild and simple." —

> " Gin ony body speer at you
> For them ye took awa',
> Ye may tell their wives and bairnies
> They're sleepin' at Harlaw."

Professor Neilson points out the use of the Highland dialect in this ballad both for characterization and for comic effect; it is a conglomerate of chronicle, pathos, and humor.

The covenanters, it has been said, do little for balladry; another sort of poem has found adequate expression for hearts that beat more fast over the graves of the martyrs. "Bothwell Bridge" has been quoted already for Earlstoun's good-night. "Loudon Hill" savors of a rude and untuneful bard; and the same may be said of "The Battle of Philiphaugh," though both are traditional ballads. A little repetition, a touch of the picturesque, fail to redeem "Bonny John Seton" from mediocrity or worse. These all form an easy bridge by which one crosses to the thorough-paced minstrel ballad and the piece which invokes printed or written authority. "Gude Wallace" [1] comes, in no long journey, from the poem attributed to Blind Harry; but its patriotic tone and the discomfiture of the English captain would make it popular and remembered. Of the actual battle-pieces, "Flodden Field," preserved by Deloney,[2] is the shortest and most traditional in tone; "the commons of England made this song,"

[1] No. 157.
[2] See above, p. 12, and nos. 168, 159, 172, 174, 175, 176, 177.

he says, "which to this day is not forgotten of many." It has been touched a little, one infers, and shortened here and there, more in repetitions than in the story; its main defect is that one fails to find the root of the matter in it; not the ballad, but its subject gave it vogue. "Durham Field," with sixty-six stanzas, has a minstrel or humble poet behind it; he is chronological in noting that Durham, Crécy, and Poitiers were all fought within one month, and he is interesting in telling us that

> "There was welthe and welfare in mery England,
>   Solaces, game and glee,
>   And every man loved other well
>   And the king loved good yeomanrie."

Another minstrel sings "Musselburgh Field" in the same vein, but the ballad is a fragment. "Earl Bothwell" tells of Riccio's and Darnley's death. "The Rising in the North," "Northumberland Betrayed by Douglas," and "The Earl of Westmoreland" are chronicle ballads composed by this or that minstrel; the third of these has a curious addition of what Child calls "imitation of stale old romance" and Professor Schofield suspects it to be drawn from "Libeaus Desconus:" we start out with Nevilles and old Master Norton, and end by cutting off the soldan's head.

So closes the unrefreshing catalogue, save for two ballads which rise from these arid foothills like peaks of the Sierras: "Otterburn"[1] and the "Cheviot." It is

---

[1] No. 161. There is even here a background of learned information. "The chronicle will not lie," says stanza 35; and the same appeal to authority is found in so artificial a ballad as *The Rose of England*.

uncertain which of them Sidney had in mind when he
praised "the old song of Percy and Douglas;" but, as
Professor Child remarks, while the quality of "Otterburn"
amply deserves such praise, the quality of "Cheviot"
deserves it better, and for that, and no other reason, one
assumes the latter ballad. If guessing is allowed, one
may go straight to the passage which breathes a spirit
as noble as Sidney's own knighthood, and must have
delighted his soul. Douglas and Percy have been fighting manfully; an arrow comes flying along and strikes
Douglas "in at the breast-bone:" —

> "Thorowe lyvar and longës bathe
>   the sharpe arrowe ys gane,
> That neuer after in all his lyffe-days
>   he spayke mo wordës but ane:
> That was, 'Fyghte ye, my myrry men, whyllys ye may,
>   for my lyff-days ben gan.'

> "The Persë leanyde on his brande,
>   and sawe the Duglas de;
> He took the dede mane by the hande,
>   and sayd, 'Wo ys me for the!

> "'To haue savyde thy lyffe, I wolde haue partyde with
>   my landes for years thre,
> For a better man, of hart nare of hande,
>   Was nat in all the north contrë.'"

So the older version, which is called the "Hunting of the
Cheviot." The younger and inferior version, "Chevy
Chase," — the only one known to Addison when he ap-
preciated it so highly in the "Spectator," calling it the

favorite ballad of the English people [1] and asserting it
to have been the object of extravagant admiration on
the part of Ben Jonson, — runs thus: —

> " With that there came an arrow keene
> out of an English bow,
> Which stroke Erle Douglas on the brest
> a deepe and deadlye blow.
>
> " Who never said more words than these:
> 'Fight on, my merry men all!
> For why, my life is at an end,
> lord Pearcy sees my fall.'
>
> " Then leaving liffe, Erle Pearcy tooke
> the dead man by the hand;
> Who said : 'Erle Dowglas, for thy life
> wold I had lost my land !
>
> " 'O Christ ! my verry hart doth bleed
> for sorrow for thy sake,
> For sure, a more redoubted knight
> mischance cold never take.' "

This version, "written over for the broadside press,"
still good in spite of the hurdy-gurdy tone, need not be
considered further. "Otterburn," however, "tran-
scendently heroic ballad" as Mr. Child calls it, though
less concentrated in effect, though it has neither dying
speech nor victor's eulogy, and though patch-verses occur
like "I tell you in certayne," must be placed beside the

[1] "You will not maintain that *Chevy Chase* is a finer poem than
Paradise Lost ?" — "I do not know what you mean by a fine poem; but
I will maintain that it gives a much deeper insight into the truth of
things." "I do not know what you mean by the truth of things." —
T. L. Peacock's *Melincourt*, chap. ix.

"Cheviot." The chivalry lies here in facts. Besieged
Percy defies invading Douglas over the walls of Newcastle, and makes a tryst to fight with him; then sends
him a pipe of wine that he and his host may drink. On
the next day, as battle is preparing, letters come to Percy
bidding him delay until his father shall arrive. "Wend
again to my lord," says Percy, in Nelson's vein, "and say
you saw me not. My troth is pledged, and no Scot shall
call me coward. So, archers, shoot, and minstrels, play;
every man think on his true-love and cross himself in the
Trinity's name: I make my vow to God this day will
I not flee!" Then high floats the Douglas standard, with
its bleeding heart, high the white lion and crescent of the
Percy; " St. Andrew! " loud shouted there, " St. George!"
here; and the fight is on. "Otterburn" should stir any
man's blood. We heed only the English ballad; there are
two inferior Scottish versions, with a famous stanza, —

> "'But I have seen a dreary dream,
>   Beyond the isle o' Sky;
> I saw a dead man won the fight,
>   And I think that man was I,'" —

which Mr. Child refuses to accept as traditional. Inferior
as they are, and in part "suspicious," they have a popular,
traditional tone and lack the broadside twang of "Chevy
Chase" in its younger form.

How shall one account for these two fine ballads of
"Otterburn" and the "Cheviot"? Where are they to
be placed? Assuming, in spite of Mr. J. W. Hales,[1] that

[1] In a paper in his *Folia Litteraria*. The battle was fought August

they describe the same actual fight, we have only to read Froissart's story of it to understand the fine note of chivalry that rings through their rough stanzas. It is the chivalry and the sentiment of men-at-arms, if not of lofty knighthood itself, rather than the work of a professional song-writer like Laurence Minot, who was almost a contemporary of these warriors and wrote exultant verses on the wars of Edward III, pouring out impetuous scorn upon the foe.[1] It is far removed, too, from the simple and rural conception of things such as one can find in ordinary traditional ballads or even in battle-pieces made "by the commons." It is the spirit characteristic of fourteenth-century Englishmen at their best, as history records it in Edward III with his sacred word of honor[2] and his generosity to the captive, as Chaucer embodies it in his knight and his squire, and as Shakespeare, with amazing sympathy, has fixed it in his Hotspur, the Percy of these ballads. Who knows, by the way, what the ballads may not have done for Shakespeare's study of this favorite, who, by the sneer of the rival, would " ride up a hill per-

19, 1388. The English version of *Otterburn* "is likely to have been modernized from a ballad current as early as 1400," and is closer to the facts. The *Cheviot*, though older in its linguistic forms, is more remote in information ; it turns the tryst of battle in England into a defiant deer-hunt in Scotland. The spirit of the piece, however, is quite contemporary with the fight. In form it has probably been submitted to many changes.

[1] See above, p. 55.

[2] This sentiment was not confined to England. The old French king, when his son escaped from Edward, felt bound to go of his own will over channel and take the hostage's place in captivity.

pendicular," and by his own account would follow honor beyond mortal bounds ? The noble speech before Shrewsbury fight, —

> " 'O gentlemen, the time of life is short,' " —

is a kind of summary of Percy's character as the balladmakers saw it.[1]

Judging them, then, by their tone, these ballads spring originally from fighting men of the better sort, and suggest the old songs of warriors by warriors and for warriors which one guesses in the background of epic. Precisely, too, as the nobler sort of rhapsode or professional poet worked old improvisations into epic shape without impairing their note of simple and hardy courage, so a border minstrel of whatever time has surely laid his hand upon the original form of these stirring verses. They are still popular, still traditional, but not in the sense that "Mary Hamilton " and "Captain Car" and the Scottish versions of "Otterburn" itself are traditional and popular. They are epic in their appeal, particularly in their habit of singling out this or that hero and naming him for especial praise, a method which is often called Homeric and which is particularly effective in the best of Anglo-Saxon battle-lays, "The Fight at Maldon." Richard Witherington, squire of Northumberland, is a worthy successor to those heroes of East Anglia, the leader Byrhtnoth, Ælfere, Maccus, Wulfmær, and the rest,

[1] So far is this sentiment to the fore that Hume of Godscroft (see Child, iii, 303) calls the *Cheviot* "a meer fiction, *perhaps to stirre up vertue.*"

immortal all. Our two ballads are matched in this respect, moreover, by songs which are not of so traditional
a cast. A very interesting song on the Battle of Agincourt,[1] printed by Wright in the second volume of his
"Political Poems," "is preserved in . . . an early chronicle of London, the writer of which was taking his narrative from the account given in the popular ballad, until,
tired of paraphrasing it, he went on copying the song
itself." In its praise of the individual warriors, it runs
parallel with "Otterburn" and the "Cheviot;" but this
is not all. These ballads break away in several instances
from the common metre and ordinary stanza; the same
rime often connects two or more stanzas; and Professor
Skeat thinks that the whole of the "Cheviot" was meant
to run in eight-line stanzas, — as Child prints it, — and
that either the task was too hard or our copy is badly
damaged. Now "Agincourt" is in interlaced eight-line
stanzas, of the *ballade* order, with a refrain; and Wright's
second volume, just cited, contains a number of poems of
this general form, all on popular subjects and tending
to "journalism" of the better class. Such, for example,
is the "Lamentacioun of the Duchess of Glossester," reported in the first person by one who "passed through a
palace" and heard her moan. "All women may be ware

---

[1] The other song *For the Victory at Agincourt*, which Percy printed
from a MS. which also contained the music, has a Latin refrain. Percy
notes that "although Henry 'had forbidden the minstrels to celebrate his
victory,' he was a patron of the 'order,' and both of his biographers mention his love of music." Wright says that this song "carried the tidings
of the victory . . . through the towns and villages of England."

by me," is unlucky Eleanor's refrain; and there is, of
course, no refrain line in our ballads. But the general
resemblance is clear. Striking is the tendency to ex-
cessive alliteration, not found in the normal traditional
ballad in such riotous force, but breaking out here and
there in our two border pieces so as to match the consistent habit of songs like "Agincourt," with its —

> "Stedes ther stumbelyd in that stownde,
> That stod stere stuffed under stele."

Instead of the modest "dale and down" or "green as
grass" of balladry, we have in "Otterburn" "styffely
in stowre can stand;" while Percy's tryst is described
as a place where —

> "The roo full rekeles ther sche rinnes
> To make the game and glee;
> The fawken and the fesaunt both
> Among the holtes on hye."

Douglas is painted finely in the "Cheviot," by good help
of "hunting the letter:" —

> "His armor glytteryde as did a glede,
> a bolder barne was never born."

These are marks of the poet, and are in line with the
characteristics of middle-English lyric in its mingling of
popular and artistic elements. Not that the humble
ballad-singer, Richard Sheale, who signs the copy of the
"Cheviot" which he had probably learned by ear and
either dictated to a poor scribe or set down in his own
blundering hand, made any line of the poem. He copied
it as part of his stock, just as a more prosperous man,

years before, set down favorite songs in a commonplace book and signed, for example, "The Nut-Brown Maid" with his own name: "explicit quod Ric. Hill." So the Tamworth minstrel wrote "expliceth, quod Rychard Sheale." That should disturb nobody. Nor should the minstrel's rendering of a transition stanza: "The first *fit* here I end; if you want any more of this Cheviot song, more is coming." Not even that is Sheale's affair. Heusler notes that remote Faroe ballads have such a division with such an announcement: "here the first *fit* ends," or "here we will begin our second *fit ;*" and it is common in medieval tales. Finally, the imperfect metre is precisely what one should expect from an illiterate copyist. Ballads sung in good rhythm are always in good metre, and in this respect not inferior, as Mr. Child once wrote in a private letter, to "any Pindaric ode by Gray or whomever else." An ignorant man sings or recites good rhythm, he cannot write or dictate it; just so children invariably observe rigorously good rhythm in saying verse, and will "make up" a good line or so. Let them take pencil and paper, try to compose and set down their lines, and the result is sad limping stuff.

It is clear, then, that these two great ballads spring from no simple countryside memory. We hear, as in Froissart, the cry of heartening or of defiance, and, as in 'Maldon," the crash of weapons and din of actual fight. Contrast with this the movement and detail of the "Baron of Brackley;" there the persons are named but incidentally; everybody knows them, and they are

neither introduced nor described. The action begins at
once. Here, though we are dealing with such a prominent
man as Harry Percy, the epic instinct asserts itself in lines
of introduction or detail: —

> "He had byn a march-man all hys dayes
> And kepte Barwyke upon Twede."

The route of the invaders is carefully given, their numbers, — with appeal to "the chronicle," — and the exact
time of year by rural calendar; [1] whereas

> "Inverey cam doun Deeside whistlin' and playin',
> He was at brave Braikley's yett ere it was dawin',"

is the incipient chronicle style, still communal in manner
and form. Moreover in "Otterburn" and the "Cheviot"
comment of the narrator is heard: "the child may rue
that is unborn," for the general, and for the particular —

> "It was a hevy syght to se
> bright swordes on basnites lyght."

Most striking is the absence of ballad commonplaces,
matching the deviation from ballad structure. In the Scottish popular fragment of "Otterburn," three stanzas are
taken from the chronicle ballad; and then enters a bonny
boy, of the regular breed, with his news, and as inevitably
he is told that if this be true he shall have the best,

---

[1] In the *Cheviot* there is a kind of antiquarian appeal, already quoted:

> "Old men that knowen the growende well yenoughe,
> Call it the battell of Otterburn."

This version is therefore a strictly local redaction of the familiar chronicle ballad material.

if false he may look to be hanged; whereupon he takes
out his "little penknife" from its right ballad place and
gives Earl Douglas "a deep wound and a sare,"—which
is the popular and traditional expression of a belief
that Douglas was not killed by the enemy, but by a re-
vengeful groom of his chamber whom he had struck
the day before and who left part of his master's armor
unfastened behind so as to strike him down in the heat
of battle.[1] In the chronicle ballad, however, not a hint of
any commonplace of typical situation ballads can be
found.

For these two are chronicle ballads, — with emphasis
on the chronicle. The fight of Otterburn was surely sung
on both sides of the border, in hall, bower, and cottage,
by the roadside and at the dance; but what we have in
the two splendid poems about it seems to come to us, in
stuff and spirit, from men-at-arms,— who, as the bishop
testifies, could make and sing their ballads readily
enough, — with more or less editing, recasting, and fresh
phrasing, by minstrels of varying degree, upon the way.
That way was not very long; both ballads are in manuscript of the sixteenth century. They are ballads of fight,
traditional, but not popular in the normal sense of the
word. There is nothing choral or concerted or dramatic
in them; they seem to have been epic from the start.
But it is useless to speculate on their far-off and conjec-
tural making; they are made, and, more to the purpose,
have been kept; they are to be taken as Dryden would

[1] Hume of Godscroft, Child, iii, 295.

have men take Chaucer, and one is glad enough to say
that here is God's plenty.[1]

VI. THE GREENWOOD BALLADS

The epic process of balladry does not culminate in
heroic pieces such as we have been noting. Of these,
indeed, it may be said that except in their traditional
ballad style, and in their compactness, their swifter and
more irregular pace, they do not differ essentially from
longer epic poems. Professor Ker has shown that the
chasm between epic and heroic song is no wide, impas-
sable affair. Still less is the difference between popular
ballad and popular epic; and this difference can be
studied at will in the various pieces which make up the
Robin Hood group as compared with the Gest, an actual
though not elaborate epic poem.[2] Its hero, of course, is
the outlaw.

[1] The "popular" *Chevy Chase* of the broadsides, though it was
worked over from traditional sources, has as little of the typical and
traditional ballad structure as the manuscript *Cheviot;* but one would
like to have heard those Scottish shepherds sing, and perhaps dance,
their *Hunttis of Chevet.* The fragment of *Otterburn* (B) combines borrowing of the chronicle ballad with its own popular stanzas not derived
from the chronicle ballad ; and the line of cleavage is evident. The
point is not only that no facts support the idea, which some critics are
fond of advancing, that a heroic tale such as the *Cheviot*, told in the
manner of romance, falls like crumbs from the knight's table among
retainers, scullions, and begging-minstrels, who cook it again into a
popular ballad with more or less pitiful repetition and other "slang,"
but that a convincing array of facts can be brought against this theory.
See Kittredge, in the Cambridge ed. of Child's *Ballads*, pp. xv f.; and
the present writer, in *Modern Philology*, 1904.

[2] These are compared, on lines laid down by Professor Ker, in

The outlaw, now as humble poacher and now as ideal champion of the rights of man against church and state, is a natural favorite of the ballad muse. She has little liking, however, for George Borrow's friend, the gypsy, who came into view too late for the best traditional song; he has just one ballad to his credit. John Faa [1] was a leading name among the gypsies; and this particular hero, so it seems, was hanged in Scotland about 1624. The ballad without warrant of fact makes the Countess of Cassilis leave her earl and elope with Johny Faa, whose people had "coost the glamer o'er her." There is plenty of repetition, and a thoroughly traditional style. Another Johnie, however, and with no trace of the vagrom blood, is more to our purpose. "This precious specimen of the unspoiled traditional ballad" is Mr. Child's eulogy of "Johnie Cock," [2] and Professor Brandl, defying tradition, has undertaken to restore the original text of the ballad; but as a matter of fact, traditional ballads have no text in the ordinary meaning of the word. "There are texts," as Professor Kittredge says, "but there is no text." Old things and new jostle each other in "Johnie Cock;" wolves roam about, and birds give information, but Johnie himself, in a version taken down in 1780, wears not only Lincoln green, but "shoes of the

A. Heusler's *Lied und Epos*, 1905, pp. 37 ff. A volume by Professor W. M. Hart, soon to be published, examines the case at length and with interesting results.

[1] See no. 200, *The Gypsy Laddie*.

[2] See, for the following, nos. 114, 115, 116, 118 to 154 inclusive, and 117, the *Gest*.

American leather." What Johnie does, however, is the same in all versions: he disregards his mother's benison and malison alike, her proffered wine and bread, and goes off to hunt the dun deer. An old palmer, or other informer, sees him and tells the seven foresters, who surprise him, wounding him badly, but are all killed save one. Johnie's indignation at the unmanly mode of attack is curiously expressed : —

> " 'The wildest wolf in aw this wood
>   Wad not ha' done so by me ;
> She'd ha' wet her foot i' th' wan water,
>   And sprinkled it o'er my bree ;
> And if that wad not ha' waken'd me,
>   She wad ha' gone and let me be.' "

It goes with a burden, this sterling old song, and has traces of an incremental repetition that has been reduced to lowest terms by impatient transcribers. But the dramatic throb is still there. Burden and repetition are still more to the front in a very old greenwood ballad preserved by a manuscript of the fifteenth century. "Robyn and Gandelyn" is not a part of the Robin Hood cycle, though it has some resemblance to the type. Robyn, or Robert, uses his namesake's oath, and he goes with Gandelyn after deer as Robin goes with Little John on other quests. Wrennok of Donne shoots Robert from ambush, — "out of the west;" whereupon Gandelyn takes vengeance, cleaving Wrennok's heart with an arrow. —

> " 'Now xalt [1] thou never yelpe,[1] Wrennok,
>   At ale ne at wyn ;

[1] Shalt; boast.

That thu hast slawe [1] goode Robyn
And his knave [1] Gandeleyn.

"'Now xalt thou never yelpe, Wrennok,
     At wyn ne at ale,
That thu hast slawe goode Robyn
And Gandeleyn his knave.'
Robin lygth in grene wode bowndyn."

Despite its beginning, "I herde a carpyng of a clerk,"
attributing the tale to a scholar's song, this bit of verse is
of indirect popular origin. At beginning and end, as in
Danish ballads, is the burden: *Robin lies in greenwood
bound ;* while the incremental repetitions in so old a copy
are valuable evidence for its primitive structure. "Adam
Bell" brings us to very different matter. Reprinted often,
a regular story in one hundred and seventy stanzas, it
has a good plot — partly used again in the ballad of
"Auld Matrons" — and situations of absorbing interest
such as the Tell episode where Cloudesley shoots the
apple from his son's head. This, like other good things,
is probably imported from abroad; to ascribe it to an
old Aryan sun-myth is futile. These ballads all praise
good archery; and such a story would fall into the outlaw's doings as to a magnet. The three heroes are sworn
brothers; and their narrative shows distinct traces of an
arranging hand in dealing with the abundant traditional
and popular material. It is treated very briefly here
because arrangements of this sort, the combination and
the interplay, are most conveniently studied in a compilation like the "Gest." Moreover, the "rescue" part of

[1] Slain; servant, squire.

"Adam Bell" is repeated in "Robin Hood and the
Monk," one of the best ballads of its kind ever made,
just as the surprised porter, the outwitted citizens, the
slain sheriff, the "complacent king," and the happy ending, return not only in the better known cycle but in the
"Gest" itself. Here, too, though in slightest compass,
we meet the "nature introduction;" we roam with merry
archers under the green leaves, and fleet the time in a
style akin to Robin's own royal way. We hear the reciter,
too, already met in the "Cheviot," with his "listen, gentlemen," and his warning of a completed "fit:"—

> "To Caerlel went these good yemen
> In a mery morning of Maye :
> Here is a fit of Cloudesli,
> And another is for to saye."

The rhapsode has arrived.

As we have said, the progress of heroic ballads through
a cycle up to a coherent epic poem lies before us in its
latter stages, although its actual beginning and its possible end cannot be seen. "The Gest of Robin Hood" is
an epic poem in that it tells its connected story about a
definite hero; and it is put together, smoothed, and completed into unity, out of sundry epic ballads which themselves make a single though not a coherent group. While
we have not the actual pieces used for the making of this
epic, we have versions which correspond very closely to
them. Had the "Gest" been composed in an unlettered
age, had its hero been national as well as popular, the
epic process would have gone on its way to higher and

wider achievement. Confined to humble tradition and the interest of a class, it reached no advanced stage, and can be called full epic only by the courtesy of anticipation. For the other extreme of the process, there is reasonable conjecture. It would be an enormous gain to the science of literature if one could follow back to their beginnings, not only actual ballads of the cycle, but also that dramatic or even ritual treatment[1] of the theme which analogy with other cases forbids us to confine to such late, incidental, and corrupted specimens of the Robin Hood plays as have been preserved. Little more than the name comes to these from greenwood tradition; Maid Marian is an impertinence, mere Marion of the French Robin, and no mate for our outlaw. Fragments, however, of the true greenwood drama occur; such is the bit of a play, preserved in a manuscript which must be older than the memorandum of 1475 on its back, with plot similar to the story of "Robin Hood and Guy of Gisborne." But the plays do little for our purpose.

A careful study of the ballads, however, makes it reasonably sure that they were sung in the first instance about some local hero in the manner of "Robin and Gandelyn" and "Johnie Cock," but with the structure of a dramatic ballad of situation.[2] Overwhelming popular favor has-

[1] The May festival claims Robin for its own, and with good reason; but these relations belong to students of our earliest drama.

[2] The language of the *Gest*, which was printed near 1500, contains some Middle English forms which may be "relics of the ballads from which this little epic was made up," or else the natural language of a poem "put together as early as 1400 or before." See Child, iii, 40.

tened the epic course. As Arthur probably began with some real chieftain and formed the nucleus for innumerable accretions of fiction and fact from every side, growing into the sovran ruler of all romance as well as "the flower of kings," so a petty fugitive of whatever name, poaching on the royal preserves, may well have grown in fame, appropriated the legends of other fugitives, and so become what Professor Child has called him, the ideal outlaw. His character is drawn in terms of eulogy. He is distinctly named as one who did poor men much good; and poor men of the fourteenth century not only needed a friend, not only were ready to hail him hero, but, in their humble song, could save that friend and hero from the fate of the unrecorded brave. The author of "Piers Plowman" yearned for a body of knights and gentlemen who would protect the poor peasant, but chivalry did nothing of this kind; what wonder that the generous outlaw should appeal to popular sympathy? Robin took from the rich and gave to the lowly, correcting sociological abuses, and gaining that gratitude which the *klephts* of modern Greece have won from the popular muse. A very pedestrian muse in our own day has taken kindly to bandits like Jesse James; but Robin was hero not of the rabble, but of the people at large, the commons of England in a wide, rural sense. Robin, again, is no old divinity, no Woden, Odin, Hooden, come upon the parish; he is just as he is sung, outlaw, archer, foe of the unco' guid and the unco' rich, the poor man's friend. Yet he is no humble person. He is lavishly generous, full of pride, —

"Robin was a proud outlaw," runs the verse, — and of exquisite courtesy. He harms no woman. The laudatory touches are general, ideal; his "milk-white side " is vaguely aristocratic, and the fact that an inch of his body was worth a whole man reminds one of the descriptions of Beowulf's hand-grip, — strong as that of thirty men. In brief, the ideal outlaw, a vividly drawn type.

With this theory of Robin's provenience agree such facts as can be gathered. The mention of him in the fourteenth century by an Englishman, and early in the fifteenth by a Scot, testifies to his vogue; and the English account is significant. Sloth, in "Piers Plowman," knows "rymes of Robyn Hood and Randolf, erle of Chester." Identification of the rank of these two, often attempted, is absurd on the face of it; for the cycles differed utterly. Sloth evidently held at command two groups of songs, one of battle and feud, in which the great earl spent his half-century full in the public eye, and one of humbler origin, which was so far complete by 1377, the earliest date for this reference, that one may assume the "Gest" itself to have been made not many years later. We should say now that Sloth had equal liking for history and for romance; nor do we admit for a moment that Sloth's taste was in question. Probably his industrious and pious friend Piers, though a rank Puritan, was fond of a good cleanly ballad, only he did not neglect his pater-noster for secular song. Those two cycles, united in Sloth's memory, have been divided by fate. The history has disappeared, the romance lives on. Randolf, second or third earl, or perhaps a compound of both, who now defied royalty and now made peace and pact, was at times an outlaw on the grand scale, and offered every inducement for immortality in song; but, like Hereward, he is for us a ballad-hero without his ballads, while the fortuitous Robin Hood, "absolutely a creation of the ballad muse," with no history to commend him, is the hero of an excellent epic and of thirty-six known individual ballads, good and bad, besides those that have gone the way of destruction. Of the thirty-six, as Child points out, four are of quite ancient form: "Robin Hood and the Monk" and "Robin Hood and the Potter," from old manuscripts of the fifteenth century, "Robin Hood and Guy of Gisborne" and "Robin Hood's Death," from the Percy Folio. The rest, mainly gathered from broadsides and garlands, while popular in some respects, often give Robin a sorry fate, bringing him down to the stupid, amicable bully whom any stray tinker or tramp can soundly thrash, and striking, in most cases, a deplorably poor note. So Charlemagne declines from the all-wise and all-powerful hero of the earliest *chansons de geste* to the weak, vassal-ruled figure of twelfth-century accounts. Most of these garlands and broadsides preserve sound old ballad stuff in its dotage, as a bit of comparison will show. In the "Gest" Little John remarks to Robin that it is time for dinner: —

"Than bespake hym gode Robyn :
'To dyne have I noo lust

Till that I have som bolde baron,
Or som unkouth gest,' "[1] —

which, as Professor Child reminds us, was King Arthur's
way. In "Robin Hood Newly Revived" the singer calls
on all "gentlemen in this bower" to listen to him, and
then plunges into the dialogue as follows: —

"'What time of the day?' quoth Robin Hood then
Quoth Little John, ''T is in the prime.'
'Why then we will to the green wood gang,
For we have no vittles to dine.'"

It is not all as deject and wretched, to be sure; but that
is too often the tone of the late "popular" ballads.[2] A
glance at these will suffice, nor is it even well to make a
list of their titles. Of the good and ancient versions, however, it may be said that nothing better of their kind can
be found in any time or place; none, says Professor Child,
"please so many and please so long." But they should
not be made over in condescending prose and mixed with
alien stuff. It is to be regretted that the original Robin
Hood of these sterling poems, the "pious founder" himself, who loves his king, though he eats the king's deer
and shoots the king's officers, who gets uneasy if he can-

---

[1] "Stranger as guest."
[2] The best of these ballads of the "secondary" period is one that may
be derived from North Country tradition, and is in the better traditional
style, — *Robin Hood and the Beggar*, ii, no. 134 in Child. See his
remarks, iii, 159. Another good ballad is no. 144, *Robin Hood and the
Bishop of Hereford*, composed by somebody on the basis of the *Gest*, but
well composed. Forty years ago it was the most popular Robin Hood
ballad sung in England.

not attend church, though he exacts huge sums from the
monks, who helps the poor everywhere and even an occasional worthy knight, who holds a kind of greenwood
assizes, and when made an official at the king's court
pines for his forest and the dun deer, and who has such
a follower as Little John, should be presented to healthy
youth along with those Maid Marians and Friar Tucks
who have no ballad rights to existence on any terms.
It is true that many of the inferior ballads about Robin
Hood had their vogue; they were often meant for singing,[1]
and have a burden. The last of them, however, "A True
Tale of Robin Hood," professing to be history, is the work
of a known author, Martin Parker, the only poem in
Child's collection which is not anonymous; and it is a
dreary compilation indeed. It ends with a supposed
epitaph from the hero's tomb in Yorkshire; and of course
Robin is Earl of Huntington. More to the purpose are
the broadsides and garlands, beloved of rural England;
yet, while a few commonplaces occur in these and incremental repetition now and then is used, the commonplaces are seldom apposite and the repetition rarely
effective. Lovers of the traditional ballad have little to
do with these broadsides, save as with studies in degeneration; while the popular heroic ballad is seen at its
best in the old and sterling pieces to which we now turn.

Striking are the differences between this group and
those ballads of situation which were assumed as normal

[1] For example, nos. 122, with traces of repetition, 123, 124, 125, 126,
132, 133, 135, 143, and 150.

and at no great distance from choral origins. "Guy,"
"The Monk," "The Potter," are long stories, epic
through and through. Each begins with description of the
greenwood, with the boon season and the singing birds.
Like the conventional May morn of so many poems, this
descriptive opening — it is echoed with variations as
overture to the Canterbury Tales — is supposed to have
been brought into vogue by medieval Latin poets,
although it seems more probable that these poets were
themselves inspired by choral summer songs of the folk.
But it is not an original traditional ballad affair; it
belongs both to pure lyric, like that old Provençal song
of the *regine Avrillouse*, and to these incipient epics of the
greenwood. Least meritorious of the four, "The Potter"
has the shortest and barest opening; and "Guy,"
though admirable, is, just a trifle too abrupt. When
shaws are sheen and copses fair, we are told, and leaves
large and long, it is merry to hear the small birds singing
in the forest. Then the tense shifts : —

> "The woodweele sang and wold not cease
> Amongst the leaves a lyne; [1]
> And it is by two wight yeomen,
> By deare God, that I meane."

And the story can begin. "The Monk," however, most
successful of these pieces, while opening in the same
way, has its conventional material under better artistic
control, runs more smoothly, and joins its scene very
prettily with its story. These beginning stanzas are

[1] Linden leaves.

already classic, — if by "classic" one means the best things in a literature : —

> "In somer, when the shawes be sheyne,
>   And leves be large and long,
> Hit is full mery in feyre foreste
>   To here the foulys song :
>
> "To se the dere draw to the dale,
>   And leve the hillës hee,
> And shadow hem in the levës grene,
>   Under the grene-wode tre.[1]
>
> "Hit befel on Whitsontide,
>   Erly in a May mornyng,
> The son up feyre can shyne,
>   And the briddis mery can syng.
>
> "'This is a mery mornyng,' seid Litull John,
>   'Be hym that dyed on tre ;
> A more mery man then I am one
>   Lyves not in Christiantë.
>
> "'Pluk up thi hert, my dere mayster,'
>   Litull John can sey,
> 'And thynk hit is a full fayre tyme
>   In a mornyng of May.'"

Here the epic opening, itself an accretion upon the old dramatic and choral ballad, is provided with an introduction beautiful for purposes of art, but superfluous in a song made up wholly of action and dialogue. Dominance of actual situation over description and story comes more into view in "Robin Hood's Death," which opens with

---

[1] The late Dr. Boynton, in an unpublished dissertation on ballad refrains, copy in Harvard College Library, pp. 237 f., thinks that this opening was once a true burden-stem such as one often finds at the beginning of Danish ballads.

a dialogue and makes no mention of time or place. Robin
is ill; he must go to Churchlees and be let blood. Danger
from a yeoman there is urged; let Robin take a sufficient
bodyguard. He will take only Little John. They shoot as
they go, and pass a black water with a plank over it where
kneels an old woman banning Robin Hood; her reasons
are lost with a lost leaf of the Percy Folio. Doubtless, as
Child says, she is a hired witch; and presently there are
women weeping for Robin's "dear body that this day
must be let blood." Omens are in the air, but Robin fears
not; dame-prior is his kin. The catastrophe is effective
enough; and the singer makes boding comment as Robin
rolls up his sleeve and the prioress prepares her blood-
irons. —

> "I hold him but an unwise man
> That will noe warning leeve."

The blood-irons are laid on; a familiar stanza, commonplace indeed, begins but is not finished, — for here at the
end, whatever the opening verses, is no mood for lingering
repetition, choral devices, or dramatic effect, but a plain
story to tell: —

> "And first it bled, the thicke, thicke blood,
> And afterwards the thinne,
> *And well then wist good Robin Hoode*
> *Treason there was within . . ."* [1]

The "Babylon" ballad would have made us infer all
this. Then there is a struggle with one Red Roger, lover

[1] One expects: —
> "And syne came out the bonny heart's blood;
> There was nae mair within,"

as in *Sir Hugh*, and elsewhere; but Robin is not dead yet, and the singer
is wary.

of the prioress, and Robin's foe; but though Red Roger wounds the weakened man, he gets swift death from him and a farewell of scorn. Dying, Robin calls for the last sacrament, forbids Little John to "burn up all Churchlee," lest "some widow" should be hurt and just blame come of it. "But take me on thy back, Little John; make me a fair grave; set my sword at my head, arrows at my feet, and my yew-bow by my side. . . ."

The rest is silence or disorder; [1] for the few missing verses can have done nothing more. The interest of this fine ballad, compared with other traditional verse, lies in its simple but appropriate art. Short as it is, it differs in quality from the dramatic and normal type. It has really but one situation, and approaches the scene individable, — but by a long and detailed introduction; its structure is narrative throughout. In the other old ballads, of course, there can be no talk of a situation; they are story, and good story, from end to end. "Guy" abounds in alliterative and proverbial phrases; but, like all these ballads, shuns incremental repetition — save for one faint echo — as a useless, outworn art. There is comment on the story; and Professor Child finds a curious parallel with Byron's lines in "Childe Harold" when one reads that he who "had been neither kith nor kin" would have enjoyed the sight of Robin's long duel with Sir Guy, — a touch of the reflective note common to all artistic

[1] No details are given at the end of the *Gest*. Robin is betrayed to death by the prioress and Syr Roger of Donkestere. The prayer for Robin's soul which concludes the *Gest* may well have ended the ballad.

poems. This fight is described in more detail than is usual. The "two hours" limit is observed; the inevitable shrewd thrust of the victim is recorded, which is followed by the victor's final blow, the "ackwarde stroke," but it is explained here that Robin "was reckless on a root," stumbled, and so exposed himself. All ballad readers know that in "Sir Guy" Robin, dressed in the slain knight's horse-hide weeds, fools the sheriff of Nottingham and releases Little John, who kills that luckless official in the last stanza. In "The Monk," Robin quarrels with Little John on the way to church, strikes him, and is left to go alone; at mass a great-headed monk ("I pray to God, woe be he!" ejaculates the singer) betrays Robin to the sheriff, and the outlaws presently hear sad news. Robin is in a dungeon, awaiting the king's order for execution. But Little John and Much slay the messenger monk and take his letters to the king. "Where is this monk?" — "He died on the way," says Little John simply. Humor, by the bye, begins to lift its head in this ballad, and increases in the "Gest." [1] Armed with the king's seal, John and Much go to Nottingham; and again, "Where is the monk?" asks the sheriff. "The king," replies John, "has created him abbot of Westminster." After the sheriff has been made drunk with wine and ale, the pair unbind Robin and escape with him to merry Sherwood. "There," says John, "I have done thee a good turn. Farewell and have

---

[1] Mainly there as humor of the situation, not of character, or, as here, of phrase.

good day!" "Nay," says Robin, "be master of my men
and me!" — "Only thy fellow," answers John; and the
quarrel is mended nobly. The king's remarks when he
hears of the trick are delightful. "Little John has beguiled
both me and the sheriff. And I gave those fellows good
money, and safe-conduct! — Well, he is true to his
master. . . .

> "'*Speke no more of this matter*,' seid oure kyng,
> 'But John has begyled us alle.'" [1]

The poet of the "Gest" does not go much beyond the
art of these ballads, versions of which he works into his

[1] There is noticeable in this passage (at stt. 86–87) a tendency,
obvious for reciters and singers of long ballads, and common in Scandinavian pieces, to repeat from one stanza into another. It occurs in the
border-ballads (*Dick o' the Cow*, 22–23, 26–27, and other cases), in *Guy*
(36–37), elsewhere in the *Monk* (77–78), and frequently in the *Gest* (24–
25; 156–157; etc.). For an example, Little John says in the *Monk* : —

> "'I have done thee a gode turne for an evill,
> Quyte the whan thou may.
>
> 'I have done thee a gode turne' said Litull John,
> Ffor sothe as I you say.'"

There is one case of incremental repetition in the *Gest* (57–58), but it is
for emphasis, and not the conventional kind. The favorite form of repetition in which the *Gest* agrees with balladry at large, and even with
writers like Layamon (Fehr, *Formelhafte Elemente in den alten Englischen Balladen*, p. 47), is the epic repetition, not without value for
reciters: "They looked east, they looked west," *Gest*, 20, is like "Sometimes she sank and sometymes she swam" in *The Twa Sisters*. Commonplaces, moreover, must be sundered from current phrases like
"Glasgerryon swore a full great othe," repeated in the *Gest*, st. 110. It
is to be wished that these "formal elements" could be studied, and not
simply catalogued as in Fehr's dissertation. Even his comparison with
old Germanic formulas is not worked out.

little epic.[1] Eight "fits" tell his story, in four hundred
and fifty-odd quatrains and less than two thousand lines.
No story was ever told to better purpose, and with better
skill; the pace is not strenuous; and all tragic suggestions
are banned. A touch of the pathetic, natural as breath-
ing, is Robin's homesickness at Edward's court; but
the rebound is quick when the outlaw fools his king for
a seven days' furlough, reaches greenwood, hears the
"small notes" of merry birds, and "lists a little for to
shoot at the dun deer." No tragic use is made of Robin's
betrayal and death; five stanzas compress the long story
of the separate ballad, and the close is a simple prayer for
the soul of a "good outlaw" who "did poor men much
good." Robin's deeds and not his death interest our poet.
His most successful work is in the story of Robin's loan
to Sir Richard on the security of Our Lady, and the
involuntary payment of the loan by a monk of St. Mary's
abbey. The dialogue is easy and straightforward,
advancing the action naturally; intervals are bridged by
a stanza or so of explanation; and there is hardly a trace
of the alternate leaping and lingering, familiar in the
normal ballad. The ballad commonplaces are absolutely
wanting; though a few standing "epic phrases" recur as
mere connectives, and there are patch-verses — "without

[1] Johnson's ridicule of ballads was only one of his friendly growls.
He had to dust Percy's jacket once or twice; but really he liked the
things. He refers twice to *Johnny Armstrong*, and quotes it once (Hill's
Boswell. v, 43); while of Ossian he says (ibid. v, 164, 389) that "it is
no better than *such an epic poem as he could make* from the song of
Robin Hood."

any leasynge" — like the phrases in "Otterburn." The
whole story of the "Gest," while told in the simplest manner and in the normal ballad measure, is quite free from
complications and repetitions of the ballad structure,
from all choral clogs, and is a precious specimen of epic
development on lines closer to the primitive and unlettered course than can be shown in any literature of any
time. A poet is behind this story, not an improvising
throng, not even, as in the case of ballads like "Babylon,"
a series of singers who derive in longer or shorter reaches
of tradition from an improvising throng; but the poet is
quite unsophisticated, and his art, even in its half-per-
sonal comment on the course of events, is only a conscious application of the simple objective epic process by
which the original ballads came to their best estate.

The fact of evolution, not in any wise a theory, con-
fronts the student of ballads from their palpably choral,
dramatic, iterating, intensifying, momentary state up to
this narrative perfection of the "Gest." Facing these
differences, not only must he regard this body of ballads
as heterogeneous, incapable of comprehensive definition in any other terms than those of origin ; not only
must he divide them into several classes; he must also
admit that these classes fall into logical if not chronological order of development, and that this order of
development is a traditional epic process working upon
material made at a primitive stage not quite within our
sight, but well within our sure inference, by the choral
throng, the "people," and not by the individual poet. A

review of the foregoing long account of actual English balladry, here brought to a close, will surely commend this reasonable view of ballad origins; and the study of ballad structure, even mere comparison of early stages in a "Babylon," a "Maid Freed from the Gallows," with later stages in the Robin Hood cycle, ought to place this view beyond denial. It is the definition by origins, without which there can be no really permanent division of English literature under the head of Popular Ballads.

CHAPTER III

THE SOURCES OF THE BALLADS

R. JOHNSON, whom we have just re-claimed as a lover of ballads, made merry over the new historical and comparative school of his day. "Hurd, sir," he remarked, "is one of a set of men who account for everything systematically;" and he instanced "scarlet breeches" as a problem not too trivial for Hurd's study of origins. Now the main source of ballads cannot be revealed by any system; for oral tradition is not a systematic affair. It is unwritten, unrecorded, capricious in its final favors, the very shadow of chance. Tenacious enough, not without instinct for the best, it runs a fairly straight course in its own way; but, when pursued by the tran-scriber and collector, it grows self-conscious or else disappears from sight. We can study it in survivals; occasionally it can be spied in remote lands by the stu-dent of ethnology; but for English and Scottish sources we know it only in its last, uncertain stage, and even that is now at an end. What the old collectors gleaned from their autumnal field, however, and what one can still learn from analogous processes among remote and isolated communities throughout the uncivilized world, are ample warrant for the assertion of tradition's an-

cient pride of power. Tradition, which could make
no literary form, and simply accepted the ballad as its
rhythmic expression, modified that form to suit epic needs,
and made the various ballads as we have them. We
must sunder here, as elsewhere, ballads from the ballad.

The impersonal character of our ballads [1] is largely
the work of this traditional process. The ballad itself,
the original choral and dramatic type, fairly well preserved in "The Maid Freed from the Gallows," derived
its impersonal note from the choral fact, from the consent of many voices, and from the dominance of dramatic
interest, so that even individual improvisation was objective in every way; but there was quite another influence at work in the slow transmission of a given piece
from generation to generation of communal memory. It
is not simply the changes from stage to stage, not simply
the local variations, though these are interesting enough
in the study of a ballad in many versions; it is the effacing
fingers of tradition herself which sweep gradually away
a hundred original marks and make, in course of time, a
new impersonality, a new objectivity. By the old logical
phrase, the ballad gets objectivity in intension from its
origins and condition of form, while the actual and separate ballads get objectivity in extension from successive
stages of the traditional process. [2]

So much for tradition as motive-power of the ballads.

[1] See also above, p. 66.
[2] See Professor Kittredge's study of this process in the one-volume ed.
of Child's *Ballads*, p. xvii.

What, however, of their material, and of the sources whence it derives? Apart from this great background of balladry, this enveloping and necessary atmosphere of it and its condition of existence, whence come the ballads as they stand? Their sources, to be sure, have been to some extent indicated in the previous chapter. We have seen the rare ballad of literary origins, so far as its narrative is concerned, taken into the traditional fold; now it changes its setting, as in "Bonnie Annie" and "Brown Robyn," — if these be really derived from the story of Jonah, — and now, as in the "Judas" group, it holds to its original character and place. We have seen the chronicle ballad, based on fact, now in the immediate epic style of "Otterburn," and now more traditionally vague, remote, and full of the incremental manner, as in "Mary Hamilton" and "Captain Car." From this traditional fact one passes easily through legend, with vague and varying names and uncertain locality, to almost wholly dramatic pieces of situation, where the names mean nothing at all, as in "Babylon," or are left out, as in the old riddle ballads.

But there are wider reaches to consider. Stories, parts of stories, episodes, and situations, which are found in our versions, are also found in the Scandinavian, the German, the French, and even in popular literature of eastern and southern Europe. Remoter parallels occur. How, then, is all this to be explained? Have we borrowed from our neighbors? Or are they and we using a common European or Aryan fund of popular tradition? Or thirdly, as Mr. Andrew Lang has urged, is there in many places spontaneous and independent production of similar narratives? Each of these three explanations is reasonable in itself, and should be tested for the particular case; the mistake is to demand that one of them must explain balladry at large. The first is easiest to apply, but needs close study of facts; hence it is the favorite method of comparative literature to-day, and has grown contemptuous of its rivals. Yet one may venture the assertion that even this debit-and-credit theory shows signs of fatigue from overwork. The second explanation, though at one time defended warmly by Gaston Paris, suffers rather from inactivity. That "common fund of Aryan popular tradition" has no very sure rating in these times; it is involved in the bankruptcy, as some view it, of the Primitive Aryan's estate, his residence, myths, — library, one might put it, — and household goods. His very plow has been seized. The theory of mutual borrowing is certainly a nearer way for the student of ballad-material than assumptions of common descent and the Aryan patrimony. It appeals to sensible minds and general experience. All the world thrives by credit, and private life is said to be merriest on such a base: *Borgt der Wirth nicht, borgt die Wirthin; und am Ende borgt die Magd.* Yet one does yearn now and then, in a gross way, for sight of grains or minerals as they wave on their native fields or come unstamped, unworked from the mine; trade presupposes production; and one tires of a perpetual adjustment of the books of borrowing unlimited, and of no-

thing original from end to end of the subject. The east
is vaguely indicated as starting-point in this series of
literary credits; but it is too far a cry from the present
point of investigation. And the theory proves too much.
Even as M. Cosquin, in his "Contes Populaires de Lorraine," justly derided the "vague vapoureux et poétique"
of the Grimms, so M. Bédier, in "Les Fabliaux," has
quite as justly derided M. Cosquin's tendency to see in
every story, anecdote, plot, something "come from the
east in the wake of the crusades." And here, surely, is
reason for at least a respectful hearing of Mr. Lang's
explanation. We have said in a previous chapter that
some few primary instincts of humanity, crossing some
few tendencies of mortal life, inevitable clashings of fate
with the heart of man, might well result in action and
suffering, in deeds and events, that could pass directly
into song without taking that oriental route. Surely, by
M. Bédier's showing there is room for a little spontaneity
here and there in the way of popular song, for a little
home production and a few native wares! Surely as with
jest and plot and popular tale, so with ballads. No one
denies the borrowing. Where the story or episode is so
striking, so crossed or complicated in motive, as to put
spontaneous suggestion from daily life and ordinary human passion out of the case, and where, moreover, this
story or episode, reproduced with fair exactness from ballad to ballad, agrees in names as well as facts with some
definite narrative of long standing and fame, then the ultimate borrowing is certain, and the explanation of patent

agreement in the ballads lies between farther borrowing or derivation from a common source, — not the Aryan or European stock, but let us say an older ballad from which the others copy. There is no doubt that the Shetland ballad of "King Orfeo" comes from its classical source through the medium of a popular tale or of another ballad. Oftener the borrowing is partial. We have seen how widespread was the habit of singing riddle ballads at the dance. How this riddle ballad itself began, whether it was "invented" somewhere and passed from land to land, or whether, like its close relative the flyting, it was developed out of conditions common to our humanity at certain stages of culture, is a question not to be asked in this place; but it is clear that a definite and particularly clever riddle, like a good story, would be carried about, used, transmitted, and so appear in ballads of many climes and times. "Impossible things" would have the same fate; this or that impossible thing, demanded by elf or maid, appears in the German and the English ballad and certainly is a case either of borrowing or of derivation from a common ballad source. This for the riddles; but an epic process makes capital of one's desire to know all about the person who guesses them, and hence rise the widespread and various stories properly grouped by the student of such matters as "The Clever Lass" or the "Wise Daughter" division; and these of course are eagerly borrowed everywhere. On the other hand, the asking of riddles at a dance, combined with choral and dramatic features, is not necessarily a borrowing or a derivation, any more than singing and dancing of a given people needed to be imported from abroad. Speaking in a general way, and repeating the conclusions gained from a study of ballad structure, we may regard all particularly epic material, when not based on a historical or local and legendary event, as mainly borrowed or derived in our English and Scottish ballads, while the dramatic material, the "action" of the choral throng, the situation which appealed to those improvising singers, and even that complication of kinship or of social relations which gives motive to so many of the old ballads, must be left in good part to the original side of the account. To be sure, a good story might be used for choral purposes, just as a good situation was developed into epic; but the original and main division is a fair one. Inasmuch, however, as our ballads have all advanced well out of the choral and improvising stage, and in the majority of cases are distinctly epic, insisting upon the narrative, it is clear that epic interests will always fill the foreground in the study of individual ballads, and the points of contact with kindred pieces in other European tongues will first claim study and explanation. Great erudition, a nice sense of proportion, and the instinct for right paths are imperatively needed in this work; for many a day the student will content himself with the splendid comparative studies made by Professor Child in his various introductions, or at best with a detail or two added, a statement here and there modified or withdrawn. To these introductions the reader should turn who wishes to know how far the narra-

tive of our ballads repeats or slightly varies the narrative
in ballads of the continent. Meanwhile Grundtvig thus
sums up the community of Germanic ballads.[1] They are
not found anywhere in their original form and original
extent; but they can be traced in Denmark, Norway,
Sweden, Iceland, the Faroe Islands, Scotland, England,
the Netherlands, and Germany. Of Scandinavian ballads, a larger number can be found in English and Scottish
versions than in German and Dutch. England and Scotland preserved none of the old heroic lays which are so
plentiful in Scandinavia, and which in Germany, though
unknown to the ballad, have been worked into national
epic. Mythic stuff is scant in England, unknown in Germany, but plentiful in Scandinavia. So far as oral tradition goes, the Faroes and Norway have kept the most and
the best; but Denmark has manuscripts, three or four
centuries old, of traditional ballads.

It is clear that ways of accounting for these facts will
differ; but the facts are there. For derivation many
scholars would substitute transmission, and would
assume a system of exchange far beyond Germanic
boundaries. The matter is not to be discussed here in any
such range of the literary world; but something may be
learned from a study of the English ballads themselves.[2]

From the nature of the case, it is clear that certain inci-

[1] In his Introduction to Rosa Warrens's *Dänische Volkslieder.*

[2] It is worth while to point out, with the aid of Professor Herford's
admirable *Studies in the Literary Relations of England and Germany in
the Sixteenth Century*, that while "wonderful strange news from Germany," reports of battles, stories of murders or monstrosities, what not,

dents, complications, an unusual outcome of the usual, would drift about and find a subordinate place in ballads of many lands. These incidents, again, fall into two classes, one general, such as the "recognition" incident, which may be said to belong to the world's common stock, and one particular, such as the test by which recognition occurs, in "Child Maurice," by sending of mantle and ring; in "Hind Horn," by the magical information of a keepsake. These particular incidents are naturally copied from a definite source, and are not, so to speak, floating in the ballad air.[1] Again, there is the accused queen or wife, and her rescue by some David of a champion, even by a child, from an all-powerful accuser; how widely this story is spread, how it stands with legend, romance, history, custom, how its details now vary and now agree, how the English ballad matches the Scandinavian, and how it differs, may be learned from the respective introductory studies.[2] Conclusions are not

came over at that time for the journalistic ballad press, nothing of Germany's heroic legend, its abounding folk song and really popular lyric, crossed the sea. Heroes of magic and their tales of horror, Faustus and Paracelsus, were eagerly welcomed in England; but nothing was desired of the old saga and myth still current among common folk. An actual ballad in German on the defeat of the Turks in 1593 was entered in the Stationers' Register for that September. On the spread of popular tales by the agency of Jews, see L. Wiener, *Yiddish Literature*, pp. 25 f.

[1] Information given by live birds, combined with the virtue of rings and other ornaments, may have begotten this idea of the silver larks. For tests of chastity, see the long list in Child's Index, v, 472 f. The ingenuity of these presupposes a literary or epic source in nearly every instance.

[2] See no. 59.

uniformly sure. Coincidence and derivation are always scuffling in the world of letters, and it is now and then a nice matter to decide which is in the right. If in several ballads a man or maid feigns death to come near the beloved, one scents a "good story" and allows borrowing or community forthwith. But it is dangerous to run down too broad a trail with particular and narrow purpose. There is a brave group of tragic poems, dramas, episodes, in which the conflict of two duties springing from kinship gives at once the initial motive and the last throb of agony. What, however, have Orestes and Hamlet and Rodrigue, and even Rüdeger in the "Nibelungen," and those two Cumberland boys in our ballad,[1] to do with any common auditing of accounts in literary bookkeeping? They belong to the clash of human lives and passions with inexorable fate, and there an end. One warning will suffice. Simrock grouped the Tristram story, Romeo and Juliet, and Pyramus and Thisbe, as a single narrative springing from the notion of hindrance to true love. They are "hindrance" stories. The hindrance, as other details gather about the different versions, splits into three; in Tristram it is a husband, in Romeo and Juliet it is a family feud, in Pyramus and Thisbe it is a wall; but there, says Simrock, is still the same story in these separate guises. Whoso wishes to follow this process with ballads has a lifetime of exhilarating work before him. He can trace analogies as remote as the feigned madness of Hamlet as told by Saxo, and the feigned

[1] *Bewick and Graham.*

idiocy of Brutus as told by Livy, handily converted into the same theme for a student of Shakespeare's sources. "Bewick and Graham," by this reckoning, is the last of its line, a beggar in ragged cloak, but descended from them of Pelops and the sceptred pall, — that is, if the plot and the kin-tragedy are impossible as outcome of conditions of English life three centuries or more ago. Mr. Hardy has found in our own day tragedies of Æschylean keenness; but they were not of Æschylean source. What shall one assert, for example, about the "relative-climax," say in the situation of "The Maid Freed from the Gallows"? Reasonably, this: a widespread group of ballads presents the common trait that a girl in dire stress appeals vainly to one relative after the other, and finally gets her salvation, at whatever cost, from the nearest and dearest. As a situation, developed under different conditions in choral song, there is nothing here that could not occur in isolated communities everywhere without hint or help from foreign sources. Where, however, there is identity between different ballads in sundry epic details, in the development of this situation along certain lines, — for example, the fact of the gallows, the judge, and so on, — then it is folly to set aside so obvious a solution as common derivation from a parent ballad, the case of the American "Hangman's Tree," and the borrowing of striking narrative details from other ballads or from epic material however transmitted. Again, the excuses for John's absence in the "Twa Brothers" are the same in kind and series, but differ in details, from one version to the other; they are clearly the same ballad. Where difference in detail ceases and difference of origin begins is often hard to decide. In many cases Professor Child has worked out these perplexing relations with wonderful accuracy and success; his sturdy common sense, too, went hand in hand with his exquisite literary tact, his technical knowledge, so as to play the iconoclast at need, and to strew the way here and there with such wrecks as the Woden theory of Robin Hood and the celestial origins of William of Cloudesley. The more one can learn of a given ballad the better, no matter how wide and far its affiliations may go; but that caution of Müllenhoff needs to be kept well in sight. Every song, he said, every tale, legend, myth, must be studied primarily on its own ground in its own local associations. Grant that the home-plot has had its proper yield; grant that human nature, and the spontaneity of utterance in stress of a common emotion which leads to common expression, must both find their account in any theory of poetry before books; and no quarrel need arise in the literary world between harvest-field and warehouse.

Borrowing, derivation, even coincidence itself, are not always applicable terms for the analogous traits of balladry in different countries. Earl Brand, it is true, looks very like a corruption of the Scandinavian Hildebrand, and we doubtless are here on the trail of a loan; so, too, with the identity of replies in Danish and English versions, "She is my sick sister;" but because ladies both in Norland and in Scottish parts are discovered in their bowers "sewing the silken seam," we should not jump to a like conclusion. Ballad commonplaces, idea and expression, belong to tradition at large. Ghost and fairy, too, traveled the high road in those days, and there is no need of tracking them to private haunts. Transformation is a favorite theme of folklore; in "Tam Lane," which Burns surely did not invent, one finds belief in the recovery of lost mortal shape by means of some kind of dipping, whether in water or milk or what not. In "The Great Silkie," interchange of seal and man is a quite local affair. The main idea, change of shape itself, leads far, and carries one up to the highest type of poetic myth as well as down to the simplest and rudest narrative told by Uncle Remus himself. Romantically treated, it reaches the group represented by the Wife of Bath's Tale in Chaucer, and by a few ballads on the same general theme. Here, of course, is a particular case. General notions of this kind point to no specific source for a given ballad unless its details go beyond the general notion involved, as, in "Kemp Owyne," with the three kisses and the three gifts. So it is with the idea that birds talk, warn a criminal, and give damaging information, as they do in "Young Hunting," or act as occasional penny-post with the "Gay Goshawk," or carry grave news in "Johnie Cock." Curious old ideas prevail about behavior on occasions such as childbirth and funeral. Minor superstitions abound which are derived from a lapsed mythology and a superseded habit of dealing with the other world.

A few of these "remaines of gentilisme"[1] may be worth remark. It is interesting to note that Aubrey holds the civil wars of his day mainly responsible for the vanishing of old superstition from England; as he says quaintly, "no suffimen is a greater fugator of phantosmes than gunpowder." But if supernatural ballads of our tongue have been lamentably lost in tradition, bits of demonology and ghost-lore are scattered about the surviving versions. Some are not "gentile," only old, like the custom of casting lots to discover a guilty person on shipboard, the gift of the arm-rings in "King Estmere," and the habit noted there of warriors who ride their horses into hall. The *comitatus*, old Germanic league of chief and liegemen in mutual bond until death and beyond it, the superb note of "Maldon Fight" and the Beowulf, is not specifically mentioned by ballads, but has left its mark in the fidelity of Border clansmen, as in "Jock o' the Side," in the Robin Hood group, and of course in that "poor squire of land" who will not look on while his captain fights in "Cheviot." Sworn-brotherhood flames up nobly for its last effort in "Bewick and Graham;" although we must remember that the three heroes of "Adam Bell" had "sworn them brethren upon a day." The ordeal is met in various forms, — fire in "Young Hunting," for example, as well as battle in "Sir Aldingar;" while the trail of once fiery heathen oaths moves harm-

[1] Aubrey intended to collect more than remains. "Get the song which is sung in the ox-house where they wassell the oxen," he notes. *Remains of Gentilisme and Judaism*, p. 9.

lessly over the ballads in Glasgerion's famous "oak and ash and thorn" and the incremental stanzas in which Young Hunting's mistress will clear herself, — now, "turning right and round about," by the corn, and again, with the same contortion, by the moon. In another version, it is "by the grass sae greene" and "by the corn." In the "Twa Magicians" the lady swears "by the mold," a heathen oath like the appeal in Anglo-Saxon charms to mother earth, and loses; while our crafty blacksmith swears "by the Mass," and wins. A commonplace line, "The king looked over his left shoulder," is referred by Child [1] to superstitious origins; possibly, as used in "Sir Andrew Barton" and elsewhere, it refers to some such custom at court as makes the master of ceremonies under Hrothgar, in the Beowulf, take stand for messages at his monarch's shoulder. This as it may be. A very poor and suspicious ballad [2] preserves the curious old custom of giving an injured, forced, or unequally mated woman the choice of sword or spindle; she could take the sword, slay the man, and so get her freedom, or she could take the spindle and accept her lot. Here it is ring for spindle, — whether "to stick him wi' the brand or wed him wi' the ring." Lady Maisry "minded" thrice to the brand; but of course "took up the ring;" and all the ladies who heard of it said she was wise. A corpse betrays the murderer by

---

[1] See v, 286.

[2] No. 268. One archaic feature of the ballads is the prominence given to a sister's son; see the present writer's essay, named above, p. 182, note.

beginning to bleed, and similar prodigies happen repeatedly; most interesting is the "singing bone" in the "Twa Sisters." Dreams are not very frequent; Douglas's "second sight," Earl Richard's dream, which bodes only flight, not death, Robin Hood's vision of disgrace, and the chamber full of swine, the bed full of blood, may be cited here. When a man dies, — in a late ballad, this, — his horses go wild and his hounds lie howling on the leash. Apparitions are fairly common; the ghost has been discussed already, but the elfin knight's horn should be heard, seductive as that gift of Oberon; and at least a touch of the uncanny is in that warning when Lord Barnard's horn sounds "away!" in Musgrave's ears. Before shipwreck there rises to the sailors' gaze a mermaid[1] with comb and glass, now silent, a mere sign, and now vocal with the true siren's taunt: —

> "'Here's a health to you, my merrie young men,
>   For you never will see dry land.'"

Another sign of shipwreck or storm is the new moon late in the evening, — quite sufficient as portent without an auld moon in her arm. Dealings with the other world have been already recorded; though we may note that Tom Potts, serving-man as he is, could be a "phisityan" at need; "he clapt his hand upon the wound," we are told, and "*with some kind of words* stauncht the blood." Sleep can be produced by charms; the venerable runes are still potent in this article, though they are mainly rationalized, just as Peter Buchan makes all his com-

[1] No. 289, A, 2; 58, J, 18.

municative birds into parrots. Stroking troth on a wand
has been noted in "Sweet William's Ghost;" it recurs
in "The Brown Girl." Ancient myth from Germanic
days still lurks in the reference to middle-earth, an
alliterative phrase of "Sir Cawline," and in those "rivers
aboon the knee" or even "red blude to the knee," of
"Thomas Rymer."

> "For a' the bluid that's shed on earth
> Rins through the springs of that countrie,"

is perhaps popular lore, too, with a glimpse of the old
Scandinavian "water-hell;" Professor J. A. Stewart
aptly compares with this verse the mention in Dante of
those infernal rivers which are fed by human tears. One
may also note the willingness of the foresters to "ride the
fords of hell" if they can catch Johnie Cock. Perhaps,
moreover, there is a shred of myth left in the description
of a "mountain . . . dreary wi' frost and snow" which
the Demon Lover declares to be his proper abode. The
red cock and the gray that call back the wife's three sons
at Usher's Well, the "milk-white and the gray" that
summon Sweet William's ghost, represent the usual
white, red, and black of folklore, and have near relatives
in old Norse myth, which heard the crowing of the dark-
red cock as warning from the underworld. In another
version of the latter ballad, it is simply the ordinary cock-
crow and the "wild fowl" boding day. One of the most
persistent echoes of an old idea is the mention in many
ballads of a more or less supernatural light that is given
out by some object. Weapons were once prone to this

service; Valhalla was said to be lighted by the gleam of swords, and readers of the Beowulf remember how the magic brand throws radiance about that hall below the sea "even as when heaven's candle shines from the sky." In "Salomon and Saturn," light beams from the barrow of a dead warrior where still lies his sword, although in the Norse lay of Helgi it is the spears that shine. Magic, to be sure, is not far away; men were wont to read the future in their gleaming swords, — *im schwerte sehen;* but for the most part this illumination is contemporary. For ballads, the little champion's sword in "Sir Aldingar" casts light over all the field; but our singer's comment is feeble to a degree: "it shone so of gilding." A late Scottish ballad is quite as superfluously rational with Charlie Macpherson's sword and targe; and Lang Johnny More's armor is also bright in mere prose, dimming the king's eye. But the rings on the fingers of Old Robin's wife are better, and "cast light through the hall;" and in "Young Lamkin" we are with good magic again. "How can I see without candle?" asks the lady; and her false nurse replies that there are two smocks in the coffer as white as a swan; "put one of them about you, it will show you light down." Lamkin cut off her head, and hung it up in the kitchen: "it made a' the ha' shine," — a weird bit of folklore. The light from clothes became a commonplace, and very common at that, copied by vulgar songs. In a ribald piece [1] about Charity the Chambermaid,

---

[1] Bodleian, 4 Rawlin., 566. Another of the deplorable sort has a line "wavers like the wind," familiar in a Scottish version of *Child Maurice*.

her poet unexpectedly tells how "such a light sprung from her clothes, as if the morning-star had rose," — more than negligible stuff, were it not for its witness to the influence of good traditional ballads upon these outcast things. That weapons and implements, even ships, are addressed as persons and respond, is an assumption at the very heart of folklore and still potent in ballad tradition. Cospatrick's sword reveals a secret;[1] but we miss in English versions not only the horror and audacity of a piece like the Danish "Hævnersværdet," where the hero has to restrain his sword's avenging thirst for blood by naming its name, but also such vivid personifications as when in the Beowulf a blade "sings eager war-song," and in the Finnsburg fragment "shield calls to shaft."

A more obvious minor source of composition lies in the constant use, and the incidental abuse, of phrases that become common property. Some of these have been noted as a part of incremental repetition. Lists of ballad "formulas," not very satisfactory so far, have been made in Germany and compared here and there with identical or similar forms which went to make up the body of Germanic traditional verse. With the lapse of alliterative poetry, however, many of the old forms lost their suggestive, almost inevitable quality, and disappeared. Ballad commonplaces, on the other hand, are mainly connected with the situation or the event, and so have a kind of permanence; their parallels in older verse consist less in

---

[1] *Gil Brenton*, B, 22: —

"And speak up, my bonny brown sword, that winna lie."

epic phrases than in conventional descriptions of battle
or the like, when gray wolf of the wood, dewy-feathered
eagle, and horny-nibbed raven follow the path of war.
To be sure, the ballads have a store of mainly alliterative
formulas that answer to the Germanic tradition; but such
a formula as "kissed her baith cheek and chin" often
takes the incremental way: —

> "'It's kiss will I your cheek, Annie,
>   And kiss will I your chin.'"

The main point is that ballad folk do the same things
under the same circumstances, and in a fairly limited
sphere of events; hence these recurring phrases, sentences, stanzas, which may well claim a page or so of
quotation.   Child Waters and Lord Lovel are introduced as combing their milk-white steeds and making
rude remarks to their sweethearts.   Chaucer's squire,[1]
gracious and graceful to a degree, keen to win his lady's
favor, would not be guilty of such talk; ballads take
the traditional and popular point of view towards the
youth of high lineage.   When met alone, our young gentleman is combing his own yellow hair.   Turning to his
aristocratic counterpart among women, if she is not one
of twenty-four maids playing ball, we find her in her bower
alone and "sewing the silken seam."   If she starts off
alone, mainly for quite serious reasons, she is sure to
kilt her green kirtle a little above her knee and braid her

---

[1] This critical parallax, so to speak, which one gets by comparing the
ballad way with Chaucer's, is invaluable in any study of our poetry as it
passes from its medieval to its modern state.

yellow hair a little above her brow. From force of habit this must be done even when, like Margaret, she pursues a vanishing ghost. She summons her lover when she pulls flower, leaf, nut, in the grove. Sometimes she must send for him from afar. Pages all run errands with the same consistency and success, getting the same promise of reward, making the same profession of devotion, swimming when they come to broken bridges, and slacking shoon to run over grass; doing things meanwhile which are quite hard to understand, such as bending the bow at rivers and using it for a pole-vault over the wall at their destination. They are apt to say that they have come through "moss and mire." The knight, husband, lover, thus summoned, if not leaning over his castle parapets to behold both dale and down, is at a table which he knocks or kicks over at the exciting news, obtained after three questions, where only the third is serious. If the news be false, the page shall be hanged; if it is true, he is to have great reward. If a letter is brought, the first line makes the hero laugh loud; the second or third calls out tears. Straightway he has three horses saddled, specifying their colors; the third, preferably white, is the choice, often after absurd trials of the other two. Consistency is not a jewel always set in these phrases. Child Waters, in a familiar formula, will have his new-born son washed in the milk, and the mother rolled in the silk; the Cruel Mother would do both for the bonnie babes she sees; [1] but Willy of

[1] In *Prince Heather*, A, 8, wash with milk and *dry* with silk.

Douglas Dale, fugitive with his wife in the greenwood, must go through the same agreeable but impossible ceremony for his son and heir. Heroes wipe their swords, not always appropriately, on grass, or straw, or their own sleeves, before making that last shrewd thrust; what, we ask, with Cicero, what is Tubero's sword doing meanwhile? Fair Annet is set aside for her poverty; but she goes to Lord Thomas's wedding in the correct dress of richest quality, on a horse caparisoned in silver and gold, and with four and twenty good knights and as many fair ladies in her train. Heroes and heroines are always yellow-haired, and blindingly blond, as becomes their Germanic pedigree; change to the brunette type is a fairly sufficient disguise. The proud porter, who, as one remembers, so irritated Matthew Arnold by talking drivel not strictly Homeric, greets the supposed harpers: —

> ". . . 'And your color were white and redd,
> As it is blacke and brown,
> I wold saye King Estmere and his brother
> Were comen untill this towne.' "

Hind Horn covers up his fair locks for disguise. Even the athletic heroes, even Robin Hood, are "white as milk;" their dress glitters, mainly red, gold, and indefinitely splendid. The ladies like Faire Ellen often wear green; Scott noted that illustrations in sundry medieval manuscripts held to this color. But there is plenty of glitter here; Annet's dress "skinkles." Fair Ellen, as Burd Ellen in a Scottish version, wears "the scarlet and brown." Willie's "milk-white weed"[1] is startling. Lady Margaret's father comes "clothed all in blue;" Lady Maisry's "wearing the gold so red." Alliterative phrases like "purple and palle," "in the royal red," are conventional; but Johnie Armstrong's men, and Will Stewart and John, are described more in detail; the latter in scarlet red, with black hats, feathers white and gold, silk stockings, garters golden trimmed, and shoes "of the cordevine," or Spanish leather. This care for details leads away from balladry, and points, though from remote distance, to Chaucer. The ballads simply give a touch of splendor, as with persons who are loaded with gold to the point of concealment, like that drowned sister; as with towers, halls, gates, gleaming with gold, like Child Waters's mansion or the hall of Hrothgar in the Beowulf; and as with horses that are silver shod before and golden shod behind, but are not further described. One deals with types. There is no attempt at the concrete, individual portrait. Occasionally contrast is employed: two heads on one pillow, — Lady Maisdrey like the molten gold, Auld Ingram like a toad! In "The Gay Goshawk," how, asks the messenger bird of the lover, how shall I your true-love know from another? The answer is not explicit, — fairest in England, and to be distinguished out of the conventional twenty-four by the gold on her skirt and on her hair. Another version at this point falls sheer out of balladry: —

[1] No. 70. See the absurd increment of color in dress quoted above, p. 88.

"The red that is in my love's cheek
Is like blood spilt among the snaw,
The white that is on her breast-bone
Is like the down on the white sea-maw."

This will never do.

The "wee pen-knife" in "Babylon," "a little wee sword" of "Young Johnstone" and other ballads, which often "hangs low down by the gare," or dress, is a curious commonplace;[1] men carry this pen-knife as well as women. It should belong by rights only to Child Maurice's schoolmasters. Babylon, however, stabs home with it; the cruel mother kills her babes with it; while Clerk Colvill uses it merely to cut cloth, drawing his good sword for serious work. Fights are much of a kind in the ballads, and are seldom described in detail. Heroes stop even then to wipe their blades. The "awkward" stroke finishes after long struggle in sweat and blood; even the potter, fighting Robin Hood, makes one of these strokes with his staff. Death is seldom a matter for lingering or comment; and the commonplace of giving the nobler or better of two dead persons the sun-side of the grave is as familiar and chivalrous as the uniting briar-and-rose from tombs of parted lovers is familiar and beautiful. The favorite characters of the old ballad of communal tradition are the knight and the lady, wife or maid, who

[1] These phrases are so common as to be used without thought of consistency. A wee pen-knife may be "three-quarters (of a yard) long." So a babe just born may be an "auld son" (no. 64, B, 6, 7); true-love comes to be any sweetheart, and "false true-love" need not shock, any more than "good" Sir Guy or "good" William a Trent, villains both and disturbers of greenwood peace.

were in the focus of communal view and represented the fairly homogeneous life of that day.

All these commonplaces, and many more, all the superstitions and customs and sayings of the folk, were in the ballad air, and involved no borrowing as we now understand the term. Stories drifted along as popular tales or as scraps of learned and literary record, and were also taken in. Nothing can be more uncertain than the actual sources and making of a ballad; it can be grouped with other ballads, and its constituent parts may be paralleled from a hundred near or remote pieces of popular literature; but just how and when and where it was put together in its present forms is seldom to be known. The date of making is hardly ever the date of record. Ballads recovered from late Scottish tradition may be older in fact, as they certainly are older in structural form, than ballads handed down in manuscripts three or four centuries old. And a further cause of confusion must be noted: not only is a ballad changed to almost any extent in tradition, not only does tradition itself largely determine the matter and the style, but there is still the possibility, often enough fact, of parts of one ballad fusing with parts of another and so forming a piece which in course of time may come to its own individual rights. It is this peculiar quality of tradition which makes the classifying of ballads difficult enough, even without reference to source and date, and which renders nugatory so many judgments of the critic who undertakes to settle questions of general origin and particular derivation by

the laws of artistic poetry. We must not forget how much
the ballad, and the dance out of which it sprang, meant
for an unlettered community, and how many strands
must be unraveled in this complicated web of traditional
verse. Even where feudal conditions are invaded by
modern ways almost to the point of extinction, as in the
Western Islands at the time of Johnson's visit, the old
impulses live on. Clan equality, homogeneous life, the
fact that all eat at the same board and bear the same
name, keep ancient custom alive. "We performed, with
much activity," says Boswell,[1] "a dance which I suppose
the emigration from Sky has occasioned. They call it
America. Each of the couples, after the common in-
volutions and evolutions, successively whirls round in
a circle till all are in motion; and the dance seems
intended to show how emigration catches till a whole
neighborhood is set afloat." It is no very far cry back
to the Frisian pirates; and while the Celtic ballad is not,
one would like to know more of the words that high-
landers and islanders must once have sung to their
choral and dramatic performances.[2] Add tradition to
these choral elements, and we have factors for the ballad

[1] Ed. Hill, v, 277.

[2] J. Darmesteter, in *English Studies*, London, 1896, p. 208, after
defining Ossian as "a combination of two independent epic cycles,
welded together against nature . . . prettyfied and airified to suit
eighteenth century tastes," goes on to give "a fine example of the essential distinction between Primitive poetry and Romantic poetry" by a
study of "the Irish Helen whom the ancient epics call Derdrin." Primitive poetry is not the term. We should have the old Celtic songs of the
dance, not the work of their epic bards, to get at the primitive stuff.

which cannot be treated by modern rules of the poetic game. What, for instance, of the text? Mindful of the great critical achievements in classical and other literature, scholars have tried to restore the "original text" of a traditional ballad.[1] As has been already asked, how can there be such a thing as this original text? There are texts, versions, now of manuscript authority and now from singing or recitation; but the very conditions of the case, the postulate that every one of these ballads must derive from tradition of the people, absolutely bars this idea of a single and authoritative source. The task of the editor is to follow back each of the versions to its particular origin, and to separate from it any "improvements" or changes due to interference from whatever hand. But when he has reached the dairymaid or the "old man," who got it by natural process in its traditional course, he has done all he can do for it; he has traced it to popular tradition. Of a large group of variant versions, he selects the best, the oldest, those which agree with the kindred ballad in other tongues, and prints them all in the order of preference. That is the only "classical" treatment of ballads. For anthologies the different versions may be combined into one; but this task is difficult, and the best of the versions, as representative, will in most cases serve the reader's turn.

Fidelity to traditional report is the collector's main virtue, although his opportunity is now mainly gone. The great harvest was reaped in Scotland a century or

---

[1] See above, p. 267.

more ago; but in colonial and remote, undisturbed nooks a degenerate version is now and then to be found, — like the North Carolina texts of " The Maid Freed from the Gallows " and "The Wife of Usher's Well." But the ballad has vanished from its old haunts. Sir George Douglas has noted that at the annual dinner of the border shepherds, held at Yetholm in the Cheviots, these old ballads are heard no more; they have found a precarious refuge, he says, among fisher-folk in the obscure little havens, but it is evident that their time is past.[1] In the eighteenth century they were still heard everywhere in rural and remote communities. Percy relied not only on his folio, but on friends and correspondents whom he inspired with the collector's zeal. Over thirty ballads collected for him in this way are now in the Harvard College Library. Scott, of course, had an even larger staff of helpers, and both his published and manuscript collections are beyond price. Before him, David Herd, distinguished for his fidelity to the material in hand, his unwillingness to improve or change, had done splendid service. Mrs. Brown[2] of Falkland is the best known of all the reciters; her versions are straight from tradition, and were set down about 1783. Sharpe, Motherwell, Kinloch, and others, were helpful in the good cause; and in our own day the diligence of Mr. Macmath, who supplied

[1] See G. L. Kittredge's sketch of Mr. Child's life, prefixed to the large edition, p. xxviii. ". . . little or nothing of value remains to be recovered in this way." See, also, *The Bitter Withy*, printed above, p. 228.

[2] She was born in 1747, and learned most of her ballads before 1759. So Mr. Macmath's information, Child, i, 455.

314 THE SOURCES OF THE BALLADS

so much of the new material to Professor Child, should be gratefully borne in mind.[1]

While the ballad remained wholly a traditional affair, the treasure of the humble, there was no danger that it would be adapted to purposes of the literary world. Towards the close of the eighteenth century, however, after Percy's collecting and Herder's preaching had dignified these fugitive songs, Cinderella was brought forth triumphantly from her nook, and was even exalted above her sisters.[2] Tradition, too, had begun to lose its vitality; and there was now room as well as incitement for the repair, the imitation, the counterfeit. Of these, indeed, the crime of counterfeit was far less damaging than the peccadillo of repair. Collectors themselves found it hard to keep their improving hands off the material which they gathered from so rude a source. Allingham, a born poet and fine critic, changes "Bonnie James Campbell," and puts an intrusive stanza of his own into "The Wife of Usher's Well." Scott himself retouched old versions, set them dancing where they limped, or seemed to limp, and in one case, "Kinmont Willie," really made up a new ballad by the best model in the world. "Katharine Jaffray," too, has many marks of Sir Walter on it. Burns

---

[1] Joseph Ritson ought to be canonized by lovers of the ballad, if only for his indomitable zeal in editing and his passionate accuracy. Full of evil were his days, and his end was dark indeed; but his services to sound learning should never be forgotten.

[2] This whole movement has been traced by the present writer in the Introduction to his *Old English Ballads;* there is no need to repeat the journey.

had a little commerce, not very extensive, with "Tam Lane;" and no one can question that all these ballads are good. In general, however, it may be said that literary imitation of the ballad, patchwork or piece, is a failure; and the possible exceptions to this rule — Mr. Andrew Lang informs me that he would count with them such a piece as old Elspeth sings [1] about "the red Harlaw" — only emphasize the wide difference between poetry of the people and poetry of art. In times before Scott, editorial improvement was common enough. Percy's feats and Ritson's rage are notorious; but it must be remembered that something of the sort was needed to secure readers. Show touches of "elegance," and you could beguile the man of taste into appreciation of the rough and the sincere. Even Herder served up his ballads and folk songs along with soliloquies from Shakespeare. The famous Percy Folio, rescued from the office of lighting fires in Humphrey Pitt's mansion, was written about 1650; it was probably a faithful transcript, but even here allowance must be made for considerable changes in the passage from tradition to record, so that with the actual text before us, and Percy's iniquities swept away, we are not dealing with absolute tradition. The later group of

---

[1] In the fortieth chapter of *The Antiquary.* "'It's a historical ballad,' said Oldbuck eagerly, 'a genuine and undoubted fragment of minstrelsy. Percy would admire its simplicity, Ritson could not impugn its authenticity.'" The prose thrown in by Elspeth is interesting; and Scott's account of the "shrill, tremulous voice . . . chanting . . . in a wild and doleful recitation" is no fiction. He had heard such voices often singing just such ballads.

collectors, just now noted, who took down ballads from singing and recitation, learned fairly well the lesson of fidelity and literal report; but here again was danger, even with such a splendid recorder as Herd, that abbreviation, forgetfulness, distortion, and outright fabrication, on the part of singer or reciter, should play havoc with the genuine traditional ballad.   Fabrication counted for much in the performances of that "wight of Homer's craft" whom Buchan hired to collect popular ballads in the north of Scotland, and a spurious, silly affair like "Young Ronald" is indefensible; but it may be said that this fabrication, however poor in quality, held fairly well to the structural and traditional form. As one can never tell where a bit of genuine traditional verse is mingled with the wight Rankin's own making, the versions have been admitted by Professor Child; it is true, moreover, that the blind beggar has had more blame than he deserved. His potations are fearfully thin; but it is real "Scotch" which one does taste in them, and he knew both the people and their songs. He ought not to have been "paid by the piece." Buchan's own feats of compilation, to be sure, must not go uncursed; his long version of "Young Waters" is called by Mr. Child "a counterfeit of the lowest description." But on the whole Peter did far more good than harm.

Other versions of ballads from recitation in Scotland seem sound; barring the accidents already named, they should represent the traditional ballad at the stage which tradition had reached in the early eighteenth century under conditions of a fairly homogeneous rural life. What they do not directly represent is the primitive and original ballad itself. That is not to be recovered, though it can be inferred. The normal type of the popular ballad is something which one must make up, as a composite photograph, from the best old manuscript versions and the versions of soundest oral tradition. The printed sources, to be sure, vary greatly in value, and open the door to far more serious chances of corruption; but in many cases they help rather than hinder the composite process. Patient sifting and testing of all this material leads to sure results, and enables the true ballad critic to throw out a vast amount of alien stuff. What he keeps is the real; but this real is not always good. Mr. Henderson makes it the reproach of Professor Child's collection that "the chaff is out of all proportion to the wheat." Possibly. But the chaff is wheat-chaff, not sawdust or other sham; and this is the triumph of the edition. For the matter of wheat and chaff, of good and bad, any selection of genuine ballads must be an affair of purely subjective judgment.

Forgeries and imitations need not detain us long. Everybody has heard of Lady Wardlaw's "Hardyknut," [1] which appeared as early as 1719, and bewrays itself at once to the ballad-reader. Clever Scottish women of the

[1] See curious remarks by T. Warton, *Observations on the Fairy Queen*, 2d ed., i, 156 (1762), on this "noble old Scottish poem" which he now hears was written "near fifty years ago" by a lady. "The late lord president Forbes was in the secret, and used to laugh at the deception of the world."

later eighteenth century wrote more than one song which
was accepted as popular; but now and then a woman of
humbler parts undertook this amiable fraud. Among
the pamphlets in the Bodleian library [1] is "The Knyghte
of the Golden Locks; an Ancyent Poem, Applicable to
the Present Times, Selected from many others in the
Possession of Mrs. Morgan." "Mary Morgan " remarks,
by way of preface, that though this ballad is in no collection, she sincerely believes it "to be an original." It is
fit, she thinks, for these times when men are going to war.
She has kindly "altered obsolete words," but gives three
stanzas in their "primitive orthography." It is deplorable
stuff, and has all the marks of a poor forgery; but in
these premises, as Sir Walter proved later, one may "lie
like a gentleman."

> " 'O happy horse,' the ladye cryd,
> And strok'd his rainbow neck."

Absolutely nothing happens in the ballad except orthography — of the primitive kind. Mrs. Morgan says she
learned to love Percy's "Reliques" when she was visiting
Admiral Sir Joseph Knight, "whose daughter, Miss
Cornelia Knight, has distinguished herself by her Continuation of Dr. Johnson's 'Rasselas.'" Besides ladies, the
clergy could take part in this pious fraud; witness the
Rev. Mr. Lamb's "Laidly Worm," which he calls "a
song five hundred years old, made by the old Mountain
Bard, Duncan Frasier, living in Cheviot, A. D., 1270.

[1] G. Pamph. 1740, no. 26. It is dated Wisbech, 1799.

From an ancient manuscript." But Mr. Lamb was no Chatterton.[1]

Imitations differ from forgeries only in the matter of morals. Scott has been mentioned for his successful work; some harmless and not very effectual imitations, made by himself and Leyden and C. K. Sharpe, he inserted in his "Minstrelsy." If these men failed, and they did fail, who should succeed? Again, there is the general imitation of the type, such as began feebly enough and at very long range; as early as Prior it is to be noted, and it appears in differing degrees of merit as the work of Shenstone, Collins, Goldsmith, and the notorious Mallet. Unlike either of these ways, the collector's and the amateur's, was that delightful robbery of a stanza or so from tradition, by Scott or Burns, so as to get a motive for a song. Thus Campbell, collecting airs, "got in the south country," from recollections of a lady's singing, two traditional stanzas of a ballad known more completely in other versions; the first stanza ran thus: [2] —

> " 'Why weep ye by the tide, ladye,
>   Why weep ye by the tide?
> I 'll wed ye to my youngest son
>   And ye sall be his bride.
> And ye sall be his bride, ladye,
>   Sae comely to be seen,' . . .
> But aye she loot the tears down fa'
>   For John o' Hazelgreen."

[1] Chambers has a formidable list of forged ballads, including some of the best pieces. The conclusions of Professor Veitch on this subject, *History and Poetry of the Scottish Border*, ii, 81, seem quite beside the mark.

[2] No. 293, E, 1.

320   THE SOURCES OF THE BALLADS

"O whaten a man is Hazelgreen?" the weeping maid is asked. "Long arms, shoulders broad, sae comely," she says, and lets the tears fall on. Scott keeps the stanza, changes the hero's name, and makes his own charming song, — far more effective for modern taste than this particular piece. But the song is not a ballad. Haunting lines can beget whole poems; we know what the ballad-fragment, "Child Roland to the dark tower came," could do for Browning, and what provocation there is in many a refrain: —

"For we'll never gang doun to the broom nae mair."

Only it must be remembered that the romantic and sentimental turn of these modern poems was quite foreign to the ballad whose fragment inspired them. Even the objective character — *hübsch objectiv*, said mocking Heine — of the literary ballad, the "Agincourts," the "Hohenlindens," the "Revenges," the "Hervé Riels," and, above all, of the refrain ballad such as Rossetti wrote so effectively and Calverley parodied with his "butter and eggs and a pound of cheese," even this severe but conscious impersonality is far removed from the communal note of tradition. The old songs were made by the people and handed down by the people; no individual author, going about his work as an artist in poetry, can make his work impersonal in the old sense. Once again be it said that "popular" as a definition by origins, as conveying the idea that ballads were really made by the people, does not mean a single, initial process of authorship on the part of a festal throng. Such a conception involves a contradiction in terms and flouts common sense, assuming the choral foundation and rejecting that epic process which is tradition itself. The ballad is a conglomerate of choral, dramatic, lyric, and epic elements which are due now to some suggestive refrain, now to improvisation, now to memory, now to individual invention, and are forced into a more or less poetic unity by the pressure of tradition in long stretches of time. In this sense they represent no individual, but are the voice of the people; and successful imitation of them by any individual, however gifted and sympathetic he may be, is a task hardly to be done. The great poems of the world are far greater than the greatest ballads; but no poet has ever had the power to compete with popular tradition on its own ground. Art can create far beyond the beauty of sea-shells, and on occasion can exactly reproduce them; but it cannot fashion or imitate their murmur of the sea.

CHAPTER IV

THE WORTH OF THE BALLADS

IN this world the question of values is imperative; and an account of the popular ballad must be rendered in terms of its achievement and its essential worth. True, what is popular is not every man's affair. "Study the people," said Goldsmith to Gray, quoting Isocrates and deprecating the exclusive, learned appeal of the Odes; but "I do not love that word 'people,'" is Bacon's way. In these opinions, however, there is nothing either bad or good for balladry. Bacon was thinking of the rabble; Goldsmith had what we call the public in his mind; but in the vital days of the ballad, it dealt with that collective power which is now absorbed with other forces in the idea of society. Social realization in art can by no conception be called common or unclean even now, but must rather be regarded as drawing the individual out of his more sordid self; what is bad in art is really antisocial.[1] If this is true in days when the individual has achieved such a command of the field, it must have meant everything for primitive times and for the more homogeneous community. What qualities, then, would pass into the ballad from its com-

[1] Some excellent consideration of this point will be found in the early pages of M. Faguet's *Propos Littéraires*, Paris, 1902.

munal and social origins, and what would it fail to receive? Briefly stated, the ballad may be said to possess the advantages and disadvantages of a cumulative appeal to the emotion of a throng, and to lack the advantages and disadvantages of suggestive appeal to individual imagination. These lines of difference are not hard and fast, but they will serve; and they may be tested by certain facts.

Writing to a friend, Taine once declared[1] that art is a general idea put into the most particular form. As for the poets, instead of fine distinctions in color and outline to express this idea, one finds in them a word, a metaphor, a sound, a suppression, a turn of phrase, which can be discovered nowhere else. Here, in the affirmation of modern poetry, is plain negation of the more primitive ballad. The ballads are conventional and formal to a degree; their chief marks are the refrain, that constant repetition of the text, those recurrent commonplaces. Rhythm itself, the communal and conventional essence of poetry, appeals to certain modern poets as too vulgar a form; and they oppose to it centrifugal devices of every sort. But before poetry grew to be the cult of the unusual, rhythm was the only vehicle for pleasant or beautiful or even entertaining words. John of Ireland, who wrote "the earliest extant example of original literary prose in Scots," apologizes in quaint phrase; "thocht my language

---

[1] *Correspond.* (May, 1854), ii, 47. One thinks of the advice to poets by Eumolpus in Petronius: *effugiendum est ab omni verborum ut ita dicam vilitate; et summendae voces a plebe summotae.*

be nocht in Ryme nor plesand to part of pepil," he says, it will nevertheless appeal to the religious sort by reason of its matter. In brief, repetition of sound, word, phrase, structure, is the soul of balladry, and is precisely what modern poetry disowns. Suppose that Dante should repeat "we read no more that day" for his next pair of lovers, and his next, repeating the event! Suppose that Shakespeare put Hamlet's soliloquy into the mouths of all his tragic heroes! In ballads we must renounce every æsthetic surprise of form and phrase. One searches them in vain for that vivid line, that memorable word, which flash out of the situation and the act, marking them forever and belonging to them alone. Ballads are full of action, and they give us situations quite as strong as that of "The Duchess of Malfi" in which the brother stands over his murdered sister; but where is "Cover her face; mine eyes dazzle; she died young," or anything approaching such a verse? It is impossible to note high-water marks of ballad achievement, as Matthew Arnold was fain to do for poetry itself, by quoting test or tonic passages. Perhaps the appeal of Fair Ellen to the surly Child, or her lullaby, both quoted on a preceding page, might go for a specimen to justify our praise; but these are inadequate, and any detached portion is inadequate. The whole ballad is the thing. One would rather bid the seeker after excellent differences of the ballads to read "Child Waters" itself, "Babylon," "Lord Randal," "Spens," "Glasgerion," "The Wife of Usher's Well;" to read "Johnie Cock," "Robin Hood and the Monk,"

"Jock o' the Side," the "Cheviot;" and to sing out loud and bold whatever else commends itself, like the lilt of "St. Stephen"[1] or the crooning air of the "Queen of Elfan's Nourice." One must live one's way into balladry, must learn to love it as a whole and not by elegant extracts. Such passages as one can call vivid and memorable to some degree are recurrent, traditional, unfixed, the very opposite of particular. Even the affecting close of "The Twa Brothers" is found elsewhere. The force of ballad style is centripetal, emotional, communal, cumulative, not suggestive, not intellectual and centrifugal. What is true of the style, the invention, is also true of the external form. Ballad airs differ, of course, although a severe simplicity marks them all; but the rhythmical scheme shows no attempt at originality. Ballad metres are almost uniform; the range is very slight; and they can all be reduced to variations of the immemorial verse of four accents [2] which savage poetry

[1] "I sing it all over the house," said Professor Child to the present writer with regard to this ballad. Readers should note an admirable summary of Child's *obiter dicta* on ballads and the ballad, collected from his various introductions and notes, by Professor Walter M. Hart, printed in the *Publications of the Modern Language Association*, xxi, 755 ff. The great scholar's judgment is almost invariably unassailable. Perhaps in the passage (v, 299) where he calls the *Fire of Frendraught* and *The Baron of Brackley* "fairly good," but adds that these and others composed in the seventeenth century are not to be compared with *Mary Hamilton*, one feels a desire to lift *Brackley* clean out of its bracket, though not to the level of *Hamilton*.

[2] Preserved in the old two-line ballad stanza, and not very remote in the *septenarius*, however this may be related to the sacred Latin verse.

prefers and which may even lie behind later developments like the hexameter and the Saturnian. The verse-scheme is simple; and has not the resources even of regular alliterative verse, which is capable of so much emphasis and change. In rime there is little variety and no originality; a few obvious combinations do yeoman work. Alliteration, common enough, is mainly a matter of traditional phrases; as conscious effort it is rare, found chiefly in the chronicle ballads and in an occasional outburst like the "fat fadge by the fire" of "Lord Thomas." The vocabulary, too, is slender; perhaps a "dissertation" will one day count all the ballad words. Inversions, meant as inversions, and antitheses are practically unknown; there is as little conscious testing of the possibilities of surprise in the order as in the choice of expression. Climax is never calculated; if it occurs, it is merely the end of the singer's material; and to modern notions, the singer sometimes fails to stop where he ought to stop, — as in Percy's beautiful speech over Douglas. So, too, divergencies from common usage [1] are generic; it is simply the traditional ballad way, as in the case of the superfluous pronoun, found even in French: —

"Le fils du roi, il a juré."

A corresponding peculiarity, omission of the relative, as

---

[1] Ballads taken from the recitation of servants and nurses, when not in marked dialect, are often disfigured with ungrammatical, silly, and vulgar phrases. This is not surprising. The surprising fact is that so many of the traditional ballads are quite free from these disfigurements, and show a simple dignity of language quite their own.

in "I holp a pore yeman, with wrong was put behind," and "sent it to Sir Patrick Spens, was walking on the strand," is not peculiar to ballads, though characteristic. The leaps and omissions of narrative have been noticed already; they form no intentional feature of style, but spring from the choral origins of the ballad and are of the essence of its tradition.

The same centripetal tendency, the same failure to suggest and to provoke the imagination, rule in what is called figurative language. All the epithets are timid, traditional, general; they do not commit themselves. Any water is "wan." Ladies are "gay," but so are rings. The hero bears himself "like a king's son," and the maid is "as leal as the moon shines on." A wife is as true "as stone in the castle wall;" but a different case, "as dead as the stones in the wall," seems to take the faithful quality away. Comparisons as a whole are few and of the smallest range; "feet as white as sleet" is the only touch of surprise. Lady Barnard's eye, turned on Little Musgrave, is "bright as the summer sun," and outlaws in their forest are "light as leaf on linden;" but these are common stuff. There is no attempt to "heighten" style as an individual and artistic feat. Convention is followed through thick and thin, even when it is at odds with the fact.

> "O wha woud wish the win' to blaw,
>   Or the green leaves fa' therewith?
> Or wha wad wish a leeler love
>   Than Brown Adam the Smith?

"His hammer's o' the beaten gold,
    His study 's [1] o' the steel,
    His fingers white are my delite,
    He blows his bellows well."

The conventional hero of ballads is bound to show the milk-white skin somewhere, and his effects must bristle with gold; hence our preposterous blacksmith. Again, the introduction of him by those pretty but irrelevant lines about wind and falling leaves only sets off the general poverty of ballads in descriptions of nature, a field where poets of all time have followed Taine's formula of the general in the particular with extraordinary zeal, and where metaphor and simile and hyperbole have achieved their worst and their best. This expression of nature in new or startling phrase is half of poetry, by the modern idea, and a good two-thirds of favorite extracts and familiar quotations. But the ballads take nature for granted, and say little or nothing about it. Delight in the May morning, in the greenwood, the deer, the birds, has been noted already along with other particulars of the Robin Hood life, and the chronicle ballad elsewhere ventures a modest allusion; but in the typical ballad of situation and dialogue and refrain, nature plays no part. Landscape is ignored. We should like to know more of that Silver Wood mentioned in "Child Maurice" and "Jellon Grame," for there is a waft of myth in it; but not a word is said. So with Wearie's Well. The "unco land, where winds never blew nor cocks ever crew," does

[1] Stithy, anvil.

little for us; and the scant notes of True Thomas's journey through the other world are disappointing. Who nowadays does not remember the description of Grendel's abode in the Beowulf, the wolf-haunted crags and windy nesses, the wild stream hurrying underground, and then the mere itself, so full of horror that even the hounded stag chooses to be torn to pieces on its brink rather than to plunge for safety into its waves? Here is strong imaginative suggestion; where is it, even faintly, in the ballads? We should have something of this sort about Wearie's Well, about other uncanny places, if the individual poet were at work with his inexhaustible treasure of comparison, metaphor, glimpse, and hint, derived from the processes of nature. "Child Waters" offers the most tempting chances for ordinary description, but they are not taken; once, indeed, there is mention of the broom, but it is only to make a rime for that increment which the Robin Hood poets would have thrown out, possibly substituting a real touch of description.

> "All this long day Child Waters rode,
>   Shee ran bare ffoote by his side;
> Yett was he never soe courteous a knight
>   To say, Ellen, will you ryde?
>
> "But all this day Child Waters rode,
>   Shee ran barffoote thorow the broome;
> Yett he was never soe courteous a knight
>   As to say, Put on your shoone."

The water which they cross is specified vaguely as flowing "from banke to brim;" at the great hall "of red gold shine the gates," and so it is with the tower, — intolerable stretch of conventional splendor. That is all. Not an adjective or epithet or description stays with us. When "romantic" scenes are mentioned, they are shorn of all romance. Moonlight is as little regarded as daylight for imaginative purposes. The shut of day means nothing for ballads but the coming of dark — no flush of sunset — no

"... reapéd harvest of the light
Bound up in sheaves of sacred fire," —

no pomp of stars; the night's face holds no "huge cloudy symbols of a high romance;" and sunrise itself, save for that scant courtesy in "The Monk," is unhonored and unsung. With the same slight allowance, too, it may be said that the seasons pass unnoticed. Even in "Spens," where the matter is vital, it is only "this time of the year;" elsewhere it is either mere calendar, as in "Car" and "Otterburn," or else the conventional manner of getting the story under way, as in "Sir Andrew Barton," which throws in a songbird or so. A refrain — "Aye as the gowans grow gay" — can start imagination; but the flora and fauna of refrains lack *tenue*.

"As the dew flies over the mulberry tree,"

is not reassuring; while

"The broom blooms bonnie and so it is fair,"

is anticlimax. Moreover, since the method of balladry, as of early epic, is cumulative and not suggestive, since its art is to give details and not provoke the imagination into creating them, one must be careful not to assume such a provocative intention where none is meant. In Motherwell's weird little version of "Sheath and Knife," the sisters ride down to the valley "when the green, green trees are budding sae gaily," hunt and hawk together, till at last one of them is buried in a wide grave; then, —

> "The hawk had nae lure, and the horse had nae master,
> And the faithless hounds thro' the woods ran faster."

This, if genuine, should not set us dreaming; it is only fact, not a beckoning of romance, not a "horn in 'Hernani.'" It was a lover and his lass, or rather one of them yearning for the other, that put nature to work in the provocative, imaginative way. At first the connection is as vague as in an Italian "flower of the vine," or what not: —

> "O western wind, when wilt thou blow
> That the small rain down can rain?
> Christ, that my love were in my arms,
> And I in my bed again!"

But it rapidly grew definite. Daybreak songs led to some of the finest touches of description; dawn, parting the lovers in Wolfram's great lyric, is a bird of prey striking fiery talons through the cloud.[1] But the rise of lyric out of folk song is apart from our subject; ballads tread the epic path.

The explanation of all this is very evident. Ballads are communal, because they spring from the community in

---

[1] The late ballad, *Grey Cock*, no. 248, noted above as an *aube*, has no touch of this sort.

their choral origins and appeal to it in their traditional career. Their source and their object, collective emotion, is centripetal in its influence; and is open only to the cumulative effect, responding readily to the familiar, the repeated, to what is both present and near. It asks the same emotional impression over and over again; it refuses the series of fresh and varied intellectual suggestions, as well as all efforts to detach it from its object. These qualities, modified in some degree, are taken over into the great epics and give the objective cumulative note. Epic poetry, however, even in such crude forms as the "Gest of Robin Hood," begins to show its centrifugal tendencies, not only by modifying this cumulative appeal of facts by the omission of refrain and verbal iteration, but in positive comment on the facts and in marked artistic control. The initial word, "listen," — emphatically "lithe and listen, gentlemen," — is significant enough. The chorus is now discharged, and the ways of the chorus are in disrepute. Our poet-reciter or singer is already on the steps of the pyramid, and looks over his hearers' heads. The Homeric rhapsode, indeed, has gone so far as to appeal to a distinct intellectual effort on the part of these hearers, making them detach themselves from the story far enough to look down on it from the flight of a simile, or from the vantage-ground of wide emotional comment. This separable quality the ballads never show; while modern epic poems stretch it to its limit. In quest of the particular our modern and artistic poetry must be capable of detachment at

every turn; only so can it gain its splendor and sweep
of phrase.

> " Flat as to an eagle's eye
> Earth lay under Attila,"

is Mr. Meredith's impressive opening of a poem where
the centrifugal, particular, and detaching method exactly
meets the definition of Taine. Hundreds of verses flash
and dart from every corner of the poetic heaven to light
up the bridals of Attila and the tragedy of this single
night. Eleven stanzas, on the other hand, for a contrast
of method, tell without a trope, without a conscious turn
of phrase, without a suggestion of the wider world or of
times past and to come, but in their own conventional
leap-and-linger style, the story of "Sir Patrick Spens,"
the tragedy of his summons, his journey, and his end.
This traditional bit of verse, smooth as it has grown, holds
to the cumulative and undetached habit of genuine ballad
style. From first to last it is at the heart of the action and
never attempts to view that action, whether by stuff or
by phrase, by figure or by comment, from without. It
moves in a straight if redoubled line to the end, — the
Scots lords lying at Sir Patrick's feet, half over to Aberdour, fifty fathoms under sea. So, to be sure, Tennyson
left his Revenge: —

> "And the little Revenge herself went down by the island crags
> To be lost evermore in the main."

But this objective note is not the objective note in
"Spens." Mr. Kipling, too, is objective and direct; in
his "Danny Deever," a stirring poem, dialogue and

refrain do all, but the method is still suggestive, not cumulative. "What 's that a-whimperin' overhead?" and "I've drunk his beer a score of times," effective as they are, are impossible in the ballad of remote choral origins and direct traditional source. The difference is obvious. All impersonal poetry has "its eye on the object;" but a ballad is the object itself, and needs no contrasts in time or place. A modern poet bears down upon his theme, circles it, and takes it finally by siege and storm. When he has it, he does not keep it; he whips his readers away from it in order that they may come back to it by another path. He stirs abrupt intellectual flights, and sets a series of trysts in dreamland. Mr. Meredith tells almost nothing of that wild bridal night as early epic would tell it; but what provocation lies in his flash of trope and figure, his hints, his shadows as from flying clouds of reminiscence, to make one see this Attila and feel the tragedy of the end! The conqueror is resting from war; that is, —

"On his people stood a frost," —

and the army is

"Like a charger cut in stone."

Suggestion after suggestion lights the pomp of bridal feasting, shades a contrast of the conquered, submissive world without, throws a deeper glare on the figures, on the bride, Attila, the warriors, —

"Those rock-faces hung with weed,"

and again the conquest, again feast, bride, king. Where

is the story? Nearly two hundred verses glitter by before the action begins, and then it only seems to begin.
When the climax comes, it is a picture by sheer simile:
the chieftain dead, —

> "Square along the couch and stark
> Like the sea-rejected thing," —

and "that" —

> "Huddled in the corner dark,
> Humped and grinning like a cat." [1]

Every epic method is suited to its own time. Ballads
hold attention to the story by repetition of its main
details; they leap or linger, but move straight. Germanic verse, tenacious of its method for a good thousand
years, as one may guess, combined repetition with variation, moving in zigzag. Modern poets move round their
subject in narrowing circles, and must not repeat. More
than this. They are bound to startle by unexpected
phrase and idea, like changing lights on the rhythmically
moving form of the dancer. In that shift of colors we
may well forget the meaning of the dance itself; but we
like the color; and *suum cuique* is an old word. What
does one remember from the fine ballad of "Robin Hood's
Death"? The story. What does one remember from
that exquisite and even noble poem, Tennyson's "Morte
d'Arthur"? The setting of it, the colors and sounds, the
haunting, provocative suggestion, the charm of words.
Each is open to praise as to blame; but the praise is what

---

[1] Compare the picture of Judith and Holofernes, as drawn by Anglo-
Saxon art.

abides. Poetry is tested by the strongest and not by the weakest links of its chain; and to call one of these poems drivel, the other mere flashlight and innuendo, is to tell the half-truth which is a lie.

Corresponding to this outer circle of differences in style and form is the inner circle, the conception of character and events. Here the ballads can bear no comparison with even early epic art. Their events have no sweep, no slow and inexorable sequence; a narrow scene, central, unchanged, or perhaps, as in the "split situation," two scenes without any careful connection, must suffice. Dramatic in origin, in setting, in dialogue, in splendid tragic possibilities, the ballads absolutely fail to develop what is now regarded as the supreme dramatic fact, — character.[1] Robin Hood looms up in fairly personal guise; but Robin is centre of a cycle and has felt the epic influences. He has been accounted for in ancestry, birth, and breeding; his whole story has been told, retold, belied by sordid contaminations, rescued; his death is nobly sung. As with Beowulf, hints are given about Robin's habits, personal strength, tastes. Contrast the ballad of situation and its limited range of character in a "Babylon"! One gets not even a motive, not a shred of fact, for solution of this tragedy; take it or leave it, — but the situation is the thing. A lightning-flash reveals it, and the dark straightway swallows it up; who can study poses, faces, expression, anything but the

[1] See the already quoted analysis of a Danish ballad and its heroic epic predecessor by Professor Ker in *Epic and Romance*, pp. 147 ff.

group and that swift climax of a merely hinted complication?

Still less is the chance for comment, the artistic aside, the comparison with larger issues. There is no proverbial wisdom — although the singer of "Robin Hood and Guy" quotes proverbs — in the older choral ballads, and none in the ballad of tradition that springs from them. The hero does not ask how man can die better than by facing fearful odds; he faces them, and dies. Even the harmless and general *contemplatio mortis* is absent.

> "For though the day be never so longe,
> At last the belles ringeth to evensonge,"

quaint and pretty sentiment, is no affair of the balladist, but the comment of Master Stephen Hawes. For "observations of a strong mind operating upon life," Johnson's reported phrase, one must go to Johnsonian verse. Religion itself is only an incidental matter, and makes no real figure in balladry.

It is time to sum up the case for ballads as a definite if closed account of our literature. The overwhelming majority of them, committed to oral tradition, have been lost; such as have been rescued, however, are probably representative in kind as well as in proportion. They tell us something of remote origins at the dance, of choral and dramatic beginnings which have survived, now merely in the mould and structural framework of traditional epic ballads, now in the actual version which still clings to situation, to repetition in dialogue, and to refrain, as its chief elements. With the remote beat of foot in the ballad is heard louder and nearer the voice of those who sing it. It is lyric in this singable quality, or has been so once. Tradition by word of mouth, mainly in isolated unlettered communities, is its vital test; and narrative is its vital fact. Its supreme art is to tell its story well; and its narrative is not to be regarded as a mere stalking-ground for more serious intentions. Entertainment is an obvious purpose; and Sidney's fine words about the poet may be as well applied to the humbler muse of English and Scottish ballads. She also "cometh to you with words set in delightful proportion, either accompanied with or prepared for the well-enchanting skill of music; and with a tale, forsooth, she cometh unto you, with a tale which holdeth children from play and old men from the chimney-corner."

What is this tale, when all is said? How is it varied? And what mood really prevails? Rarely is it the thing which ought not to be heard; the ballad muse is cleanly. Perhaps five and twenty ballads come under the light or comic class, and only a few of these are distinctly coarse. "The Keach in the Creel" of the new, "Crow and Pie" of the old, are sooty things; to "The Jolly Beggar," readers, like certain editors, will give a buffet nicely weighted with equal parts of liking and reproof. At its best, this pure entertainment, this delight of tales well told, meets us in the Robin Hood ballads, as in that unrivaled story of the monk's discomfiture in the "Gest," and more seriously in the thrill and deeper interest of

"Child Waters." But here we begin, as with a certain
stage in all poetry, to work below the surface and to find
deeper meanings whether consciously or unconsciously
expressed. "Child Waters" is on the tragic marches; it
hovers at the brink of that sea of troubles which a majority of the best ballads are quite willing to face without the
"happy ending" interposed. This statement can be
based on statistics. By a rough but apt division, out of
the three hundred-odd ballads we may call twenty by
this title of "the happy ending;" with them tragedy is
averted, but often, as in "The Fair Maid of Northumberland," escape from death is no boon. Often, again, the
happy ending is unavailing to remove a tragic impression
which is upon us almost to the final stanza; it is like
"Measure for Measure," put only by courtesy on the
"comic" file. The "entertaining" narrative, of course,
lies between the light things already noted, and these
semi-tragic pieces which lead up to tragedy pure. There
are about seventy-five of the chronicle or epic type, which
includes at once the sterling Robin Hood and other outlaw
ballads, and also a long list of the poor, the doubtful,
and the abject; and there are seventy ballads which may
be credited, with large use of the word, to romance,
ranging for scene from a throne to a kitchen, and for
heroes from King Arthur to Tom Potts. Beyond those
happy-ending tales, finally, which just avert tragedy at
their close, is the fiery gate; and through this one goes
to what is really the citadel. A round hundred of ballads,
the longest list, are purely and simply tragic; and to these

must be added "Otterburn" and "Cheviot" from the
chronicles. And what a list it is! There is less chaff here
for the wheat than in the other catalogues; the best, the
most characteristic, the oldest, the most haunting and
persuasive ballads are here. Count all the ballads, and
tragedy is well to the fore; weigh them, and the odds are
still greater on its side. The combination of tragedy and
antiquity in the two-line refrain ballads is of great significance. They and the other tragic pieces suggest not
Wordsworth's definition of poetry at large as "emotion
recollected in tranquillity," but rather Emerson's account
of it as the litanies of nations, coming, —

> "Like the volcano's tongue of flame,
> Up from the burning core below,
> The canticles of love and woe."

They echo without comment the clash of man and fate.
If any lesson is to be learned from them, it is by implication: the old lesson that while destiny is inevitable, inexorable, the victim is there neither to whimper nor
to mock over his plight, but simply to play the man.
Tragedy, but not pessimism, is their last word. Their
deepest value is that they revive to some extent the impression which primitive and communal poetry could
make by means now impossible for any poet to command.
They are not primitive verse, — far from it; they are
crossed and interwoven with the poetry of art, only by
such support surviving to our day; but they bring with
them something of the old choral appeal, and still speak,
however faintly, with the voice of tradition. That is their

value; and it is not merely the value of a survival. In the old Quaker phrase, they speak to the condition of modern men and women, and can be counted as a permanent possession of the race. Surely there is some common poetic ground for the primitive survival in "Babylon" and the modern achievement in "Hamlet," different as these are, and inferior as one is to the other by our own standards of taste. The ballad at its best, and the great poems of the world, are akin in many ways and walk one path. We must judge both of them by their relation to poetry in its whole course as a social art, as expression, not of yesterday, not of to-day, not of the young man in a library, and not of the festal throng, but of the rhythmic and emotional elements common to individual and mass. In rhythmic instinct the "Babylons" and the "Hamlets" are alike, and the degree of excellence is of slight account, just as the noblest piece of music has room for chorus as well as solo. For the emotional and sympathetic part, the actual stuff of poetry as distinguished from its pattern, the union of ballad and artistic poem lies in shadow. But it can be seen. In each case, life deepest and strongest is reported at first hand and with that high seriousness of which Matthew Arnold had so much to say. The main work of civilization for the onlooker in life has been to detach the notes of agony, misery, grief, weariness, from the notes of fighting, of victory and defiance and defeat, and to make literature the reflection upon life instead of life itself. Barred from this reflective note, the old poetry was devoid of humor.

The humorist is left behind; for comedy, after all, must be the affair of prose. The last word of the great poem, like that last word of the ballads, expresses life in its tragedy; and only the tragic can be finally true.

The cause of our liking for tragedy, or rather of our need of it, has often been discussed; but there is a very simple explanation of this need as a craving for truth. Day in, day out, it is pleasanter to keep the screen of comedy before us, and to take the curtain for the play; but to every man come times when he desires to see the thing as it is, and what he then sees is tragedy. Comedy at its best is the conventional "poetic justice," say of "Hind Horn" in balladry and of "As You Like It" in art, all things working together for those delightful but preposterous pairs. No one wishes to cut the part of our comedian or to dismiss the very clown; but it must be borne in mind that comedy began in Greece under the patronage of Bacchus as a roaring farcical song, a phallic revel, and that every "happy ending" is at heart a kind of drunkard's paradise in dream. Our very English word "dream" has curious origins, synonymous once with beer. Humor is potent enough, and Pantagruel's mood is enviable, *certaine gaieté d'ésprit*, its master defines it, *conficte en mespris des choses fortuites;*[1] but it does not have that last word which belongs to tragedy and echoes in all great verse, echoes even in these humble

[1] Or one may take to heart the motto of the Paris *Figaro*, quoted of course from Beaumarchais: "Je me hâte de rire de tout . . . de peur d'étre obligé d'en pleurer."

traditional songs. Cynicism, the recoil of humor upon sentiment, ballads never know. Everybody can quote Omar's great "forgiveness" stanza; but Heine's climax is not so well known. We keep asking, he says, why the just suffer, why the evil thrive, keep asking, asking, "until at last a handful of earth stops our mouths: *but is that an answer?*" This cannot be the last word, for it is mere resignation and protest against the odds. Tragedy plays the game, without complaint, and with no thought beyond the limits of the scene. Primitive ballads, however inadequate they would seem for our needs, came from men who knew life at its hardest, faced it, accepted it, well aware that a losing fight is at the end of every march. A modern writer has pointed out that Germanic popular poetry, along with Celtic and Slavic, has always loved the beaten cause and echoed the tragedy of life. Who, moreover, does not recall that large simplicity in which doom is announced, as if to a Greek tragic chorus, at the close of the Nibelungen Lay? Who does not feel the same spirit, playing in smaller bounds, at the close of "Sir Patrick Spens"?

Primitive men transcribed their tragic experience by a process which psychology may call either gymnastic preparation or æsthetic impulse, which Aristotle called imitated action, and which, like most human performances, really sprang from no conscious purpose but from the interplay of social instincts and the conditions of earliest social life. Through all the changes due to long tradition, through changes of stuff, form, appeal, this primitive way of life still speaks, though with very faint and far-away tones, in the ballads. One must make no preposterous claim for such survivals as we find in them. The majority of them must be classed as inferior poems. The best, even, cannot compete with great poems of art; but there is a greatness of their own in their attitude towards life, in their summary and transcript of it. They know, as the lords of tragedy in Hellas knew, as Shakespeare knew, that only the anguish of some inevitable conflict is worth while. They know by instinct, as lyric poets have known in their "recollected emotion," that while tragedy is insoluble, it holds the solution of existence in its own mystery, and that only from death springs the meaning of life. Without the unfixed but certain parting for eternity there could be no human love. The ballad does not say these things; far from that. Its makers and transmitters would balk at the name of tragedy, and would be helpless to understand the greatest definition that tragedy has yet found, the close of Milton's "Samson Agonistes." But they give the spirit of that close in their simple verses, which tell of traffic with danger and defeat. They report the battle of life as soldiers, not as the captain, with eyes and ears for the fighting alone, and no thought of plan and campaign and allies and the unseen leader of the foe. That, after all, is the main difference. It is no individual that speaks out his thoughts, his hopes, his fears, in the ballads. If their very name tells of external origin at the communal dance, Herder's title for them as Voices of the Nations, of the People, goes to their essence and their heart; his beautiful dedication remains the best commentary ever made upon popular song. The people are now fairly passive in the poetic function; their deputy, the poet, acts as lord of verse to the extent of forgetting the suffrages that made him what he is. But ethnology, history, and the long career of poetry itself, testify beyond reasonable doubt to a time when individuals counted for very little in rhythmic expression, and when the choral element was over all. A faint echo of this imperious choral can still be heard in the ballads, a murmur of voices in concert, borne over great stretches of space and through many changes of time.

BIBLIOGRAPHICAL NOTES

MOST of the literature dealing with the "ballad question" is recorded, up to the year 1894, in the present writer's *Old English Ballads;* subsequent editions are unchanged. A summary of later investigation is made by H. Hecht, "Neuere Literatur zur englisch-schottischen Balladendichtung," in *Englische Studien*, xxxvi (1906), 370 ff. The best short discussions of the matter are those of G. L. Kittredge, Introduction to the one-volume edition of Child's *English and Scottish Popular Ballads*, 1904, and Andrew Lang, new edition Chambers's *Cyclopædia of English Literature*, 1902, i, 520 ff. Opposed to the idea of popular origins are W. J. Courthope, chapter on "Decay of English Minstrelsy," in *History of English Poetry* (1895), i, 426 ff.; T. F. Henderson, *Scottish Vernacular Literature* (1898), pp. 355 ff., and new edition of Scott's *Minstrelsy* (1902), Introduction; G. Gregory Smith, *The Transition Period* (1900), pp. 180 ff. — Professor Child's opinions on ballads and the ballad have been gathered by W. M. Hart, *Publications Modern Language Association*, xxi (1906), 755 ff. — With regard to *Auld Maitland* (above, pp. 14 f.), Mr. Lang now says, *Sir Walter Scott*, Literary Lives Series, 1906, pp. 33 f.: "I lean to a theory that *Auld Maitland* and the *Outlaw Murray* are literary imitations of the ballads, compiled late in the seventeenth century, on some Maitland and Murray traditions." — For negative conclusions about the Anglo-Saxon historical "ballads," see Abegg, *Zur Entwickelung der historischen Dichtung bei den Angelsachsen*, Strassburg, 1894. — Two papers need special mention in their bearing on the ballad problem of origins. George Morey Miller, in *The Drama-*

tic Element in the Popular Ballad, University of Cincinnati Bulletin, No. 19, has very properly insisted on a closer study of the mimetic and dramatic features; while Arthur Beatty, in "The St. George, or Mummers' Plays; a Study in the Protology of the Drama," *Transactions Wisconsin Acad.*, xv (1906), 273 ff., has pointed out the importance of ritual elements in popular poetry, and has made noteworthy additions to the valuable work of E. K. Chambers in the often cited *Mediaeval Stage*, 2 vols., Oxford, 1903. — A very old and almost unique case of Incremental Repetition, the kind familiar in ballads and certain tales, occurs in "The Descent of Ishtar," as translated into German by Jensen, in Schrader's *Sammlung von Assyrischen und Babylonischen Texten*, vi, i, *Assyrisch-Babylonische Mythen und Epen*, Berlin, 1900, pp. 80–91: seven sets of three verses each describe the spoiling of Ishtar as she passes through the seven gates into the underworld, and the process is detailed in reversed order at her release. The analogy with ballad structure is striking. On page 87 is an interesting case of the repetition of a message.

For the ballads themselves, as set forth in the second chapter, Child's great work remains, of course, practically unaffected: *The English and Scottish Popular Ballads*, ten parts, two to a volume, 1882–98, the final part, containing all the apparatus of investigation, edited by G. L. Kittredge. Work goes on, to be sure, with regard to special groups like the Robin Hood Cycle; Heusler's *Lied und Epos*, for example, and the dissertation, now in press, of W. M. Hart on *Ballad and Epic*. Görbing, *Anglia*, xxiii (1900), 1 ff., "Beispiele von realisierten Mythen in den englischen und schottischen Balladen," hardly keeps the promise of his title. — An extremely interesting companion study to Professor Child's various introductions is the account and summary of Danish ballads given by Axel Olrik in his *Danske Folkeviser i Udvalg*, Copenhagen, 1899.

For the sources of the ballads, Ewald Flügel has done good work (*Anglia*, xxi, 312 ff.) *zur Chronologie der englischen Balladen*. Supplementing the list of *Sources of the Texts*, in the fifth volume of Child, compactly given in the one-volume edition, pp. 677 ff., Professor Flügel makes a chronological index, from which one easily gathers the facts of the ballad record. *Judas,* in the Trinity Coll. MS., goes back to the thirteenth century; *Robin and Gandelyn* dates from about 1450, — and so do *Robin Hood and the Monk* and *St. Stephen, Robin Hood and the Potter* following about 1500. Then come the Edinburgh printed fragments of the *Gest* and the edition of Wynkyn de Worde. Of sixteenth-century texts may be mentioned the printed *Adam Bell* and the MSS. of *Otterburn, Cheviot, Captain Car, Sir Andrew Barton.* In the seventeenth century a few printed ballads are overshadowed by the Percy Folio MS., often described, and edited by Hales and Furnivall, 1867–68, in 3 vols. and supplement. Percy collected liberally, and his *Reliques,* 1765, in spite of its faults in omission and commission, deserved its vogue. The collectors were now in the field, and their transcripts, good or bad, along with broadside rescues, complete the record. A word should be said in recognition of the labors of Mr. Macmath, who helped Professor Child in the latest gathering of material; through Mr. Macmath's zeal was recovered what Scott called "the collection of an old lady's complete set of ballads." It has furnished valuable readings.

On the recitation and chanting of ballads, the old love of repetition, and the connection of these two phases of balladry, may be quoted here some words of Goethe about his way of telling stories to children. Werther, of course, cutting bread and butter for Lotte's charges, is the poet himself. "Weil ich manchmal einen Incidentpunkt erfinde muss, den ich beim zweitenmal vergesse, sagen sie [the children] gleich, das vorigemal wär' es anders gewesen, so dass ich mich jetzt übe,

sie unveränderlich *in einem singenden Sylbenfall* an einem
Schnürchen weg zu recitiren." — In regard to ballad com-
monplaces, the point of departure for comparison with older
Germanic *formulae* is the admirable collection by Sievers at
the end of his edition of the *Héliand*, Halle, 1878, pp. 391 ff.
Fehr's dissertation, *Die Formelhaften Elemente in den Alten
Englischen Balladen*, Zossen b. Berlin, 1900, needs continuation
and elaboration. — In treating the characteristics of the ballad,
I should have noted the contrast with medieval literature in
that total ignorance of "examples" which all ballads reveal.
"What know I of the quene Niobe?" the balladist could cry
with Troilus; "lat be thine olde ensaumples!" — Little, perhaps too little, has been said of the borrowing of narrative
elements in individual cases; but that subject is endless. Perhaps a study of the haphazard statements about more "literary" sources would yield good results; for example, when The
Man of Law says, *C. T.*, B, 132 f., that he got his tale years
before from "a marchant." But this kind of investigation needs
no stimulants, and is in good hands. — This mention of Chaucer,
finally, may serve to remind us that all appreciation of the
ballads ranges between Professor Child's constant praise for
the best of them as good stories, told with as much success
by folk afoot and afield as was attained by his other favorites,
the pilgrim company on horseback, and the sweep of Herder's
eulogy in that untranslatable dedication. Behind the splendid
elegiacs, the appeal for "die Stimme des Volks der zerstreue-
ten Menschheit" is sufficient shelter for any one who is accused
of finding qualities in balladry which balladry never knew.

BALLADS CITED OR QUOTED

INDEX

Dream-opening, 67.
Dreams, 301.
Dress, color of, 129, 132, 308 f.

Eoiae, 79.
Epic, 36 f., 42 f., 69, 78 f., 83, 92, 135, 270, 284.
Epic methods, 335 f.
Epic preface, 92 f.
Epic process, 79 ff., 109 f., 118 f., 141, 147, 150, 243, 260, 266, 270, 291.
Ethnological evidence, 21 ff.

Fabyan's chronicle, 55.
Fairy ballads, 215 ff.
Faroe Islands, ballads in the, 24, 26, 69, 105, 107, 109, 146 f., 150, 263.
Father, the, 173.
Figurative language, 72, 327 f.
Flytings, 55, 137 f., 143.
Folklore in ballads, 299 ff.
Folk song, 66.
Fontenelle, 1.
Forgery, *see Ballad*.
Frankish ballad, 48 f.
Frazer, J. G., 45, 94.
Fulk Fitz-Warine, 8.
Funeral songs, 46, 95.
Furnivall, F. J., 207.

Games, 80, 108 f.
German ballad in England, 294.
Germanic ballads, 36, 293, 343.
Gerould, G. H., 228.
Ghosts, 200, 220 ff., 301 f.
Goldsmith, 322.
Good-nights, 211 ff., 252.
Goths, 44, 46.
Gray, 73, 181.
Greek ballads, modern, 172.
Greenwood ballads, 266 ff.
Grundtvig, 15, 60, 100, 204, 293.
Guenillon, 150.

Hales, J. W., 258.
Halewijn, 124, 154.
Happy ending, 339.

Hardy, T., 9, 248.
Harpens Kraft, 70.
Hart, W. M., 267, 325.
Hebrew ballads, 48.
Heine, 171, 179, 198.
Helgi, Lay of, 221.
Henderson, T. F., 16, 192, 317.
Henley, W. E., 63.
Henry of Huntingdon, 50.
Herd, D., 313.
Herder, 17 f., 344 f.
Hereward, ballads of, 30, 49 f., 274.
Herford, C. H., 293.
Hero and Leander, 86 ff., 92, 223 f.
Heusler, A., 263.
Highland dialect, 254.
Hilde saga, 151.
Hildebrand and Hilde, 151.
History perverted, 234.
Holstein dances, 97 f., 139 f., 147 f.
Humor, 177 f., 233 f., 281 f., 341 f.
Husband and wife, 176 ff.

"I," the, of ballads, 66 f.
Icelandic saga, 113.
Imitations, 314.
Impersonal quality, 66, 287.
Impossible things, 139 f., 142, 291.
Imprecation, 144 f.
Improvisation, 14, 22, 24 f., 48, 58 ff., 73 ff., 101, 249 f., 260, 287; by warriors, 37, 40 f., 57.
Incest, 192.
Incremental, *see Repetition*.
Indecent ballads, 65, 203, 232 f., 338 f.
Informers, 197.

Jacobs, J., 107.
Jealousy, ballads of, 177, 189 f.
Jeanroy, 140.
John of Bridlington, 52.
John of Ireland, 323.
Johnson, Dr., 73, 283, 286, 337.
Jordanis, 46.
Journalism, 4, 10, 13, 32 f., 40, 52 f., 56, 238; degenerate, 159, 235, 261.
Judith and Holofernes, 153, 335.

CATALOGUE OF DOVER BOOKS

Books Explaining Science and Mathematics

WHAT IS SCIENCE?, N. Campbell. The role of experiment and measurement, the function of mathematics, the nature of scientific laws, the difference between laws and theories, the limitations of science, and many similarly provocative topics are treated clearly and without technicalities by an eminent scientist. "Still an excellent introduction to scientific philosophy," H. Margenau in PHYSICS TODAY. "A first-rate primer . . . deserves a wide audience," SCIENTIFIC AMERICAN. 192pp. 5⅜ x 8.   S43 Paperbound **$1.25**

THE NATURE OF PHYSICAL THEORY, P. W. Bridgman. A Nobel Laureate's clear, non-technical lectures on difficulties and paradoxes connected with frontier research on the physical sciences. Concerned with such central concepts as thought, logic, mathematics, relativity, probability, wave mechanics, etc. he analyzes the contributions of such men as Newton, Einstein, Bohr, Heisenberg, and many others. "Lucid and entertaining . . . recommended to anyone who wants to get some insight into current philosophies of science," THE NEW PHILOSOPHY. Index. xi + 138pp. 5⅜ x 8.   S33 Paperbound **$1.25**

EXPERIMENT AND THEORY IN PHYSICS, Max Born. A Nobel Laureate examines the nature of experiment and theory in theoretical physics and analyzes the advances made by the great physicists of our day: Heisenberg, Einstein, Bohr, Planck, Dirac, and others. The actual process of creation is detailed step-by-step by one who participated. A fine examination of the scientific method at work. 44pp. 5⅜ x 8.   S308 Paperbound **75¢**

THE PSYCHOLOGY OF INVENTION IN THE MATHEMATICAL FIELD, J. Hadamard. The reports of such men as Descartes, Pascal, Einstein, Poincaré, and others are considered in this investigation of the method of idea-creation in mathematics and other sciences and the thinking process in general. How do ideas originate? What is the role of the unconscious? What is Poincaré's forgetting hypothesis? are some of the fascinating questions treated. A penetrating analysis of Einstein's thought processes concludes the book. xiii + 145pp. 5⅜ x 8.   T107 Paperbound **$1.25**

THE NATURE OF LIGHT AND COLOUR IN THE OPEN AIR, M. Minnaert. Why are shadows sometimes blue, sometimes green, or other colors depending on the light and surroundings? What causes mirages? Why do multiple suns and moons appear in the sky? Professor Minnaert explains these unusual phenomena and hundreds of others in simple, easy-to-understand terms based on optical laws and the properties of light and color. No mathematics is required but artists, scientists, students, and everyone fascinated by these "tricks" of nature will find thousands of useful and amazing pieces of information. Hundreds of observational experiments are suggested which require no special equipment. 200 illustrations; 42 photos. xvi + 362pp. 5⅜ x 8.   T196 Paperbound **$2.00**

THE UNIVERSE OF LIGHT, W. Bragg. Sir William Bragg, Nobel Laureate and great modern physicist, is also well known for his powers of clear exposition. Here he analyzes all aspects of light for the layman: lenses, reflection, refraction, the optics of vision, x-rays, the photoelectric effect, etc. He tells you what causes the color of spectra, rainbows, and soap bubbles, how magic mirrors work, and much more. Dozens of simple experiments are described. Preface. Index. 199 line drawings and photographs, including 2 full-page color plates. x + 283pp. 5⅜ x 8.   T538 Paperbound **$1.85**

SOAP-BUBBLES: THEIR COLOURS AND THE FORCES THAT MOULD THEM, C. V. Boys. For continuing popularity and validity as scientific primer, few books can match this volume of easily-followed experiments, explanations. Lucid exposition of complexities of liquid films, surface tension and related phenomena, bubbles' reaction to heat, motion, music, magnetic fields. Experiments with capillary attraction, soap bubbles on frames, composite bubbles, liquid cylinders and jets, bubbles other than soap, etc. Wonderful introduction to scientific method, natural laws that have many ramifications in areas of modern physics. Only complete edition in print. New Introduction by S. Z. Lewin, New York University. 83 illustrations; 1 full-page color plate. xii + 190pp. 5⅜ x 8½.   T542 Paperbound **95¢**

CATALOGUE OF DOVER BOOKS

THE STORY OF X-RAYS FROM RONTGEN TO ISOTOPES, A. R. Bleich, M.D. This book, by a member of the American College of Radiology, gives the scientific explanation of x-rays, their applications in medicine, industry and art, and their danger (and that of atmospheric radiation) to the individual and the species. You learn how radiation therapy is applied against cancer, how x-rays diagnose heart disease and other ailments, how they are used to examine mummies for information on diseases of early societies, and industrial materials for hidden weaknesses. 54 illustrations show x-rays of flowers, bones, stomach, gears with flaws, etc. 1st publication. Index. xix + 186pp. 5⅜ x 8. **T622 Paperbound $1.35**

SPINNING TOPS AND GYROSCOPIC MOTION, John Perry. A classic elementary text of the dynamics of rotation — the behavior and use of rotating bodies such as gyroscopes and tops. In simple, everyday English you are shown how quasi-rigidity is induced in discs of paper, smoke rings, chains, etc., by rapid motions; why a gyrostat falls and why a top rises; precession; how the earth's motion affects climate; and many other phenomena. Appendix on practical use of gyroscopes. 62 figures. 128pp. 5⅜ x 8. **T416 Paperbound $1.00**

SNOW CRYSTALS, W. A. Bentley, M. J. Humphreys. For almost 50 years W. A. Bentley photographed snow flakes in his laboratory in Jericho, Vermont; in 1931 the American Meteorological Society gathered together the best of his work, some 2400 photographs of snow flakes, plus a few ice flowers, windowpane frosts, dew, frozen rain, and other ice formations. Pictures were selected for beauty and scientific value. A very valuable work to anyone in meteorology, cryology; most interesting to layman; extremely useful for artist who wants beautiful, crystalline designs. All copyright free. Unabridged reprint of 1931 edition. 2453 illustrations. 227pp. 8 x 10½. **T287 Paperbound $3.00**

A DOVER SCIENCE SAMPLER, edited by George Barkin. A collection of brief, non-technical passages from 44 Dover Books Explaining Science for the enjoyment of the science-minded browser. Includes work of Bertrand Russell, Poincaré, Laplace, Max Born, Galileo, Newton; material on physics, mathematics, metallurgy, anatomy, astronomy, chemistry, etc. You will be fascinated by Martin Gardner's analysis of the sincere pseudo-scientist, Moritz's account of Newton's absentmindedness, Bernard's examples of human vivisection, etc. Illustrations from the Diderot Pictorial Encyclopedia and De Re Metallica. 64 pages. **FREE**

THE STORY OF ATOMIC THEORY AND ATOMIC ENERGY, J. G. Feinberg. A broader approach to subject of nuclear energy and its cultural implications than any other similar source. Very readable, informal, completely non-technical text. Begins with first atomic theory, 600 B.C. and carries you through the work of Mendelejeff, Röntgen, Madame Curie, to Einstein's equation and the A-bomb. New chapter goes through thermonuclear fission, binding energy, other events up to 1959. Radioactive decay and radiation hazards, future benefits, work of Bohr, moderns, hundreds more topics. "Deserves special mention . . . not only authoritative but thoroughly popular in the best sense of the word," Saturday Review. Formerly, "The Atom Story." Expanded with new chapter. Three appendixes. Index. 34 illustrations. vii + 243pp. 5⅜ x 8. **T625 Paperbound $1.45**

THE STRANGE STORY OF THE QUANTUM, AN ACCOUNT FOR THE GENERAL READER OF THE GROWTH OF IDEAS UNDERLYING OUR PRESENT ATOMIC KNOWLEDGE, B. Hoffmann. Presents lucidly and expertly, with barest amount of mathematics, the problems and theories which led to modern quantum physics. Dr. Hoffmann begins with the closing years of the 19th century, when certain trifling discrepancies were noticed, and with illuminating analogies and examples takes you through the brilliant concepts of Planck, Einstein, Pauli, Broglie, Bohr, Schroedinger, Heisenberg, Dirac, Sommerfeld, Feynman, etc. This edition includes a new, long postscript carrying the story through 1958. "Of the books attempting an account of the history and contents of our modern atomic physics which have come to my attention, this is the best," H. Margenau, Yale University, in "American Journal of Physics." 32 tables and line illustrations. Index. 275pp. 5⅜ x 8. **T518 Paperbound $1.50**

SPACE AND TIME, E. Borel. Written by a versatile mathematician of world renown with his customary lucidity and precision, this introduction to relativity for the layman presents scores of examples, analogies, and illustrations that open up new ways of thinking about space and time. It covers abstract geometry and geographical maps, continuity and topology, the propagation of light, the special theory of relativity, the general theory of relativity, theoretical researches, and much more. Mathematical notes. 2 Indexes. 4 Appendices. 15 figures. xvi + 243pp. 5⅜ x 8. **T592 Paperbound $1.45**

FROM EUCLID TO EDDINGTON: A STUDY OF THE CONCEPTIONS OF THE EXTERNAL WORLD, Sir Edmund Whittaker. A foremost British scientist traces the development of theories of natural philosophy from the western rediscovery of Euclid to Eddington, Einstein, Dirac, etc. The inadequacy of classical physics is contrasted with present day attempts to understand the physical world through relativity, non-Euclidean geometry, space curvature, wave mechanics, etc. 5 major divisions of examination: Space; Time and Movement; the Concepts of Classical Physics; the Concepts of Quantum Mechanics; the Eddington Universe. 212pp. 5⅜ x 8. **T491 Paperbound $1.35**

Nature, Biology

NATURE RECREATION: Group Guidance for the Out-of-doors, William Gould Vinal. Intended for both the uninitiated nature instructor and the education student on the college level, this complete "how-to" program surveys the entire area of nature education for the young. Philosophy of nature recreation; requirements, responsibilities, important information for group leaders; nature games; suggested group projects; conducting meetings and getting discussions started; etc. Scores of immediately applicable teaching aids, plus completely updated sources of information, pamphlets, field guides, recordings, etc. Bibliography. 74 photographs. + 310pp. 5⅜ x 8½.   T1015 Paperbound **$1.75**

HOW TO KNOW THE WILD FLOWERS, Mrs. William Starr Dana. Classic nature book that has introduced thousands to wonders of American wild flowers. Color-season principle of organization is easy to use, even by those with no botanical training, and the genial, refreshing discussions of history, folklore, uses of over 1,000 native and escape flowers, foliage plants are informative as well as fun to read. Over 170 full-page plates, collected from several editions, may be colored in to make permanent records of finds. Revised to conform with 1950 edition of Gray's Manual of Botany. xlii + 438pp. 5⅜ x 8½.   T332 Paperbound **$1.85**

HOW TO KNOW THE FERNS, F. T. Parsons. Ferns, among our most lovely native plants, are all too little known. This classic of nature lore will enable the layman to identify almost any American fern he may come across. After an introduction on the structure and life of ferns, the 57 most important ferns are fully pictured and described (arranged upon a simple identification key). Index of Latin and English names. 61 illustrations and 42 full-page plates. xiv + 215pp. 5⅜ x 8.   T740 Paperbound **$1.35**

MANUAL OF THE TREES OF NORTH AMERICA, Charles Sprague Sargent. Still unsurpassed as most comprehensive, reliable study of North American tree characteristics, precise locations and distribution. By dean of American dendrologists. Every tree native to U.S., Canada, Alaska, 185 genera, 717 species, described in detail—leaves, flowers, fruit, winterbuds, bark, wood, growth habits etc. plus discussion of varieties and local variants, immaturity variations. Over 100 keys, including unusual 11-page analytical key to genera, aid in identification. 783 clear illustrations of flowers, fruit, leaves. An unmatched permanent reference work for all nature lovers. Second enlarged (1926) edition. Synopsis of families. Analytical key to genera. Glossary of technical terms. Index. 783 illustrations, 1 map. Two volumes. Total of 982pp. 5⅜ x 8.   T277 Vol. I Paperbound **$2.00**
                                                                   T278 Vol. II Paperbound **$2.00**
                                                                   The set **$4.00**

TREES OF THE EASTERN AND CENTRAL UNITED STATES AND CANADA, W. M. Harlow. A revised edition of a standard middle-level guide to native trees and important escapes. More than 140 trees are described in detail, and illustrated with more than 600 drawings and photographs. Supplementary keys will enable the careful reader to identify almost any tree he might encounter. xiii + 288pp. 5⅜ x 8.   T395 Paperbound **$1.35**

GUIDE TO SOUTHERN TREES, Ellwood S. Harrar and J. George Harrar. All the essential information about trees indigenous to the South, in an extremely handy format. Introductory essay on methods of tree classification and study, nomenclature, chief divisions of Southern trees, etc. Approximately 100 keys and synopses allow for swift, accurate identification of trees. Numerous excellent illustrations, non-technical text make this a useful book for teachers of biology or natural science, nature lovers, amateur naturalists. Revised 1962 edition. Index. Bibliography. Glossary of technical terms. 920 illustrations; 201 full-page plates. ix + 709pp. 4⅝ x 6⅜.   T945 Paperbound **$2.25**

FRUIT KEY AND TWIG KEY TO TREES AND SHRUBS, W. M. Harlow. Bound together in one volume for the first time, these handy and accurate keys to fruit and twig identification are the only guides of their sort with photographs (up to 3 times natural size). "Fruit Key": Key to over 120 different deciduous and evergreen fruits. 139 photographs and 11 line drawings. Synoptic summary of fruit types. Bibliography. 2 Indexes (common and scientific names). "Twig Key": Key to over 160 different twigs and buds. 173 photographs. Glossary of technical terms. Bibliography. 2 Indexes (common and scientific names). Two volumes bound as one. Total of xvii + 126pp. 5⅝ x 8⅜.   T511 Paperbound **$1.25**

INSECT LIFE AND INSECT NATURAL HISTORY, S. W. Frost. A work emphasizing habits, social life, and ecological relations of insects, rather than more academic aspects of classification and morphology. Prof. Frost's enthusiasm and knowledge are everywhere evident as he discusses insect associations and specialized habits like leaf-rolling, leaf-mining, and case-making, the gall insects, the boring insects, aquatic insects, etc. He examines all sorts of matters not usually covered in general works, such as: insects as human food, insect music and musicians, insect response to electric and radio waves, use of insects in art and literature. The admirably executed purpose of this book, which covers the middle ground between elementary treatment and scholarly monographs, is to excite the reader to observe for himself. Over 700 illustrations. Extensive bibliography. x + 524pp. 5⅜ x 8.   T517 Paperbound **$2.45**

CATALOGUE OF DOVER BOOKS

COMMON SPIDERS OF THE UNITED STATES, J. H. Emerton. Here is a nature hobby you can pursue right in your own cellar! Only non-technical, but thorough, reliable guide to spiders for the layman. Over 200 spiders from all parts of the country, arranged by scientific classification, are identified by shape and color, number of eyes, habitat and range, habits, etc. Full text, 501 line drawings and photographs, and valuable introduction explain webs, poisons, threads, capturing and preserving spiders, etc. Index. New synoptic key by S. W. Frost. xxiv + 225pp. 5⅜ x 8.   T223 Paperbound **$1.35**

THE LIFE STORY OF THE FISH: HIS MANNERS AND MORALS, Brian Curtis. A comprehensive, non-technical survey of just about everything worth knowing about fish. Written for the aquarist, the angler, and the layman with an inquisitive mind, the text covers such topics as evolution, external covering and protective coloration, physics and physiology of vision, maintenance of equilibrium, function of the lateral line canal for auditory and temperature senses, nervous system, function of the air bladder, reproductive system and methods—courtship, mating, spawning, care of young—and many more. Also sections on game fish, the problems of conservation and a fascinating chapter on fish curiosities. "Clear, simple language . . . excellent judgment in choice of subjects . . . delightful sense of humor," New York Times. Revised (1949) edition. Index. Bibliography of 72 items. 6 full-page photographic plates. xii + 284pp. 5⅜ x 8.   T929 Paperbound **$1.50**

BATS, Glover Morrill Allen. The most comprehensive study of bats as a life-form by the world's foremost authority. A thorough summary of just about everything known about this fascinating and mysterious flying mammal, including its unique location sense, hibernation and cycles, its habitats and distribution, its wing structure and flying habits, and its relationship to man in the long history of folklore and superstition. Written on a middle-level, the book can be profitably studied by a trained zoologist and thoroughly enjoyed by the layman. "An absorbing text with excellent illustrations. Bats should have more friends and fewer thoughtless detractors as a result of the publication of this volume," William Beebe, Books. Extensive bibliography. 57 photographs and illustrations. x + 368pp. 5⅜ x 8½.
T984 Paperbound **$2.00**

BIRDS AND THEIR ATTRIBUTES, Glover Morrill Allen. A fine general introduction to birds as living organisms, especially valuable because of emphasis on structure, physiology, habits, behavior. Discusses relationship of bird to man, early attempts at scientific ornithology, feathers and coloration, skeletal structure including bills, legs and feet, wings. Also food habits, evolution and present distribution, feeding and nest-building, still unsolved questions of migrations and location sense, many more similar topics. Final chapter on classification, nomenclature. A good popular-level summary for the biologist; a first-rate introduction for the layman. Reprint of 1925 edition. References and index. 51 illustrations. viii + 338pp. 5⅜ x 8½.   T957 Paperbound **$1.85**

LIFE HISTORIES OF NORTH AMERICAN BIRDS, Arthur Cleveland Bent. Bent's monumental series of books on North American birds, prepared and published under auspices of Smithsonian Institute, is the definitive coverage of the subject, the most-used single source of information. Now the entire set is to be made available by Dover in inexpensive editions. This encyclopedic collection of detailed, specific observations utilizes reports of hundreds of contemporary observers, writings of such naturalists as Audubon, Burroughs, William Brewster, as well as author's own extensive investigations. Contains literally everything known about life history of each bird considered: nesting, eggs, plumage, distribution and migration, voice, enemies, courtship, etc. These not over-technical works are musts for ornithologists, conservationists, amateur naturalists, anyone seriously interested in American birds.

BIRDS OF PREY. More than 100 subspecies of hawks, falcons, eagles, buzzards, condors and owls, from the common barn owl to the extinct caracara of Guadaloupe Island. 400 photographs. Two volume set. Index for each volume. Bibliographies of 403, 520 items. 197 full-page plates. Total of 907pp. 5⅜ x 8½.   Vol. I T931 Paperbound **$2.50**
Vol. II T932 Paperbound **$2.50**

WILD FOWL. Ducks, geese, swans, and tree ducks—73 different subspecies. Two volume set. Index for each volume. Bibliographies of 124, 144 items. 106 full-page plates. Total of 685pp. 5⅜ x 8½.   Vol. I T285 Paperbound **$2.50**
Vol. II T286 Paperbound **$2.50**

SHORE BIRDS. 81 varieties (sandpipers, woodcocks, plovers, snipes, phalaropes, curlews, oyster catchers, etc.). More than 200 photographs of eggs, nesting sites, adult and young of important species. Two volume set. Index for each volume. Bibliographies of 261, 188 items. 121 full-page plates. Total of 860pp. 5⅜ x 8½.   Vol. I T933 Paperbound **$2.35**
Vol. II T934 Paperbound **$2.35**

THE LIFE OF PASTEUR, R. Vallery-Radot. 13th edition of this definitive biography, cited in Encyclopaedia Britannica. Authoritative, scholarly, well-documented with contemporary quotes, observations; gives complete picture of Pasteur's personal life; especially thorough presentation of scientific activities with silkworms, fermentation, hydrophobia, inoculation, etc. Introduction by Sir William Osler. Index. 505pp. 5⅜ x 8.   T632 Paperbound **$2.00**

Puzzles, Mathematical Recreations

SYMBOLIC LOGIC and THE GAME OF LOGIC, Lewis Carroll. "Symbolic Logic" is not concerned with modern symbolic logic, but is instead a collection of over 380 problems posed with charm and imagination, using the syllogism, and a fascinating diagrammatic method of drawing conclusions. In "The Game of Logic" Carroll's whimsical imagination devises a logical game played with 2 diagrams and counters (included) to manipulate hundreds of tricky syllogisms. The final section, "Hit or Miss" is a lagniappe of 101 additional puzzles in the delightful Carroll manner. Until this reprint edition, both of these books were rarities costing up to $15 each. Symbolic Logic: Index. xxxi + 199pp. The Game of Logic: 96pp. 2 vols. bound as one. 5⅜ x 8. **T492 Paperbound $1.50**

PILLOW PROBLEMS and A TANGLED TALE, Lewis Carroll. One of the rarest of all Carroll's works, "Pillow Problems" contains 72 original math puzzles, all typically ingenious. Particularly fascinating are Carroll's answers which remain exactly as he thought them out, reflecting his actual mental process. The problems in "A Tangled Tale" are in story form, originally appearing as a monthly magazine serial. Carroll not only gives the solutions, but uses answers sent in by readers to discuss wrong approaches and misleading paths, and grades them for insight. Both of these books were rarities until this edition, "Pillow Problems" costing up to $25, and "A Tangled Tale" $15. Pillow Problems: Preface and Introduction by Lewis Carroll. xx + 109pp. A Tangled Tale: 6 illustrations. 152pp. Two vols. bound as one. 5⅜ x 8. **T493 Paperbound $1.50**

AMUSEMENTS IN MATHEMATICS, Henry Ernest Dudeney. The foremost British originator of mathematical puzzles is always intriguing, witty, and paradoxical in this classic, one of the largest collections of mathematical amusements. More than 430 puzzles, problems, and paradoxes. Mazes and games, problems on number manipulation, unicursal and other route problems, puzzles on measuring, weighing, packing, age, kinship, chessboards, joiners', crossing river, plane figure dissection, and many others. Solutions. More than 450 illustrations. vii + 258pp. 5⅜ x 8. **T473 Paperbound $1.25**

THE CANTERBURY PUZZLES, Henry Dudeney. Chaucer's pilgrims set one another problems in story form. Also Adventures of the Puzzle Club, the Strange Escape of the King's Jester, the Monks of Riddlewell, the Squire's Christmas Puzzle Party, and others. All puzzles are original, based on dissecting plane figures, arithmetic, algebra, elementary calculus and other branches of mathematics, and purely logical ingenuity. "The limit of ingenuity and intricacy," The Observer. Over 110 puzzles. Full Solutions. 150 illustrations. vii + 225pp. 5⅜ x 8. **T474 Paperbound $1.25**

MATHEMATICAL EXCURSIONS, H. A. Merrill. Even if you hardly remember your high school math, you'll enjoy the 90 stimulating problems contained in this book and you will come to understand a great many mathematical principles with surprisingly little effort. Many useful shortcuts and diversions not generally known are included: division by inspection, Russian peasant multiplication, memory systems for pi, building odd and even magic squares, square roots by geometry, dyadic systems, and many more. Solutions to difficult problems. 50 illustrations. 145pp. 5⅜ x 8. **T350 Paperbound $1.00**

MAGIC SQUARES AND CUBES, W. S. Andrews. Only book-length treatment in English, a thorough non-technical description and analysis. Here are nasik, overlapping, pandiagonal, serrated squares; magic circles, cubes, spheres, rhombuses. Try your hand at 4-dimensional magical figures! Much unusual folklore and tradition included. High school algebra is sufficient. 754 diagrams and illustrations. viii + 419pp. 5⅜ x 8. **T658 Paperbound $1.85**

CALIBAN'S PROBLEM BOOK: MATHEMATICAL, INFERENTIAL AND CRYPTOGRAPHIC PUZZLES, H. Phillips (Caliban), S. T. Shovelton, G. S. Marshall. 105 ingenious problems by the greatest living creator of puzzles based on logic and inference. Rigorous, modern, piquant; reflecting their author's unusual personality, these intermediate and advanced puzzles all involve the ability to reason clearly through complex situations; some call for mathematical knowledge, ranging from algebra to number theory. Solutions. xi + 180pp. 5⅜ x 8. **T736 Paperbound $1.25**

MATHEMATICAL PUZZLES FOR BEGINNERS AND ENTHUSIASTS, G. Mott-Smith. 188 mathematical puzzles based on algebra, dissection of plane figures, permutations, and probability, that will test and improve your powers of inference and interpretation. The Odic Force, The Spider's Cousin, Ellipse Drawing, theory and strategy of card and board games like tit-tat-toe, go moku, salvo, and many others. 100 pages of detailed mathematical explanations. Appendix of primes, square roots, etc. 135 illustrations. 2nd revised edition. 248pp. 5⅜ x 8. **T198 Paperbound $1.00**

MATHEMAGIC, MAGIC PUZZLES, AND GAMES WITH NUMBERS, R. V. Heath. More than 60 new puzzles and stunts based on the properties of numbers. Easy techniques for multiplying large numbers mentally, revealing hidden numbers magically, finding the date of any day in any year, and dozens more. Over 30 pages devoted to magic squares, triangles, cubes, circles, etc. Edited by J. S. Meyer. 76 illustrations. 128pp. 5⅜ x 8. **T110 Paperbound $1.00**

CATALOGUE OF DOVER BOOKS

THE BOOK OF MODERN PUZZLES, G. L. Kaufman. A completely new series of puzzles as fascinating as crossword and deduction puzzles but based upon different principles and techniques. Simple 2-minute teasers, word labyrinths, design and pattern puzzles, logic and observation puzzles — over 150 braincrackers. Answers to all problems. 116 illustrations. 192pp. 5⅜ x 8.
T143 Paperbound **$1.00**

NEW WORD PUZZLES, G. L. Kaufman. 100 ENTIRELY NEW puzzles based on words and their combinations that will delight crossword puzzle, Scrabble and Jotto fans. Chess words, based on the moves of the chess king; design-onyms, symmetrical designs made of synonyms; rhymed double-crostics; syllable sentences; addle letter anagrams; alphagrams; linkograms; and many others all brand new. Full solutions. Space to work problems. 196 figures. vi + 122pp. 5⅜ x 8.
T344 Paperbound **$1.00**

MAZES AND LABYRINTHS: A BOOK OF PUZZLES, W. Shepherd. Mazes, formerly associated with mystery and ritual, are still among the most intriguing of intellectual puzzles. This is a novel and different collection of 50 amusements that embody the principle of the maze: mazes in the classical tradition; 3-dimensional, ribbon, and Möbius-strip mazes; hidden messages; spatial arrangements; etc.—almost all built on amusing story situations. 84 illustrations. Essay on maze psychology. Solutions. xv + 122pp. 5⅜ x 8.
T731 Paperbound **$1.00**

MAGIC TRICKS & CARD TRICKS, W. Jonson. Two books bound as one. 52 tricks with cards, 37 tricks with coins, bills, eggs, smoke, ribbons, slates, etc. Details on presentation, misdirection, and routining will help you master such famous tricks as the Changing Card, Card in the Pocket, Four Aces, Coin Through the Hand, Bill in the Egg, Afghan Bands, and over 75 others. If you follow the lucid exposition and key diagrams carefully, you will finish these two books with an astonishing mastery of magic. 106 figures. 224pp. 5⅜ x 8. T909 Paperbound **$1.00**

PANORAMA OF MAGIC, Milbourne Christopher. A profusely illustrated history of stage magic, a unique selection of prints and engravings from the author's private collection of magic memorabilia, the largest of its kind. Apparatus, stage settings and costumes; ingenious ads distributed by the performers and satiric broadsides passed around in the streets ridiculing pompous showmen; programs; decorative souvenirs. The lively text, by one of America's foremost professional magicians, is full of anecdotes about almost legendary wizards: Dede, the Egyptian; Philadelphia, the wonder-worker; Robert-Houdin, "the father of modern magic;" Harry Houdini; scores more. Altogether a pleasure package for anyone interested in magic, stage setting and design, ethnology, psychology, or simply in unusual people. A Dover original. 295 illustrations; 8 in full color. Index. viii + 216pp. 8⅜ x 11¼.
T774 Paperbound **$2.25**

HOUDINI ON MAGIC, Harry Houdini. One of the greatest magicians of modern times explains his most prized secrets. How locks are picked, with illustrated picks and skeleton keys; how a girl is sawed into twins; how to walk through a brick wall — Houdini's explanations of 44 stage tricks with many diagrams. Also included is a fascinating discussion of great magicians of the past and the story of his fight against fraudulent mediums and spiritualists. Edited by W.B. Gibson and M.N. Young. Bibliography. 155 figures, photos. xv + 280pp. 5⅜ x 8.
T384 Paperbound **$1.25**

MATHEMATICS, MAGIC AND MYSTERY, Martin Gardner. Why do card tricks work? How do magicians perform astonishing mathematical feats? How is stage mind-reading possible? This is the first book length study explaining the application of probability, set theory, theory of numbers, topology, etc., to achieve many startling tricks. Non-technical, accurate, detailed! 115 sections discuss tricks with cards, dice, coins, knots, geometrical vanishing illusions, how a Curry square "demonstrates" that the sum of the parts may be greater than the whole, and dozens of others. No sleight of hand necessary! 135 illustrations. xii + 174pp. 5⅜ x 8.
T335 Paperbound **$1.00**

EASY-TO-DO ENTERTAINMENTS AND DIVERSIONS WITH COINS, CARDS, STRING, PAPER AND MATCHES, R. M. Abraham. Over 300 tricks, games and puzzles will provide young readers with absorbing fun. Sections on card games; paper-folding; tricks with coins, matches and pieces of string; games for the agile; toy-making from common household objects; mathematical recreations; and 50 miscellaneous pastimes. Anyone in charge of groups of youngsters, including hard-pressed parents, and in need of suggestions on how to keep children sensibly amused and quietly content will find this book indispensable. Clear, simple text, copious number of delightful line drawings and illustrative diagrams. Originally titled "Winter Nights Entertainments." Introduction by Lord Baden Powell. 329 illustrations. v + 186pp. 5⅜ x 8½.
T921 Paperbound **$1.00**

STRING FIGURES AND HOW TO MAKE THEM, Caroline Furness Jayne. 107 string figures plus variations selected from the best primitive and modern examples developed by Navajo, Apache, pygmies of Africa, Eskimo, in Europe, Australia, China, etc. The most readily understandable, easy-to-follow book in English on perennially popular recreation. Crystal-clear exposition; step-by-step diagrams. Everyone from kindergarten children to adults looking for unusual diversion will be endlessly amused. Index. Bibliography. Introduction by A. C. Haddon. 17 full-page plates. 960 illustrations. xxiii + 401pp. 5⅜ x 8½.
T152 Paperbound **$2.00**

Entertainments, Humor

ODDITIES AND CURIOSITIES OF WORDS AND LITERATURE, C. Bombaugh, edited by M. Gardner. The largest collection of idiosyncratic prose and poetry techniques in English, a legendary work in the curious and amusing bypaths of literary recreations and the play technique in literature—so important in modern works. Contains alphabetic poetry, acrostics, palindromes, scissors verse, centos, emblematic poetry, famous literary puns, hoaxes, notorious slips of the press, hilarious mistranslations, and much more. Revised and enlarged with modern material by Martin Gardner. 368pp. 5⅜ x 8. T759 Paperbound **$1.50**

A NONSENSE ANTHOLOGY, collected by Carolyn Wells. 245 of the best nonsense verses ever written, including nonsense puns, absurd arguments, mock epics and sagas, nonsense ballads, odes, "sick" verses, dog-Latin verses, French nonsense verses, songs. By Edward Lear, Lewis Carroll, Gelett Burgess, W. S. Gilbert, Hilaire Belloc, Peter Newell, Oliver Herford, etc., 83 writers in all plus over four score anonymous nonsense verses. A special section of limericks, plus famous nonsense such as Carroll's "Jabberwocky" and Lear's "The Jumblies" and much excellent verse virtually impossible to locate elsewhere. For 50 years considered the best anthology available. Index of first lines specially prepared for this edition. Introduction by Carolyn Wells. 3 indexes: Title, Author, First lines. xxxiii + 279pp.
T499 Paperbound **$1.35**

THE BAD CHILD'S BOOK OF BEASTS, MORE BEASTS FOR WORSE CHILDREN, and A MORAL ALPHABET, H. Belloc. Hardly an anthology of humorous verse has appeared in the last 50 years without at least a couple of these famous nonsense verses. But one must see the entire volumes—with all the delightful original illustrations by Sir Basil Blackwood—to appreciate fully Belloc's charming and witty verses that play so subacidly on the platitudes of life and morals that beset his day—and ours. A great humor classic. Three books in one. Total of 157pp. 5⅜ x 8. T749 Paperbound **$1.00**

THE DEVIL'S DICTIONARY, Ambrose Bierce. Sardonic and irreverent barbs puncturing the pomposities and absurdities of American politics, business, religion, literature, and arts, by the country's greatest satirist in the classic tradition. Epigrammatic as Shaw, piercing as Swift, American as Mark Twain, Will Rogers, and Fred Allen, Bierce will always remain the favorite of a small coterie of enthusiasts, and of writers and speakers whom he supplies with "some of the most gorgeous witticisms of the English language" (H. L. Mencken). Over 1000 entries in alphabetical order. 144pp. 5⅜ x 8. T487 Paperbound **$1.00**

THE PURPLE COW AND OTHER NONSENSE, Gelett Burgess. The best of Burgess's early nonsense, selected from the first edition of the "Burgess Nonsense Book." Contains many of his most unusual and truly awe-inspiring pieces: 36 nonsense quatrains, the Poems of Patagonia, Alphabet of Famous Goops, and the other hilarious (and rare) adult nonsense that place him in the forefront of American humorists. All pieces are accompanied by the original Burgess illustrations. 123 illustrations. xiii + 113pp. 5⅜ x 8. T772 Paperbound **$1.00**

MY PIOUS FRIENDS AND DRUNKEN COMPANIONS and MORE PIOUS FRIENDS AND DRUNKEN COMPANIONS, Frank Shay. Folksingers, amateur and professional, and everyone who loves singing: here, available for the first time in 30 years, is this valued collection of 132 ballads, blues, vaudeville numbers, drinking songs, sea chanties, comedy songs. Songs of pre-Beatnik Bohemia; songs from all over America, England, France, Australia; the great songs of the Naughty Nineties and early twentieth-century America. Over a third with music. Woodcuts by John Held, Jr. convey perfectly the brash insouciance of an era of rollicking unabashed song. 12 illustrations by John Held, Jr. Two indexes (Titles and First lines and Choruses). Introductions by the author. Two volumes bound as one. Total of xvi + 235pp. 5⅜ x 8½.
T946 Paperbound **$1.00**

HOW TO TELL THE BIRDS FROM THE FLOWERS, R. W. Wood. How not to confuse a carrot with a parrot, a grape with an ape, a puffin with nuffin. Delightful drawings, clever puns, absurd little poems point out far-fetched resemblances in nature. The author was a leading physicist. Introduction by Margaret Wood White. 106 illus. 60pp. 5⅜ x 8.
T523 Paperbound **75¢**

PECK'S BAD BOY AND HIS PA, George W. Peck. The complete edition, containing both volumes, of one of the most widely read American humor books. The endless ingenious pranks played by bad boy "Hennery" on his pa and the grocery man, the outraged pomposity of Pa, the perpetual ridiculing of middle class institutions, are as entertaining today as they were in 1883. No pale sophistications or subtleties, but rather humor vigorous, raw, earthy, imaginative, and, as folk humor often is, sadistic. This peculiarly fascinating book is also valuable to historians and students of American culture as a portrait of an age. 100 original illustrations by True Williams. Introduction by E. F. Bleiler. 347pp. 5⅜ x 8.
T497 Paperbound **$1.35**

CATALOGUE OF DOVER BOOKS

THE HUMOROUS VERSE OF LEWIS CARROLL. Almost every poem Carroll ever wrote, the largest collection ever published, including much never published elsewhere: 150 parodies, burlesques, riddles, ballads, acrostics, etc., with 130 original illustrations by Tenniel, Carroll, and others. "Addicts will be grateful . . . there is nothing for the faithful to do but sit down and fall to the banquet," N. Y. Times. Index to first lines. xiv + 446pp. 5⅜ x 8.
T654 Paperbound **$1.85**

DIVERSIONS AND DIGRESSIONS OF LEWIS CARROLL. A major new treasure for Carroll fans! Rare privately published humor, fantasy, puzzles, and games by Carroll at his whimsical best, with a new vein of frank satire. Includes many new mathematical amusements and recreations, among them the fragmentary Part III of "Curiosa Mathematica." Contains "The Rectory Umbrella," "The New Belfry," "The Vision of the Three T's," and much more. New 32-page supplement of rare photographs taken by Carroll. x + 375pp. 5⅜ x 8.
T732 Paperbound **$1.65**

THE COMPLETE NONSENSE OF EDWARD LEAR. This is the only complete edition of this master of gentle madness available at a popular price. A BOOK OF NONSENSE, NONSENSE SONGS, MORE NONSENSE SONGS AND STORIES in their entirety with all the old favorites that have delighted children and adults for years. The Dong With A Luminous Nose, The Jumblies, The Owl and the Pussycat, and hundreds of other bits of wonderful nonsense. 214 limericks, 3 sets of Nonsense Botany, 5 Nonsense Alphabets, 546 drawings by Lear himself, and much more. 320pp. 5⅜ x 8.
T167 Paperbound **$1.00**

THE MELANCHOLY LUTE, The Humorous Verse of Franklin P. Adams ("FPA"). The author's own selection of light verse, drawn from thirty years of FPA's column, "The Conning Tower," syndicated all over the English-speaking world. Witty, perceptive, literate, these ninety-six poems range from parodies of other poets, Millay, Longfellow, Edgar Guest, Kipling, Masefield, etc., and free and hilarious translations of Horace and other Latin poets, to satiric comments on fabled American institutions—the New York Subways, preposterous ads, suburbanites, sensational journalism, etc. They reveal with vigor and clarity the humor, integrity and restraint of a wise and gentle American satirist. Introduction by Robert Hutchinson. vi + 122pp. 5⅜ x 8½.
T108 Paperbound **$1.00**

SINGULAR TRAVELS, CAMPAIGNS, AND ADVENTURES OF BARON MUNCHAUSEN, R. E. Raspe, with 90 illustrations by Gustave Doré. The first edition in over 150 years to reestablish the deeds of the Prince of Liars exactly as Raspe first recorded them in 1785—the genuine Baron Munchausen, one of the most popular personalities in English literature. Included also are the best of the many sequels, written by other hands. Introduction on Raspe by J. Carswell. Bibliography of early editions. xliv + 192pp. 5⅜ x 8.
T698 Paperbound **$1.00**

THE WIT AND HUMOR OF OSCAR WILDE, ed. by Alvin Redman. Wilde at his most brilliant, in 1000 epigrams exposing weaknesses and hypocrisies of "civilized" society. Divided into 49 categories—sin, wealth, women, America, etc.—to aid writers, speakers. Includes excerpts from his trials, books, plays, criticism. Formerly "The Epigrams of Oscar Wilde." Introduction by Vyvyan Holland, Wilde's only living son. Introductory essay by editor. 260pp. 5⅜ x 8.
T602 Paperbound **$1.00**

MAX AND MORITZ, Wilhelm Busch. Busch is one of the great humorists of all time, as well as the father of the modern comic strip. This volume, translated by H. A. Klein and other hands, contains the perennial favorite "Max and Moritz" (translated by C. T. Brooks), Plisch and Plum, Das Rabennest, Eispeter, and seven other whimsical, sardonic, jovial, diabolical cartoon and verse stories. Lively English translations parallel the original German. This work has delighted millions, since it first appeared in the 19th century, and is guaranteed to please almost anyone. Edited by H. A. Klein, with an afterword. x + 205pp. 5⅝ x 8½.
T181 Paperbound **$1.00**

HYPOCRITICAL HELENA, Wilhelm Busch. A companion volume to "Max and Moritz," with the title piece (Die Fromme Helena) and 10 other highly amusing cartoon and verse stories, all newly translated by H. A. Klein and M. C. Klein: Adventure on New Year's Eve (Abenteuer in der Neujahrsnacht), Hangover on the Morning after New Year's Eve (Der Katzenjammer am Neujahrsmorgen), etc. English and German in parallel columns. Hours of pleasure, also a fine language aid. x + 205pp. 5⅝ x 8½.
T184 Paperbound **$1.00**

THE BEAR THAT WASN'T, Frank Tashlin. What does it mean? Is it simply delightful wry humor, or a charming story of a bear who wakes up in the midst of a factory, or a satire on Big Business, or an existential cartoon-story of the human condition, or a symbolization of the struggle between conformity and the individual? New York Herald Tribune said of the first edition: ". . . a fable for grownups that will be fun for children. Sit down with the book and get your own bearings." Long an underground favorite with readers of all ages and opinions. v + 51pp. Illustrated. 5⅜ x 8½.
T939 Paperbound **75¢**

RUTHLESS RHYMES FOR HEARTLESS HOMES and MORE RUTHLESS RHYMES FOR HEARTLESS HOMES, Harry Graham ("Col. D. Streamer"). Two volumes of Little Willy and 48 other poetic disasters. A bright, new reprint of oft-quoted, never forgotten, devastating humor by a precursor of today's "sick" joke school. For connoisseurs of wicked, wacky humor and all who delight in the comedy of manners. Original drawings are a perfect complement. 61 illustrations. Index. vi + 69pp. Two vols. bound as one. 5⅜ x 8½.
T930 Paperbound **75¢**

CATALOGUE OF DOVER BOOKS

Say It language phrase books

These handy phrase books (128 to 196 pages each) make grammatical drills unnecessary for an elementary knowledge of a spoken foreign language. Covering most matters of travel and everyday life each volume contains:

> Over 1000 phrases and sentences in immediately useful forms — foreign language plus English.
>
> Modern usage designed for Americans. Specific phrases like, "Give me small change," and "Please call a taxi."
>
> Simplified phonetic transcription you will be able to read at sight.
>
> The only completely indexed phrase books on the market.
>
> Covers scores of important situations: — Greetings, restaurants, sightseeing, useful expressions, etc.

These books are prepared by native linguists who are professors at Columbia, N.Y.U., Fordham and other great universities. Use them independently or with any other book or record course. They provide a supplementary living element that most other courses lack. Individual volumes in:

Russian 75¢	Italian 75¢	Spanish 75¢	German 75¢
Hebrew 75¢	Danish 75¢	Japanese 75¢	Swedish 75¢
Dutch 75¢	Esperanto 75¢	Modern Greek 75¢	Portuguese 75¢
Norwegian 75¢	Polish 75¢	French 75¢	Yiddish 75¢
Turkish 75¢		English for German-speaking people 75¢	
English for Italian-speaking people 75¢		English for Spanish-speaking people 75¢	

Large clear type. 128-196 pages each. 3½ x 5¼. Sturdy paper binding.

Listen and Learn language records

LISTEN & LEARN is the only language record course designed especially to meet your travel and everyday needs. It is available in separate sets for FRENCH, SPANISH, GERMAN, JAPANESE, RUSSIAN, MODERN GREEK, PORTUGUESE, ITALIAN and HEBREW, and each set contains three 33⅓ rpm long-playing records—1½ hours of recorded speech by eminent native speakers who are professors at Columbia, New York University, Queens College.

Check the following special features found only in LISTEN & LEARN:

- **Dual-language recording. 812 selected phrases and sentences, over 3200 words,** spoken first in English, then in their foreign language equivalents. A suitable pause follows each foreign phrase, allowing you time to repeat the expression. You learn by unconscious assimilation.
- **128 to 206-page manual** contains everything on the records, plus a simple phonetic pronunciation guide.
- **Indexed for convenience. The only set on the market** that is completely indexed. No more puzzling over where to find the phrase you need. Just look in the rear of the manual.
- **Practical.** No time wasted on material you can find in any grammar. LISTEN & LEARN covers central core material with phrase approach. Ideal for the person with limited learning time.
- **Living, modern expressions,** not found in other courses. Hygienic products, modern equipment, shopping—expressions used every day, like "nylon" and "air-conditioned."
- **Limited objective.** Everything you learn, no matter where you stop, is immediately useful. You have to finish other courses, wade through grammar and vocabulary drill, before they help you.
- **High-fidelity recording.** LISTEN & LEARN records equal in clarity and surface-silence any record on the market costing up to $6.

"Excellent . . . the spoken records . . . impress me as being among the very best on the market," **Prof. Mario Pei,** Dept. of Romance Languages, Columbia University. "Inexpensive and well-done . . . it would make an ideal present," CHICAGO SUNDAY TRIBUNE. "More genuinely helpful than anything of its kind which I have previously encountered," **Sidney Clark,** well-known author of "ALL THE BEST" travel books.

UNCONDITIONAL GUARANTEE. Try LISTEN & LEARN, then return it within 10 days for full refund if you are not satisfied.

Each set contains three twelve-inch 33⅓ records, manual, and album.

SPANISH	the set $5.95	GERMAN	the set $5.95
FRENCH	the set $5.95	ITALIAN	the set $5.95
RUSSIAN	the set $5.95	JAPANESE	the set $5.95
PORTUGUESE	the set $5.95	MODERN GREEK	the set $5.95
MODERN HEBREW	the set $5.95		

Americana

THE EYES OF DISCOVERY, J. Bakeless. A vivid reconstruction of how unspoiled America appeared to the first white men. Authentic and enlightening accounts of Hudson's landing in New York, Coronado's trek through the Southwest; scores of explorers, settlers, trappers, soldiers. America's pristine flora, fauna, and Indians in every region and state in fresh and unusual new aspects. "A fascinating view of what the land was like before the first highway went through," Time. 68 contemporary illustrations, 39 newly added in this edition. Index. Bibliography. x + 500pp. 5⅜ x 8.
T761 Paperbound **$2.00**

AUDUBON AND HIS JOURNALS, J. J. Audubon. A collection of fascinating accounts of Europe and America in the early 1800's through Audubon's own eyes. Includes the Missouri River Journals —an eventful trip through America's untouched heartland, the Labrador Journals, the European Journals, the famous "Episodes", and other rare Audubon material, including the descriptive chapters from the original letterpress edition of the "Ornithological Studies", omitted in all later editions. Indispensable for ornithologists, naturalists, and all lovers of Americana and adventure. 70-page biography by Audubon's granddaughter. 38 illustrations. Index. Total of 1106pp. 5⅜ x 8.
T675 Vol I Paperbound **$2.25**
T676 Vol II Paperbound **$2.25**
The set **$4.50**

TRAVELS OF WILLIAM BARTRAM, edited by Mark Van Doren. The first inexpensive illustrated edition of one of the 18th century's most delightful books is an excellent source of first-hand material on American geography, anthropology, and natural history. Many descriptions of early Indian tribes are our only source of information on them prior to the infiltration of the white man. "The mind of a scientist with the soul of a poet," John Livingston Lowes. 13 original illustrations and maps. Edited with an introduction by Mark Van Doren. 448pp. 5⅜ x 8.
T13 Paperbound **$2.00**

GARRETS AND PRETENDERS: A HISTORY OF BOHEMIANISM IN AMERICA, A. Parry. The colorful and fantastic history of American Bohemianism from Poe to Kerouac. This is the only complete record of hoboes, cranks, starving poets, and suicides. Here are Pfaff, Whitman, Crane, Bierce, Pound, and many others. New chapters by the author and by H. T. Moore bring this thorough and well-documented history down to the Beatniks. "An excellent account," N. Y. Times. Scores of cartoons, drawings, and caricatures. Bibliography. Index. xxviii + 421pp. 5⅝ x 8⅜.
T708 Paperbound **$1.95**

THE EXPLORATION OF THE COLORADO RIVER AND ITS CANYONS, J. W. Powell. The thrilling first-hand account of the expedition that filled in the last white space on the map of the United States. Rapids, famine, hostile Indians, and mutiny are among the perils encountered as the unknown Colorado Valley reveals its secrets. This is the only uncut version of Major Powell's classic of exploration that has been printed in the last 60 years. Includes later reflections and subsequent expedition. 250 illustrations, new map. 400pp. 5⅝ x 8⅜.
T94 Paperbound **$2.00**

THE JOURNAL OF HENRY D. THOREAU, Edited by Bradford Torrey and Francis H. Allen. Henry Thoreau is not only one of the most important figures in American literature and social thought; his voluminous journals (from which his books emerged as selections and crystallizations) constitute both the longest, most sensitive record of personal internal development and a most penetrating description of a historical moment in American culture. This present set, which was first issued in fourteen volumes, contains Thoreau's entire journals from 1837 to 1862, with the exception of the lost years which were found only recently. We are reissuing it, complete and unabridged, with a new introduction by Walter Harding, Secretary of the Thoreau Society. Fourteen volumes reissued in two volumes. Foreword by Henry Seidel Canby. Total of 1888pp. 8⅜ x 12¼.
T312-3 Two volume set, Clothbound **$20.00**

GAMES AND SONGS OF AMERICAN CHILDREN, collected by William Wells Newell. A remarkable collection of 190 games with songs that accompany many of them; cross references to show similarities, differences among them; variations; musical notation for 38 songs. Textual discussions show relations with folk-drama and other aspects of folk tradition. Grouped into categories for ready comparative study: Love-games, histories, playing at work, human life, bird and beast, mythology, guessing-games, etc. New introduction covers relations of songs and dances to timeless heritage of folklore, biographical sketch of Newell, other pertinent data. A good source of inspiration for those in charge of groups of children and a valuable reference for anthropologists, sociologists, psychiatrists. Introduction by Carl Withers. New indexes of first lines, games. 5⅜ x 8½. xii + 242pp.
T354 Paperbound **$1.75**

Art, History of Art, Antiques, Graphic Arts, Handcrafts

ART STUDENTS' ANATOMY, E. J. Farris. Outstanding art anatomy that uses chiefly living objects for its illustrations. 71 photos of undraped men, women, children are accompanied by carefully labeled matching sketches to illustrate the skeletal system, articulations and movements, bony landmarks, the muscular system, skin, fasciae, fat, etc. 9 x-ray photos show movement of joints. Undraped models are shown in such actions as serving in tennis, drawing a bow in archery, playing football, dancing, preparing to spring and to dive. Also discussed and illustrated are proportions, age and sex differences, the anatomy of the smile, etc. 8 plates by the great early 18th century anatomic illustrator Siegfried Albinus are also included. Glossary. 158 figures, 7 in color. x + 159pp. 5⅝ x 8⅜.   T744 Paperbound **$1.50**

AN ATLAS OF ANATOMY FOR ARTISTS, F Schider. A new 3rd edition of this standard text enlarged by 52 new illustrations of hands, anatomical studies by Cloquet, and expressive life studies of the body by Barcsay. 189 clear, detailed plates offer you precise information of impeccable accuracy. 29 plates show all aspects of the skeleton, with closeups of special areas, while 54 full-page plates, mostly in two colors, give human musculature as seen from four different points of view, with cutaways for important portions of the body. 14 full-page plates provide photographs of hand forms, eyelids, female breasts, and indicate the location of muscles upon models. 59 additional plates show how great artists of the past utilized human anatomy. They reproduce sketches and finished work by such artists as Michelangelo, Leonardo da Vinci, Goya, and 15 others. This is a lifetime reference work which will be one of the most important books in any artist's library. "The standard reference tool," AMERICAN LIBRARY ASSOCIATION. "Excellent," AMERICAN ARTIST. Third enlarged edition. 189 plates, 647 illustrations. xxvi + 192pp. 7⅞ x 10⅝.   T241 Clothbound **$6.00**

AN ATLAS OF ANIMAL ANATOMY FOR ARTISTS, W. Ellenberger, H. Baum, H. Dittrich. The largest, richest animal anatomy for artists available in English. 99 detailed anatomical plates of such animals as the horse, dog, cat, lion, deer, seal, kangaroo, flying squirrel, cow, bull, goat, monkey, hare, and bat. Surface features are clearly indicated, while progressive beneath-the-skin pictures show musculature, tendons, and bone structure. Rest and action are exhibited in terms of musculature and skeletal structure and detailed cross-sections are given for heads and important features. The animals chosen are representative of specific families so that a study of these anatomies will provide knowledge of hundreds of related species. "Highly recommended as one of the very few books on the subject worthy of being used as an authoritative guide," DESIGN. "Gives a fundamental knowledge," AMERICAN ARTIST. Second revised, enlarged edition with new plates from Cuvier, Stubbs, etc. 288 illustrations. 153pp. 11⅜ x 9.   T82 Clothbound **$6.00**

THE HUMAN FIGURE IN MOTION, Eadweard Muybridge. The largest selection in print of Muybridge's famous high-speed action photos of the human figure in motion. 4789 photographs illustrate 162 different actions: men, women, children—mostly undraped—are shown walking, running, carrying various objects, sitting, lying down, climbing, throwing, arising, and performing over 150 other actions. Some actions are shown in as many as 150 photographs each. All in all there are more than 500 action strips in this enormous volume, series shots taken at shutter speeds of as high as 1/6000th of a second! These are not posed shots, but true stopped motion. They show bone and muscle in situations that the human eye is not fast enough to capture. Earlier, smaller editions of these prints have brought $40 and more on the out-of-print market. "A must for artists," ART IN FOCUS. "An unparalleled dictionary of action for all artists," AMERICAN ARTIST. 390 full-page plates, with 4789 photographs. Printed on heavy glossy stock. Reinforced binding with headbands. xxi + 390pp. 7⅞ x 10⅝.
T204 Clothbound **$10.00**

ANIMALS IN MOTION, Eadweard Muybridge. This is the largest collection of animal action photos in print. 34 different animals (horses, mules, oxen, goats, camels, pigs, cats, guanacos, lions, gnus, deer, monkeys, eagles—and 21 others) in 132 characteristic actions. The horse alone is shown in more than 40 different actions. All 3919 photographs are taken in series at speeds up to 1/6000th of a second. The secrets of leg motion, spinal patterns, head movements, strains and contortions shown nowhere else are captured. You will see exactly how a lion sets his foot down; how an elephant's knees are like a human's—and how they differ; the position of a kangaroo's legs in mid-leap; how an ostrich's head bobs; details of the flight of birds—and thousands of facets of motion only the fastest cameras can catch. Photographed from domestic animals and animals in the Philadelphia zoo, it contains neither semiposed artificial shots nor distorted telephoto shots taken under adverse conditions. Artists, biologists, decorators, cartoonists, will find this book indispensable for understanding animals in motion. "A really marvelous series of plates," NATURE (London). "The dry plate's most spectacular early use was by Eadweard Muybridge," LIFE. 3919 photographs, 380 full pages of plates. 440pp. Printed on heavy glossy paper. Deluxe binding with headbands. 7⅞ x 10⅝.   T203 Clothbound **$10.00**

CATALOGUE OF DOVER BOOKS

THE AUTOBIOGRAPHY OF AN IDEA, Louis Sullivan. The pioneer architect whom Frank Lloyd Wright called "the master" reveals an acute sensitivity to social forces and values in this passionately honest account. He records the crystallization of his opinions and theories, the growth of his organic theory of architecture that still influences American designers and architects, contemporary ideas, etc. This volume contains the first appearance of 34 full-page plates of his finest architecture. Unabridged reissue of 1924 edition. New introduction by R. M. Line. Index. xiv + 335pp. 5⅜ x 8.   T281 Paperbound **$2.00**

THE DRAWINGS OF HEINRICH KLEY. The first uncut republication of both of Kley's devastating sketchbooks, which first appeared in pre-World War I Germany. One of the greatest cartoonists and social satirists of modern times, his exuberant and iconoclastic fantasy and his extraordinary technique place him in the great tradition of Bosch, Breughel, and Goya, while his subject matter has all the immediacy and tension of our century. 200 drawings. viii + 128pp. 7¾ x 10¾.   T24 Paperbound **$1.85**

MORE DRAWINGS BY HEINRICH KLEY. All the sketches from Leut' Und Viecher (1912) and Sammel-Album (1923) not included in the previous Dover edition of Drawings. More of the bizarre, mercilessly iconoclastic sketches that shocked and amused on their original publication. Nothing was too sacred, no one too eminent for satirization by this imaginative, individual and accomplished master cartoonist. A total of 158 illustrations. lv + 104pp. 7¾ x 10¾.   T41 Paperbound **$1.85**

PINE FURNITURE OF EARLY NEW ENGLAND, R. H. Kettell. A rich understanding of one of America's most original folk arts that collectors of antiques, interior decorators, craftsmen, woodworkers, and everyone interested in American history and art will find fascinating and immensely useful. 413 illustrations of more than 300 chairs, benches, racks, beds, cupboards, mirrors, shelves, tables, and other furniture will show all the simple beauty and character of early New England furniture. 55 detailed drawings carefully analyze outstanding pieces. "With its rich store of illustrations, this book emphasizes the individuality and varied design of early American pine furniture. It should be welcomed," ANTIQUES. 413 illustrations and 55 working drawings. 475. 8 x 10¾.   T145 Clothbound **$10.00**

THE HUMAN FIGURE, J. H. Vanderpoel. Every important artistic element of the human figure is pointed out in minutely detailed word descriptions in this classic text and illustrated as well in 430 pencil and charcoal drawings. Thus the text of this book directs your attention to all the characteristic features and subtle differences of the male and female (adults, children, and aged persons), as though a master artist were telling you what to look for at each stage. 2nd edition, revised and enlarged by George Bridgman. Foreword. 430 illustrations. 143pp. 6⅛ x 9¼.   T432 Paperbound **$1.50**

LETTERING AND ALPHABETS, J. A. Cavanagh. This unabridged reissue of LETTERING offers a full discussion, analysis, illustration of 89 basic hand lettering styles — styles derived from Caslons, Bodonis, Garamonds, Gothic, Black Letter, Oriental, and many others. Upper and lower cases, numerals and common signs pictured. Hundreds of technical hints on make-up, construction, artistic validity, strokes, pens, brushes, white areas, etc. May be reproduced without permission! 89 complete alphabets; 72 lettered specimens. 121pp. 9¾ x 8.   T53 Paperbound **$1.25**

STICKS AND STONES, Lewis Mumford. A survey of the forces that have conditioned American architecture and altered its forms. The author discusses the medieval tradition in early New England villages; the Renaissance influence which developed with the rise of the merchant class; the classical influence of Jefferson's time; the "Mechanicsvilles" of Poe's generation; the Brown Decades; the philosophy of the Imperial facade; and finally the modern machine age. "A truly remarkable book," SAT. REV. OF LITERATURE. 2nd revised edition. 21 illustrations. xvii + 228pp. 5⅜ x 8.   T202 Paperbound **$1.60**

THE STANDARD BOOK OF QUILT MAKING AND COLLECTING, Marguerite Ickis. A complete easy-to-follow guide with all the information you need to make beautiful, useful quilts. How to plan, design, cut, sew, appliqué, avoid sewing problems, use rag bag, make borders, tuft, every other aspect. Over 100 traditional quilts shown, including over 40 full-size patterns. At-home hobby for fun, profit. Index. 483 illus. 1 color plate. 287pp. 6¾ x 9½.   T582 Paperbound **$2.00**

THE BOOK OF SIGNS, Rudolf Koch. Formerly $20 to $25 on the out-of-print market, now only $1.00 in this unabridged new edition! 493 symbols from ancient manuscripts, medieval cathedrals, coins, catacombs, pottery, etc. Crosses, monograms of Roman emperors, astrological, chemical, botanical, runes, housemarks, and 7 other categories. Invaluable for handicraft workers, illustrators, scholars, etc., this material may be reproduced without permission. 493 illustrations by Fritz Kredel. 104pp. 6½ x 9¼.   T162 Paperbound **$1.00**

PRIMITIVE ART, Franz Boas. This authoritative and exhaustive work by a great American anthropologist covers the entire gamut of primitive art. Pottery, leatherwork, metal work, stone work, wood, basketry, are treated in detail. Theories of primitive art, historical depth in art history, technical virtuosity, unconscious levels of patterning, symbolism, styles, literature, music, dance, etc. A must book for the interested layman, the anthropologist, artist, handicrafter (hundreds of unusual motifs), and the historian. Over 900 illustrations (50 ceramic vessels, 12 totem poles, etc.). 376pp. 5⅜ x 8.   T25 Paperbound **$2.00**

Fiction

FLATLAND, E. A. Abbott. A science-fiction classic of life in a 2-dimensional world that is also a first-rate introduction to such aspects of modern science as relativity and hyperspace. Political, moral, satirical, and humorous overtones have made FLATLAND fascinating reading for thousands. 7th edition. New introduction by Banesh Hoffmann. 16 illustrations. 128pp. 5⅜ x 8. T1 Paperbound **$1.00**

THE WONDERFUL WIZARD OF OZ, L. F. Baum. Only edition in print with all the original W. W. Denslow illustrations in full color—as much a part of "The Wizard" as Tenniel's drawings are of "Alice in Wonderland." "The Wizard" is still America's best-loved fairy tale, in which, as the author expresses it, "The wonderment and joy are retained and the heartaches and nightmares left out." Now today's young readers can enjoy every word and wonderful picture of the original book. New introduction by Martin Gardner. A Baum bibliography. 23 full-page color plates. viii + 268pp. 5⅜ x 8. T691 Paperbound **$1.45**

THE MARVELOUS LAND OF OZ, L. F. Baum. This is the equally enchanting sequel to the "Wizard," continuing the adventures of the Scarecrow and the Tin Woodman. The hero this time is a little boy named Tip, and all the delightful Oz magic is still present. This is the Oz book with the Animated Saw-Horse, the Woggle-Bug, and Jack Pumpkinhead. All the original John R. Neill illustrations, 10 in full color. 287 pp. 5⅜ x 8. T692 Paperbound **$1.45**

FIVE GREAT DOG NOVELS, edited by Blanche Cirker. The complete original texts of five classic dog novels that have delighted and thrilled millions of children and adults throughout the world with their stories of loyalty, adventure, and courage. Full texts of Jack London's "The Call of the Wild"; John Brown's "Rab and His Friends"; Alfred Ollivant's "Bob, Son of Battle"; Marshall Saunders's "Beautiful Joe"; and Ouida's "A Dog of Flanders." 21 Illustrations from the original editions. 495pp. 5⅜ x 8. T777 Paperbound **$1.75**

TO THE SUN? and OFF ON A COMET!, Jules Verne. Complete texts of two of the most imaginative flights into fancy in world literature display the high adventure that have kept Verne's novels read for nearly a century. Only unabridged edition of the best translation, by Edward Roth. Large, easily readable type. 50 illustrations selected from first editions. 462pp. 5⅜ x 8. T634 Paperbound **$1.75**

FROM THE EARTH TO THE MOON and ALL AROUND THE MOON, Jules Verne. Complete editions of 2 of Verne's most successful novels, in finest Edward Roth translations, now available after many years out of print. Verne's visions of submarines, airplanes, television, rockets, interplanetary travel; of scientific and not-so-scientific beliefs; of peculiarities of Americans; all delight and engross us today as much as when they first appeared. Large, easily readable type. 42 illus. from first French edition. 476pp. 5⅜ x 8. T633 Paperbound **$1.75**

THE CRUISE OF THE CACHALOT, Frank T. Bullen. Out of the experiences of many years on the high-seas, First Mate Bullen created this novel of adventure aboard an American whaler, shipping out of New Bedford, Mass., when American whaling was at the height of its splendor. Originally published in 1899, the story of the round-the-world cruise of the "Cachalot" in pursuit of the sperm whale has thrilled generations of readers. A maritime classic that will fascinate anyone interested in reading about the sea or looking for a solid old-fashioned yarn, while the vivid recreation of a brief but important chapter of Americana and the British author's often biting commentary on nineteenth-century Yankee mores offer insights into the colorful era of America's coming of age. 8 plates. xiii + 271pp. 5⅜ x 8½. T774 Paperbound **$1.00**

28 SCIENCE FICTION STORIES OF H. G. WELLS. Two full unabridged novels, MEN LIKE GODS and STAR BEGOTTEN, plus 26 short stories by the master science-fiction writer of all time! Stories of space, time, invention, exploration, future adventure—an indispensable part of the library of everyone interested in science and adventure. PARTIAL CONTENTS: Men Like Gods, The Country of the Blind, In the Abyss, The Crystal Egg, The Man Who Could Work Miracles, A Story of the Days to Come, The Valley of Spiders, and 21 more! 928pp. 5⅜ x 8. T265 Clothbound **$4.50**

DAVID HARUM, E. N. Westcott. This novel of one of the most lovable, humorous characters in American literature is a prime example of regional humor. It continues to delight people who like their humor dry, their characters quaint, and their plots ingenuous. First book edition to contain complete novel plus chapter found after author's death. Illustrations from first illustrated edition. 192pp. 5⅜ x 8. T580 Paperbound **$1.15**

GESTA ROMANORUM, trans. by Charles Swan, ed. by Wynnard Hooper. 181 tales of Greeks, Romans, Britons, Biblical characters, comprise one of greatest medieval story collections, source of plots for writers including Shakespeare, Chaucer, Gower, etc. Imaginative tales of wars, incest, thwarted love, magic, fantasy, allegory, humor, tell about kings, prostitutes, philosophers, fair damsels, knights, Noah, pirates, all walks, stations of life. Introduction. Notes. 500pp. 5⅜ x 8. T535 Paperbound **$1.85**

Music

A GENERAL HISTORY OF MUSIC, Charles Burney. A detailed coverage of music from the Greeks up to 1789, with full information on all types of music: sacred and secular, vocal and instrumental, operatic and symphonic. Theory, notation, forms, instruments, innovators, composers, performers, typical and important works, and much more in an easy, entertaining style. Burney covered much of Europe and spoke with hundreds of authorities and composers so that this work is more than a compilation of records . . . it is a living work of careful and first-hand scholarship. Its account of thoroughbass (18th century) Italian music is probably still the best introduction on the subject. A recent NEW YORK TIMES review said, "Surprisingly few of Burney's statements have been invalidated by modern research . . . still of great value." Edited and corrected by Frank Mercer. 35 figures. Indices. 1915pp. 5⅜ x 8. 2 volumes. **T36 The Set, Clothbound $12.50**

A DICTIONARY OF HYMNOLOGY, John Julian. This exhaustive and scholarly work has become known as an invaluable source of hundreds of thousands of important and often difficult to obtain facts on the history and use of hymns in the western world. Everyone interested in hymns will be fascinated by the accounts of famous hymns and hymn writers and amazed by the amount of practical information he will find. More than 30,000 entries on individual hymns, giving authorship, date and circumstances of composition, publication, textual variations, translations, denominational and ritual usage, etc. Biographies of more than 9,000 hymn writers, and essays on important topics such as Christmas carols and children's hymns, and much other unusual and valuable information. A 200 page double-columned index of first lines — the largest in print. Total of 1786 pages in two reinforced clothbound volumes. 6¼ x 9¼. **The set, T333 Clothbound $17.50**

MUSIC IN MEDIEVAL BRITAIN, F. Ll. Harrison. The most thorough, up-to-date, and accurate treatment of the subject ever published, beautifully illustrated. Complete account of institutions and choirs; carols, masses, and motets; liturgy and plainsong; and polyphonic music from the Norman Conquest to the Reformation. Discusses the various schools of music and their reciprocal influences; the origin and development of new ritual forms; development and use of instruments; and new evidence on many problems of the period. Reproductions of scores, over 200 excerpts from medieval melodies. Rules of harmony and dissonance; influence of Continental styles; great composers (Dunstable, Cornysh, Fairfax, etc.); and much more. Register and index of more than 400 musicians. Index of titles. General Index. 225-item bibliography. 6 Appendices. xix + 491pp. 5⅝ x 8¾. **T705 Clothbound $10.00**

THE MUSIC OF SPAIN, Gilbert Chase. Only book in English to give concise, comprehensive account of Iberian music; new Chapter covers music since 1941. Victoria, Albéniz, Cabezón, Pedrell, Turina, hundreds of other composers; popular and folk music; the Gypsies; the guitar; dance, theatre, opera, with only extensive discussion in English of the Zarzuela; virtuosi such as Casals; much more. "Distinguished . . . readable," Saturday Review. 400-item bibliography. Index. 27 photos. 383pp. 5⅜ x 8. **T549 Paperbound $2.00**

ON STUDYING SINGING, Sergius Kagen. An intelligent method of voice-training, which leads you around pitfalls that waste your time, money, and effort. Exposes rigid, mechanical systems, baseless theories, deleterious exercises. "Logical, clear, convincing . . . dead right," Virgil Thomson, N.Y. Herald Tribune. "I recommend this volume highly," Maggie Teyte, Saturday Review. 119pp. 5⅜ x 8. **T622 Paperbound $1.25**

Prices subject to change without notice.

Dover publishes books on art, music, philosophy, literature, languages, history, social sciences, psychology, handcrafts, orientalia, puzzles and entertainments, chess, pets and gardens, books explaining science, intermediate and higher mathematics, mathematical physics, engineering, biological sciences, earth sciences, classics of science, etc. Write to:

Dept. catrr.
Dover Publications, Inc.
180 Varick Street, N.Y. 14, N.Y.